Mobile Capital
and
Latin American Development

James E. Mahon, Jr.

Mobile Capital
and
Latin American Development

The Pennsylvania State University Press
University Park, Pennsylvania

To Ma and Pa

Library of Congress Cataloging-in-Publication Data

Mahon, James E., Jr. 1955–
    Mobile capital and Latin American development /
James E. Mahon, Jr.
        p.   cm.
    Includes bibliographical references and index.
    ISBN 0-271-01525-X (cloth : alk. paper)
    ISBN 0-271-01526-8 (pbk. : alk. paper)
    1. Capital movements—Latin America.   2. Foreign exchange—Latin
America.   3. Latin America—Economic policy.   4. Debts, External
—Latin America.   I. Title.
    HG3891.M34   1996
    332'.042—dc20   95-17440
                                                                                      CIP

Contents

List of Tables

List of Figures

Preface

Any book on a single topic, with such broad historical and regional scope, runs the risk of reductionism and superficiality. I do not have a monomaniacal obsession with mobile money. But I am also not the only one to judge it to be of fundamental importance to contemporary politics. Latin American presidents and finance ministers found themselves buffeted by the scale and power of international capital movements in the early 1980s and the mid-1990s, while international bankers such as Walter Wriston find in the international mobility of capital a beneficial force for governmental discipline. I have sought to understand why the presidents and ministers went wrong and to see if observers like Walter Wriston are right or self-serving, or both. These are the sort of questions that, when I began the project, I felt needed a comparative approach, even though this meant a sacrifice of detail and narrative continuity in the name of making an argument.

My interest in the issue began modestly, while helping South American friends avoid exchange controls in the late 1970s. Why would someone go through so much trouble to place most of his savings abroad? Was the decision driven by low interest rates at home, political insecurity, the children studying in the United States, the periodic shopping trips, or the occasionally expressed desire to emigrate? My interest later grew as, like everyone else who watched the 1982 debt crisis explode, I was amazed by the waves of capital flight from Latin America. I began serious study of the issue after two conversations with Jesús Silva Herzog, who had recently retired as Mexico's minister of finance. The first product of this was a dissertation that examined the roots of the different policies that led some Latin American debtors to suffer a great deal of capital flight while others experienced relatively little. Vastly reduced and much revised, my dissertation corresponds to some of Chapter 1, most of Chapter 2, and all of Chapter 3.

Other parts of the puzzle also nagged me as I conducted research in Mexico City, Buenos Aires, Caracas, Bogotá, and Santiago. Chief among them was, what did the presence of so much domestically owned capital abroad mean for politics and policy in Latin America? After some delay I returned to my notes and began new research, just as free-market policy reforms swept much of the region and flight capital began to return. I completed revisions on the book three months into the crisis that began with the Mexican devaluation of 20 December 1994.

For financial support I thank the Tinker Foundation, the Institute for the Study of World Politics, the Institute of International Studies at the University of California, Berkeley, and the Nils Anderson Fund and the Department of Political Science at Williams College. Thanks also to Vinod Aggarwal, Leslie Armijo, Ralph Bradburd, David Collier, Paula Consolini, George T. Crane, Albert Fishlow, Mary Geske, and John Sheahan for their comments and encouragement at various stages of the enterprise, and to several anonymous referees for useful criticism.

List of Abbreviations

AD	Acción Democrática [Venezuela]
ANALDEX	Asociación Nacional de Exportadores [Colombia]
ANDI	Asociación Nacional de Industriales [Colombia]
ANIF	Asociación Nacional de Instituciones Financieras [Colombia]
BCRA	Banco Central de la República Argentina
BCV	Banco Central de Venezuela
BIS	Bank for International Settlements
BONEX	Bon[os de cambio] ex[terior] (Foreign-exchange-linked bonds) [Argentina]
BoP	Balance of payments
CAP	Carlos Andrés Pérez
CARBAP	Confederación de Asociaciones Rurales de Buenos Aires y la Pampa
CCE	Consejo Coordinador Empresarial (Business Coordinating Council) [Mexico]
CEPAL	Comisión Económica para América Latina (=ECLA) y el Caribe (=ECLAC)
CMHN	Consejo Mexicano de Hombres de Negocios (Mexican Businessmen's Council)
COPARMEX	Confederación Patronal Mexicana (Mexican Employers' Federation)
COPEI	Comité de Organización Política Electoral Independiente [Venezuela]
CTM	Confederación de Trabajadores de México (Federation of Mexican Labor)

CTV	Confederación de Trabajadores de Venezuela (Federation of Venezuelan Labor)
ECLA (ECLAC)	Economic Commission for Latin America (and the Caribbean) (= CEPAL)
FDI	Foreign direct investment
FEDECAFE	Federación Nacional de Cafeteros de Colombia (National Federation of Coffee Growers of Colombia)
FICORCA	Fideicomiso para la Cobertura del Riesgo Cambiario [Mexico]
FIESP	Federação das Indústrias do Estado de São Paulo (Federation of Industries of São Paulo state)
FNC	Fondo Nacional de Café [Colombia]
FOB	Free on board (no transit charges added)
GATT	General Agreement on Tariffs and Trade
IAPI	Instituto Argentino para la Promoción del Intercambio (Argentine Trade Promotion Institute)
IDB	Inter-American Development Bank
IFIs	International financial institutions (e.g., IMF, World Bank, IDB)
INDEC	Instituto Nacional de Estadística y Censos [Argentina]
ISI	Import-substituting industrialization
LIBOR	London interbank offer rate
MNCs	Multinational corporations
NAFINSA	Nacional Financiera, S.A. [Mexico]
NAFTA	North American Free Trade Agreement
NICs	Newly industrializing countries
PAN	Partido Acción Nacional [Mexico]
PDVSA	Petróleos de Venezuela, S.A.
PEMEX	Petróleos Mexicanos
PRI	Partido Revolucionario Institucional [Mexico]
REER	Real effective exchange rate
SNA	Sociedad Nacional de Agricultura [Chile]
SRA	Sociedad Rural Argentina
UDN	União Democrática Nacional [Brazil]
WPI	Wholesale price index
YPF	Yacimientos Petrolíferos Fiscales (Public Oil Deposits) [Argentina]

1

Introduction

When Jesús Silva Herzog flew to Washington in August 1982 and explained that Mexico could not meet its impending debt obligations, the immediate cause of his predicament was a rapid and massive capital outflow. A few years later, in November 1985, the minister again faced a crippling flight of capital. During negotiations over debt rescheduling two months afterward, foreign bankers confronted him with the question, "How can you ask us to help you when you can't even get your own nationals to keep their money in Mexico?"[1] A decade later, in the midst of another financial crisis, the head of Mexico's umbrella group for big business lamented that Mexican nationals were moving their capital out of the country much more quickly than were foreign investors.[2]

1. Interview, 11 February 1987.
2. Luis Germán Cárcoba García, head of the Consejo Coordinador Empresarial

In these stories can be found the major concerns of this work. As capital flight played midwife to the Latin American debt crisis, banks and domestic asset holders made similar, mutually reinforcing decisions during boom and bust. Flight continued as the crisis dragged on, making its solution more difficult. And the bankers' sentiment above, though somewhat disingenuous (the largest banks were handling large volumes of Latin American deposits while most of the rest were looking for reasons not to commit fresh funds), nevertheless bespoke an expectation about the local destination of local assets that has often gone unfulfilled in Latin America.

If modern confidence about economic progress rests in large part upon the idea that capital naturally moves from rich countries to poor ones, anyone looking at Latin America in the 1980s would have had his or her confidence shaken.[3] Without any strike waves or revolutions to drive investors away, private funds fled recurrently and in large amounts. More fled after the crisis broke in 1982 than did so before, and this accelerated a downward spiral that convinced informed observers that without the capital flight the pains of the region's "lost decade" would have been avoided or greatly alleviated.[4] If this were not enough, flight also has had a regressive distributional effect, as governments enforced austerity on the poor to pay debts that arose as counterparts to the foreign deposits, securities, and real estate of the rich.[5]

(Business Coordinating Council), *El Nacional* (Mexico City), 31 December 1994, pp. 1, 21. His impression was shared by John Liegey, president of the Weston Group, a brokerage house specializing in emerging markets. See Rosa Elba Arroyo, "El Capital Extranjero No Huyó Masivamente de México: Liegey," *El Financiero* (Mexico City), 11 August 1995, p. 8.

3. I make this statement acknowledging that this idea may overstate the requirements of economic progress. Cf. the idea that "capital" should refer to investment capital, not to the net flow of funds servicing debt or investment. Arnold Harberger has argued that good loans (or investments) benefit a country even in periods when the net flow turns negative, if they are funding activities that provide surplus above the interest (or remitted-profit) rate. See John Williamson, ed., *Latin American Adjustment: How Much Has Happened?* (Washington, D.C.: Institute for International Economics, 1990), p. 328.

4. "Latin America's disastrous performance in the 1980s is in large measure the result of capital flight." See Rudiger Dornbusch, *Capital Flight: Theory, Measurement, and Policy Issues*, Occasional Paper no. 2 (Washington, D.C.: Interamerican Development Bank, 1990), p. 28.

5. In many places it resembled, as an acute observer put it, a case "where the contractor absconds with the mortgage money, the banker who helped him take it out now comes to collect from the owner of the empty lot and no one will lend the lot owner any more money because his 'debts' are too high." See James Henry, "The New Philippines: Revolution, Recovery, and Reality," *International Development Review* 2,

Still, it is possible, as many have done, to find nothing to fear and little to regret in these trends. From this point of view, capital flight is a way of preserving savings against the depredations of bad politicians. As investors around the world diversify their portfolios, they improve the efficiency of capital markets and, since they can shift assets at the first hint of statist excess, keep governments honest. This view expects the whittling-away of state economic sovereignty to bring a bright future to the world's poorer countries, one that includes responsible monetary policies, balanced budgets, productive foreign investment, and even institutional development.

No matter how we view the effects of international capital flows, one thing is clear: they are more rapid and proportionally larger today than ever before. The world's foreign exchange markets are broad, deep, less and less regulated, and (in terms of costs per trade) amazingly efficient. A 1989 survey found that about 95 percent of the transactions in the three major financial centers took place among financial institutions, which suggests that only a tiny proportion of market activity is now connected with trade in goods and services.[6] By 1992 the total market had expanded another 37 percent over its 1989 volume.[7] As developing countries build domestic capital markets and tie them more closely with those of the centers, their bonds, shares, and currencies will come into play in greater amounts. The events of 1980–83 and 1994–95 testified that Latin America had joined an international financial order in which capital moved very quickly— and often in the "wrong" direction—among geographically dispersed assets.

Apart from the economic and social damage from the last decade's debt crisis, there are more general reasons to investigate the contemporary politics of mobile capital in Latin America. While mobile capital appears to have placed new constraints on states' choice of

---

no. 1 (1989): 82, cited in James K. Boyce, "The Revolving Door? External Debt and Capital Flight: A Philippine Case Study," *World Development* 20, no. 3 (1992): 345.

6. Based on April 1989 surveys in New York, Tokyo, and London by the Federal Reserve Bank of New York, cited in Jeffrey A. Frankel and Kenneth A. Froot, "Chartists, Fundamentalists, and Trading in the Foreign Exchange Market," *American Economic Review* 80, no. 2 (May 1990): 182. See also the conclusions of the Bank for International Settlements (BIS) from a June 1992 survey of twenty-six central banks, cited in Bank for International Settlements, *Annual Report* 63 (June 1993): 196.

7. IMF, *International Capital Markets: Part I. Exchange Rate Management and International Capital Flows* (Washington, D.C.: International Monetary Fund, 1992), p. 24. Bank for International Settlements, *Annual Report,* calculates from the 1992 survey an adjusted total global turnover of foreign exchange of $880 billion per day (p. 196).

economic policy, its special implications for the political economy of development have not been well explored. Beyond this, we have in the events of the last fifteen years the intersection of two important phenomena: not only the rapid movement of financial capital internationally but also the fact that in Latin American countries most of the movable wealth belongs to a few thousand households and firms closely linked to the global financial marketplace. If the coming years see the persistence of current trends toward greater capital mobility and more narrowly distributed wealth in many parts of the world, then Latin America's recent experience in this regard may be instructive.

This book examines the causes, consequences, political context, and general implications of international capital movements in Latin America during the last decade and a half. As international capital flows grew and became more private from Bretton Woods into the 1970s, they exposed developing countries to the possibility that capital would behave procyclically, aggravating trends on the trade balance. Latin American countries were especially vulnerable to this, since their exports were usually concentrated in few commodities and their openness to capital movements, including those by domestic wealth holders, was greater than their openness to trade. Governments that responded to export stagnation and repeated exchange crises by undertaking exchange policy reforms in the 1960s (and keeping them in place) would later suffer less capital flight while borrowing abroad.

Outward private capital flows from Latin America after 1982 made the debt crisis longer and more profound. Governments faced rising inflation and fiscal crises, while resident wealth holders, fearing taxes and other consequences of the debt burden, placed large amounts of capital abroad. In part because of this continued capital flight, by the end of the decade even leaders elected as populists embraced "realism" and undertook sweeping neoliberal reforms, to the loud approval of the international financial community. But as the 1994–95 Mexican peso crisis and its regional impact showed, even exemplary reformers remained quite vulnerable to rapid international capital movements.

In view of these experiences, the book also discusses broader issues about the influence of global market forces on institutional development, democracy, and dependence. In particular, it notes how many governments have deepened financial markets and created institutional safeguards for mobile international capital. Still, it questions the degree to which one can be optimistic about the effect of mobile capital on strengthening political institutions and the rule of law in Latin America.

*I. Use 1st few pages to set
stage for capital flight
II. Def.*   Introduction   5

Definitions, Magnitudes, and Immediate Causes of Capital Outflows from Latin America

Since the idea of this book is to take up where economic studies leave off, it will be necessary to determine approximately where this is. A substantial economic literature on capital flight arose in the wake of the 1982 debt crisis.

For present purposes, let us define capital flight as the acquisition of foreign assets, including foreign currency, based on an agent's perception of rising locally generated risk.[8] The main obstacle to a universally accepted definition has been the difficulty of connecting any such motivational definition with a feasible method of measurement: accounting entries in the balance of payments do not discriminate according to motivations. Some studies, like Charles Kindleberger's valuable early treatment of short-term capital movements,[9] have concentrated on definition without attempting to measure; others, such as the 1986 study by Morgan Guaranty Trust, have avoided the question of motivations while providing estimates of flight for eighteen countries;[10] still others, like John Cuddington's 1986 monograph and the later, more comprehensive contribution of Cumby and Levich, have attempted both measurement and a motivational definition while acknowledging the difficulties involved in combining them.[11]

8. "Capital flight" has somewhat distinctive usages, with the difference corresponding in part to one between flows of short- and long-term capital. The former are usually noteworthy because of currency-market turmoil, the latter, insofar as they refer to shifts in fixed investment patterns, because of job losses.

9. *International Short-Term Capital Movements* (New York: Columbia University Press, 1937).

10. Morgan Guaranty Trust Company of New York, "LDC Capital Flight," *World Financial Markets,* March 1986, p. 13.

11. Cuddington emphasizes the speculative and risk-avoiding character of capital flight, while for the purposes of estimation, he defines it according to categories in balance-of-payments statistics ("net errors and omissions" plus, in about half the cases, other categories) on a country-by-country basis. See John T. Cuddington, *Capital Flight: Estimates, Issues, and Explanations,* Princeton Studies in International Finance, no. 58 (Princeton: Princeton University Press, December 1986). Robert Cumby and Richard Levich also includes a discussion of Michael Dooley's method, which overcomes the definition/measurement gap by defining flight in terms more amenable to standard BoP categories—the change in the stock of claims on nonresidents that do not generate reported income. See "On the Definition and Magnitude of Recent Capital Flight," in *Capital Flight and Third World Debt,* ed. Donald R. Lessard and John Williamson (Washington, D.C.: Institute for International Economics, 1987), pp. 32–33. This definition yields interesting results but will not be used here. On definition, Lessard and

As defined, the term implies a dominance of "push" factors (from within a country) over "pull" factors (out toward the rest of the world). This is what separates capital flight from "ordinary" capital outflows. Whereas capital flight arises from the perception of new domestic risks, ordinary capital flows respond to international factors, mainly rising foreign interest rates, but also new opportunities to diversify internationally.

An important empirical point relates to this distinction. If, viewing the same "push" factors, many agents make the same decision to sell domestic assets, and these decisions together increase the overall risk, capital flight can be self-propagating. For example, if agents worry that the central bank will not have enough reserves to defend the current exchange rate, an ongoing capital outflow raises their expectations of a devaluation and makes it more likely they will join the flight of capital. If asset holders fear political instability and their capital flight helps bring about a politically explosive devaluation, their fears are confirmed, again provoking flight. The same can happen with expectations of future tax liability: capital that flees the prospect of taxes leaves behind a reduced base and thus (assuming constant budgets) a higher expected rate on those remaining, who then seek to avoid tax, and so on. In these instances of dynamic interaction, flight of capital often takes on the character of a run on the central bank's foreign exchange reserves. The process contrasts with the pursuit of an attractive international interest-rate differential. Here, a net flow of funds toward the higher-interest asset tends to reduce the differential. It is true arbitrage, and therefore stabilizing. We might also expect such "ordinary" flows to occur steadily and unobtrusively in balance-of-payment statistics and to be less bothersome to central bankers, whereas capital flight will take place in fairly well defined and often tumultuous episodes.

Measuring something that people are trying to hide always presents problems. Big money prefers secrecy. The detection of capital flight has an advantage, however, in that the phenomenon is international. Hence it can appear as a residual of other, explicitly counted international flows of goods and money. Two base estimates are used here. One (the "World Bank" estimate in Figures 1.1A–F) is a residual based on the sources and uses of funds, including debt, trade, and

---

Williamson argue, as I do, for consistency with normal English usage of "flight" and for the central importance of risk ("a diagnosis of capital flight . . . reflects a judgment that the deviant factor propelling the outflow is the level of domestic risk perceived by some or all residents"). However, they then measure "resident capital outflows" (pp. 202–4).

direct investment, in the balance of payments. It then adds the figure for private nongovernmental foreign holdings. The other ("Hot money" in Figures 1.1A–F) estimate sums the "errors and omissions" entry (the central bank's own residual) with short-term private capital flows. Each base estimate is further combined with an estimate of the capital flow that takes place by another route, the misinvoicing of trade. The latter draws upon annual direction of trade statistics and consists of the disparities between the reporting of trade from one country to the next. All of these figures come from a World Bank data set.[12]

Let us now examine the causes of capital outflows. Even having classified "flight" as motivated by domestic risks, there might be several macroeconomic variables creating the sense of risk. While economists have pointed to many—accumulated foreign debt, excessive monetary growth, overvalued currencies, low domestic interest rates, inflation, lack of (or threat of) exchange controls, and class conflict—they disagree about which has been the most important cause of Latin American capital flight. Part of this is obviously due to the fact that the main cause of flight varies from one episode to the next. To illustrate, let us examine a few of the imputed causes in turn.

Clearly, accumulation of huge foreign debts had some correlation with flight before 1982 and in 1994–95. It could be said to have been a necessary condition for such massive outflows: the borrowing allowed fiscal deficits, expansive monetary policy, and highly appreciated currencies to persist, often affirming such policies in the eyes of the officials responsible for them.[13] The causal significance of borrowing has also been established econometrically for the period leading up to 1982.[14] Yet if interpreted as a given period's *increase* in total external liabilities, borrowing looks less persuasive as an explanation of the varying rates of capital flight across the region after 1982, notable in

12. The IECDI Capital Flight Estimates, available on floppy disk from the World Bank, whose methodology and summary results appear in Stijn Claessens and David Naudé, "Recent Estimates of Capital Flight," World Bank, 30 July 1993, photocopy.

13. This will be argued again in Chapter 2 and with reference to specific policies and officials in Chapter 3. See Eduardo Wiesner, "Latin American Debt: Lessons and Pending Issues," *American Economic Review* 75, no. 2 (May 1985): 193; David T. Llewellyn, "The International Capital Transfer Mechanism of the 1970s: A Critique," in *The International Financial Regime,* ed. Graham Bird (London: Surrey University, 1990), p. 38.

14. Manuel Pastor, Jr., "Capital Flight from Latin America," *World Development* 18, no. 1 (1990): 8–10; for a more detailed treatment of the relationship between debt and flight for the Philippines, see Boyce, "The Revolving Door?"

Figures 1.1A–F, below. None of the studies that establish its signifi-cance add the net results of trade misinvoicing to their estimates, nor do they include the large Brazilian flight of 1987–88. Hence, while unprecedented borrowing does seem to have been responsible for the equally unprecedented magnitudes of outflows in the late 1970s, as well as for the enduring financial fragility of the region, it is also true that many indebted countries did not suffer much capital flight, and for at least the decade after 1982 the relationship between additional debt and additional flight was weak.

Monetary and fiscal policies may have played a fundamental role. Jeffrey Sachs has argued that the "conjunction of heavy public debt and large private assets is mainly a reflection of the loose fiscal policies," asserting that the "predominant mechanism" during the 1976–82 borrowing period involved increased government transfer payments, which raised the money supply to the private sector, which in turn converted much of its excess cash into foreign assets. Mean-while, the central bank's defense of the currency value required it to sell foreign assets out of its reserves. Sachs makes a similar argument, referring not to fiscal deficits but to an expansion of bank credit, to account for the Mexican capital flight of 1994.[15] In this view exchange-rate overvaluation is a mere symptom, a consequence of accelerating inflation, which in turn derives from a budget deficit or a credit expansion financed by printing money. The Chilean figures support this idea clearly.[16]

15. "Introduction," to Jeffrey D. Sachs, ed., *Developing Country Debt and the World Economy* (Chicago: University of Chicago Press, 1989), p. 12; *The Economist*, 18 March 1995, pp. 74–75.

16. The Chilean case is more complicated than it first appears. In 1972–73, on the hot money measure for both years and the residual measure for the latter, Chile recorded its highest inflow of funds, relative to exports, of any during the entire period, including the prosperous times of 1990–91. Were people and firms madly circumventing Allende's exchange controls in order to invest in his socialist experiment? The data appear to confirm the massive scale of CIA funding to the anti-Allende opposition. (This was reported as $8 million between 1970 and 1973, which clearly accounts for very little of the net inflow of $459 or $157 million [according to the hot money or World Bank residual measures, respectively] calculated for 1972.) Ian Roxborough, Philip O'Brien, and Jackie Roddick, assisted by Michael Gonzalez, *Chile: The State and Revolution* (New York: Holmes and Meier, 1977), p. 152, citing testimony of William Colby to U.S. Senate. Various authors have reported that the inflows in October 1972 managed to push the black market dollar far down until it traded at a discount—in the face of multiple and overvalued official exchange rates, accelerating inflation, and growing instability. North American Congress on Latin America, *Chile: The Story Behind the Coup*, cited in Roxborough et al., *Chile: The State and Revolution*, p. 153; Barbara Stallings, *Class Conflict and Economic Development in Chile, 1958–1973* (Stanford:

Fiscal concerns inhabit another model of capital flight that posits an asymmetry of perceived risks between local and foreign asset holders. This picture allows a prediction about why local asset holders would buy foreign assets even as foreign banks continued to lend: the former could expect to face a greater future tax liability as debts piled up, while the latter could expect the opposite—government guarantees issued even after the fact. Compared to exchange-rate overvaluation alone, this model can more easily explain the persistence of flight after the large devaluations of the early 1980s and its reversal under conditions of currency appreciation later.[17]

A related model views capital flight as the result of sectoral conflict within the real economy. It posits a noncooperative differential game between organized workers (who affect the wage share) and capitalists.[18] This model finds one of the equilibrium solutions to be "reminiscent of the experience of several developing countries."[19] It could be seen as prior to fiscal deficits, and it also offers a reason why devaluations could actually induce flight even after they have corrected an accumulated overvaluation. By delivering a large discrete push to inflation, they would raise the issue of how to divide the cost of attenuating it—thus raising the possibility of a noncooperative result as labor and capital tried to shift this cost.

Stanford University Press, 1978), pp. 141–42. The remarkable scale of these net inflows also leads one to wonder to what extent the inflow figures for 1974–77, particularly significant by the hot money measure, include continued covert aid to the Pinochet regime. However, the general conclusion that fiscal orthodoxy helps prevent a net capital outflow is safe, especially in view of the inflows to other Latin American countries over the 1989–93 period, usually accompanying reduced deficits or significant fiscal surpluses (the main exception is Brazil).

17. The model has been elaborated significantly since its initial presentation by Khan and Ul-Haque, who used "expropriation risk" but defined it in a rather general way. See Mohsin S. Khan and Nadeem Ul-Haque, "Foreign Borrowing and Capital Flight," *IMF Staff Papers* 32, no. 4 (1985): 606–8. Subsequent improvements are due to Michael P. Dooley, "Capital Flight: A Response to Differences in Financial Risks," IMF, July 1986, photocopy, esp. p. 28; on the point of government guarantees, see Jonathan Eaton, "Public Debt Guarantees and Private Capital Flight," NBER Working Paper 2172 (Cambridge, Mass.: National Bureau of Economic Research, March 1987); the summary here agrees with Liliana Rojas-Suárez in "Risk and Capital Flight in Developing Countries," in *Determinants and Systemic Consequences of International Capital Flows*, IMF Occasional Paper 77 (Washington, D.C.: International Monetary Fund, March 1991), pp. 83–92, and, I believe, with the model of Manuel Pastor, Jr., in "Capital Flight from Latin America," p. 7.

18. Andrés Velasco and Aarón Tornell, "Wages, Profits, and Capital Flight," Economic Research Report 90-21, C. V. Starr Center for Applied Economics (New York: New York University, May 1990), abstract.

19. Ibid., p. 18.

Another view argues the independent importance of exchange rates. Testing several economic variables with post-1970 data for indebted developing countries, Cuddington found expected depreciation to be the most important correlate of flight. Lessard and Williamson concur.[20] Advocates of this view sometimes argue against the idea that fiscal deficits are the cause. For example, Miguel Rodríguez concludes from the Venezuelan case that such explanations constitute a "big fallacy": between 1972 and 1982, he says, the public sector was the big national net saver; state companies were sent to borrow in order to pay for transfers to the private sector through the central bank.[21] For Argentina, Dornbusch and de Pablo conclude that "both the fact of and the motivation for the wave of capital flight in the late 1970s are very clear. . . . mismanagement of the exchange rate combined with an opening of the capital account are the almost exclusive explanations for the massive debt accumulation."[22] According to this argument, attributing capital flight to excessive money creation amounts to assuming that governments *could* let the money base shrink as a result of capital flight, with the deflation, recession, bank failures, and debt-service costs that this would entail. From this viewpoint, overvaluation (not money expansion) was the realistically corrigible mistake.

A final important issue concerns exchange restrictions, the policies governing legal access to the market for foreign currency assets. According to Lessard and Williamson,

> . . . among Latin American countries, at least, there is an exact correspondence between the countries that had no exchange control at the turn of the decade [1980] and those that suffered capital flight on a massive scale. Argentina, Mexico, Uruguay, and Venezuela all experienced massive outflows; in all of them the outflows were perfectly legal. In contrast, outflows were relatively modest from Brazil, Chile, Colombia, and Peru, all of which maintained restrictions.[23]

Although the authors go on to note qualifying circumstances like indexed assets and local foreign exchange bank accounts, and mention the failure

20. Cuddington, *Capital Flight: Estimates, Issues, and Explanations;* Lessard and Williamson, eds., *Capital Flight and Third World Debt,* pp. 228–29.

21. "El Verdadero Origen del Endeudamiento Externo Venezolano" (Caracas: Instituto de Estudios Superiores de Administración, August 1984), photocopy, pp. 1, 4.

22. Rudiger Dornbusch and Juan Carlos de Pablo, "Debt and Macroeconomic Instability in Argentina, in *Developing Country Debt and the World Economy,* ed. Jeffrey D. Sachs (Chicago: University of Chicago Press, 1989), p. 44.

23. Lessard and Williamson, eds., *Capital Flight and Third World Debt,* p. 233.

of controls in 1982 in Mexico and France, they conclude that the degree of overvaluation experienced by Brazil, Chile, and Colombia in this period would probably have led to flight in the absence of controls.[24] Moreover, Japan, South Korea, and Taiwan, all geographically well equipped for exchange controls, have had strong ones in place until very recently, and the latter two countries also avoided capital flight while borrowing. By raising transaction costs and thus also affecting expectations of volatility, they are supposed to provide greater "friction" in the exchange market and to facilitate an adequate policy response.[25] Still, the issue is more complicated. Bankers usually dismiss controls as statist and counterproductive; others have argued that free foreign exchange markets allow private agents to compensate for inconsistent policies, in a sense preserving the national patrimony by placing it out of reach of bad rulers.[26] Where controls are absent, the expectation of their emplacement may itself provoke capital flight, perhaps because it signals the escalation of a political conflict over property.

Critics of the search for macroeconomic determinants of flight point out that the persuasiveness of the case for fiscal deficits, exchange rates, or controls as determinants of flight depends on the method of measurement and the period under scrutiny.[27] This is true. For example, "hot money" flows, those examined by Cuddington and given the most prominence by Lessard and Williamson, exhibit a much stronger relationship to exchange rates and controls than do the residual estimates of the World Bank. The latter often peak later, perhaps a year after the large devaluation that followed the "hot money" attack in the currency market (Figures 1.1A–F). Moreover, "hot money"

24. Ibid., p. 234. See also the discussion by Miguel Rodríguez in a footnote to his article in the same volume (p. 135 n. 7).

25. Miguel Urrutia, in ibid., pp. 194–95.

26. One bank publication correctly blamed capital flight on "overvalued exchange rates, artificially low interest rates, and political uncertainties"—but stopped there. It went on to recommend a reduced role for the state in order to free resources for the private sector and exports. See Morgan Guaranty Trust Company, *World Financial Markets*, February 1984, pp. 9 and 11. The latter argument is Leonardo Auernheimer, "On the Outcome of Inconsistent Policies Under Exchange Rate and Monetary Rules: Or, Allowing the Market to Compensate for Government Mistakes," *Journal of Monetary Economics* 19 (1987): 279–305.

27. David B. Gordon and Ross Levine, "The 'Problem' of Capital Flight—A Cautionary Note," *World Economy* 12, no. 2 (June 1989): 237–52. The authors argue that "the rich array of 'healthy' capital flows associated with the diversification of portfolios and the financing of international activities cannot be reliably disentangled from 'abnormal' flows associated with political instability and distortionary policies" (p. 273). However, the fact that one has to look closer at a period in a country's history to make an interpretation does not, to my mind, render the interpretation impossible.

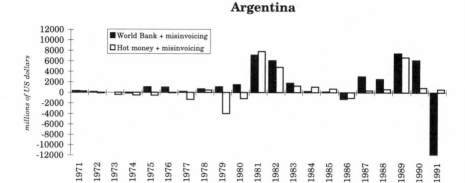

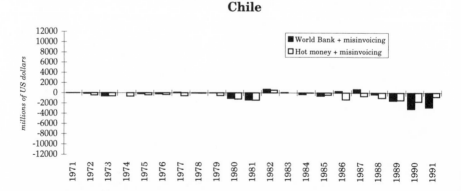

Figs. 1.1A–F.   Net capital outflows, 1971–1991, in millions of U.S. dollars. Two estimates, both from World Bank IECDI database, for each year. Negative numbers denote net capital inflows.

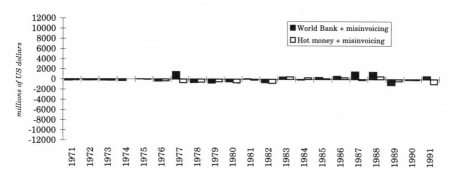

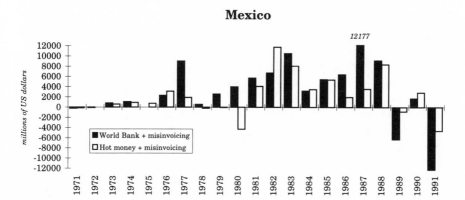

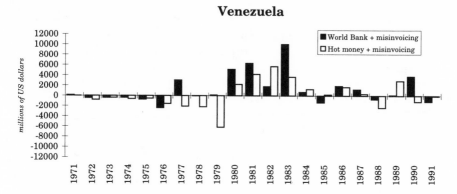

Figs. 1.1A–F.   (continued)

measures seem consistently to estimate a lower level of outflows from Brazil than do residual measures; much of the case for the effectiveness of controls is lost if we take seriously the World Bank residual estimates for Brazil in 1977 or 1987–88.[28] The former episode did not show up in hot money figures and the latter took place mostly after the Lessard and Williamson volume was published.

Let us sum up the importance of the main macroeconomic variables discussed so far. In 1978–82 both public deficits (driving money creation) and overvalued currencies (and in 1994 the latter) were clearly facilitated by abundant foreign finance. Public-sector deficits soaked up borrowed money and appear to have correlated quite well with the level of *total* capital outflows over the 1976–82 period. Monetary expansion has also been implicated in the Mexican peso crisis of 1994. Yet the spectacular flights of capital during the critical years of 1980–82 clearly involved an element of dynamic interaction among agents, often climaxing in situations of true panic. This seems to point to a different proximate cause. Where we attribute an outflow to the market acting on knowledge of macroeconomic disequilibria, the exchange rate or inflation seem more plausible candidates than the money base, even though the latter may be ultimately responsible for their disequilibrium. It is easier for people to judge the dollar too cheap or to be unnerved by price hikes than to obtain current, reliable information on money creation or the revenue shortfall of the government. (The main, important exception: sudden, massive outlays for deposit insurance during a banking crisis.) And, in fact, fears of devaluation were what usually moved people to stand in line outside the *casas de cambio*. The most significant episodes of flight during 1980–82 (especially if deflated by exports, as in Figures 1.2A–F) occurred in Argentina, Mexico, and Venezuela, countries distinguished by their combination of overvalued currencies and free exchange markets. While the underlying policy mistake was one of inconsistency—fixed exchange rates and a wildly expanding money base do not mix—in most instances of panic the focus has been the exchange rate, and the exchange market was relatively free.

After 1982 a variety of factors contributed to capital flight from Latin America. There was actually *more* capital outflow during

28. Puzzlingly, the World Bank's figures for 1977 for Brazil, Colombia, and Mexico are much higher than macroeconomic or political conditions would have led us to expect.

1983–89 than during 1976–82 (Table 1.1).[29] Why? First, real devaluations cut down at one blow the revenues of the region's large nontradeables sectors, the financial institutions tied to them, and (apart from governments with state-owned exports) the real resources available to states from these sources. Moreover, in many cases—Mexico 1982 and 1994 prominent among them—the collapse of a fixed exchange rate shattered the prestige of the government.[30] As noted above, the large discrete push to inflation presented a risk of destructive capital-labor conflict. The pattern disconfirmed the hypothesis that capital flows would respond symmetrically to exchange-rate and interest-rate incentives, coming back when these were reversed.[31] One reason was that the debt itself also undermined confidence. Latin American asset holders could regard the foreign and domestic debts as large and growing prior claims on foreign exchange and public monies, and this implied a greater risk of future tax exposure.[32] Finally, transaction

29. In part this reflects the massive Brazilian flight of 1988–89. Yet even here the debt overhang and its fiscal burden made the situation precarious; and, like Brazil, every debtor country's balance of payments had become extremely vulnerable to interest rate changes, reluctant creditors, commodity price declines, and so on.

30. Wealthy Mexican exiles saw devaluation and exchange controls, not overvaluation, as primary causes of flight; this may testify to both the timing and motivation of their own asset movements. See Valdemar De Murguía, *Capital Flight and Economic Crisis: Mexican Post-Devaluation Exiles in a California Community,* Center for U.S.-Mexican Studies Research Report no. 44 (San Diego: UCSD, 1986), p. 23.

31. Cuddington, *Capital Flight: Estimates, Issues, and Explanations,* App. A. Cuddington also notes that confidence is easier to lose than to regain (p. 13). This is surely true, but confidence is a slippery term, hard to measure except with reference to some of the variables sometimes taken to provoke flight in the first place.

32. In the 1980s the link between the debt burden and private capital movements became an important topic of debate. The banks generally saw the return of capital as a prerequisite for recovery, while others considered it the "caboose" on the train of debt relief. See the comments of Rimmer De Vries (the bank view) and Rudiger Dornbusch in Lessard and Williamson, eds., *Capital Flight and Third World Debt;* for the view that the burden deterred recovery and capital reflow, see the inaugural speech of Carlos Salinas de Gortari, 1 December 1988, or the testimony of David Mulford, Nora Lustig, Albert Fishlow, and John Williamson in *Impact of Capital Flight on Latin American Debt,* Senate Finance Committee, Subcommittee on Deficits, Debt Management, and International Debt, 102d Cong., 1st sess., 12 June 1991 (Washington, D.C.: U.S. Government Printing Office, 1991), pp. 8, 14, 16, 56. Jeffrey Sachs, "Introduction," to Sachs, ed., *Developing Country Debt and Economic Performance: The International Financial System,* NBER Project Report (Chicago: University of Chicago Press, 1989), 1:21–23; Dornbusch and de Pablo, "Debt and Macroeconomic Instability," pp. 44–46; Williamson in *Impact of Capital Flight on Latin American Debt,* p. 56. On the Mexican debt reduction as a spur to capital return see Ricardo Campos, *El FMI y la Deuda Externa Mexicana: Crisis y Estabilización* (Mexico City: Plaza y Valdés, 1993), p. 240. Similarly,

Argentina

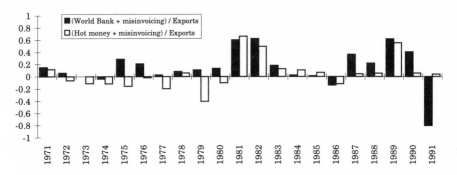

Brazil

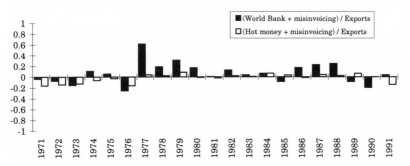

Chile

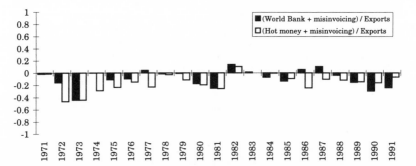

Figs. 1.2A–F.   Net capital outflows, 1971–1991, as a proportion of exports. Based on the two estimates used in Figures 1.1A–F and same-year exports FOB from IMF, *Balance of Payments Yearbook* (Washington, D.C.: IMF), various issues. Negative numbers denote net capital inflows.

Colombia

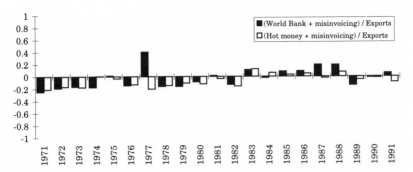

Mexico

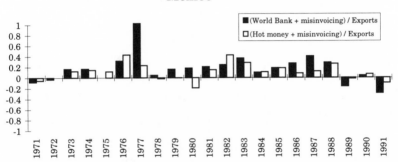

Venezuela

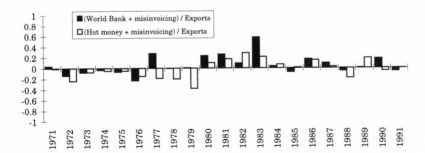

Figs. 1.2A–F. (continued)

costs had fallen and the United States began to offer favorable tax treatment for flight capital in order to fund its fiscal deficit.

Before continuing, we should note how politics can and should have a place even in narrowly focused econometric analyses of capital flight. A test based only on macroeconomic variables, such as Cuddington's, misses the significant political influences on expectations. Why? Cuddington uses real appreciation (over an arbitrary base year) as a statistical proxy for expected depreciation.[33] But the concept implies a time period in which depreciation is expected, not just an estimate of its eventual magnitude: otherwise it would be like contemplating the purchase of a bond whose yield was known but whose maturity was not.[34] This implies that a fully specified model of expectations needs to consider agents' views about policy sustainability. These, in turn, derive as much from an assessment of the capabilities and future of the existing political regime as they do from estimates of economic disequilibria: see, for example, Chile 1981–82 or Argentina 1994–95.[35]

Politics and Capital Movements

Apart from the political component of expectations noted above, there are three other ways in which outward capital movements often may be said to have a political side. The first involves corruption, the second the use of capital outflows deliberately as a tool of political pressure, and the last the relationship between capital flows and wealth distribution. Let us explore these in turn.

Pedro-Pablo Kuczynski has argued that the repatriation of capital depends on confidence, and that the main ingredient of confidence is growth. See "Panel on Policy Issues," in Lessard and Williamson, eds., *Capital Flight and Third World Debt,* p. 91.

33. In Cuddington's study, overvaluation is the degree to which the real effective exchange rate (REER) exceeds an estimated equilibrium (he uses the REER for 1977); when this is added to the nominal return on foreign assets, the sum is the expected return on such assets in terms of domestic currency (*Capital Flight: Estimates, Issues, and Explanations,* pp. 18–19, 25, 27).

34. Hence the expected value of one's loss from devaluation in the next period is a function that sums, over the period, the product of expected loss ("overvaluation") and the probability that this loss will be taken at any given moment.

35. The discussion in Chapter 3 will argue that the relative lack of capital flight from Chile during 1978–81, despite the weakening of controls on outflows, illustrates the important role of politically informed expectations about "sustainability." This differs from Lessard and Williamson, although it is true that, except for a few months in 1982, exchange purchase controls in Chile *were* somewhat stricter than in Argentina during 1980 and early 1981.

Table 1.1   Aggregated Estimates of Capital Flight for 1976–1982 and 1983–1989 (millions of U.S. dollars)

			Latin America and the Caribbean		
Period	World Bank Residual	Hot Money	Misinvoicing	World Bank + Misinvoicing	Hot Money + Misinvoicing
1976–82	113,166	41,965	−57,520	55,646	−15,555
1983–89	95,999	48,022	−31,564	64,435	16,458
			Six Countries		
1976–82				79,209	22,018
1983–89				84,108	50,785

SOURCE: World Bank IECDI database. Data Extracts System (DX) version 1.0 (Washington, D.C.: World Bank, Debt and International Finance Division, 1993), floppy disk. See also Figures 1.1A–F.

Anyone who gets a large sum of money illegally often finds it convenient to transfer the gains out of the jurisdiction in which they were obtained.[36] While this applies to all of the underground economy and to tax evasion generally, corrupt public officials face the need most acutely, since the mere appearance of large bank balances or unusual spending may provoke an investigation that could threaten their careers (and they may wish to prepare for a comfortable exile anyway). This kind of activity is not likely to show up clearly on the balance of payments unless it is extremely pervasive, perhaps in a system deserving of the term "kleptocracy."[37]

Certainly, the Latin American episodes of capital flight featured plenty of official corruption. The evidence of graft among the upper ranks of Mexico's Partido Revolucionario Institucional (PRI), and of

36. See the discussion in Ingo Walter, "The Mechanisms of Capital Flight," in Lessard and Williamson, eds., *Capital Flight and Third World Debt.*

37. This term became current in the 1980s. Trevor Parfitt defines it as "a mode of rulership based on universal and systemic corruption" and applies it to the Mobutu regime in Zaire. See "Corruption, Adjustment, and the African Debt," *Corruption and Reform* 6 (1991): 28. See also its application to the Marcos regime in the Philippines in Aurora Carbonell-Catilo, "The Philippines: The Politics of Plunder," *Corruption and Reform* 1 (1986): 235–43. It could also be largely applied to the most dramatic case of capital flight anywhere, in the Sudan, from which an estimated $10–15 billion fled during 1978–84 (from a country of 11 million people). See Richard P. C. Brown, *Public Debt and Private Wealth: Debt, Capital Flight, and the IMF in Sudan* (London: Macmillan, 1992).

the foreign destination of much of the loot, has been abundant. The same goes for outflows from Venezuela, Argentina, and Brazil. Indeed, this may be one of the reasons why reaction against capital flight included a reaction against leaders who chastised the private sector while putting funds abroad themselves. Yet in Latin America, shady dealings have not been confined to hypocritical presidents and grasping bureaucrats: there were also the businessmen who arranged with foreign banks to borrow amounts completely covered by corresponding balances, later to ask the government for foreign exchange subsidies in order to pay their debts.

Capital movements more clearly deserve the label "political" when they involve some kind of negotiation. For all the varieties of capital flow mentioned in the last section, we considered the magnitude of the incentive to move assets to be unaffected by the actions of individual agents. When a fiscal deficit looks like it will end in hyperinflation or higher taxes, or an overvalued currency appears ready to collapse, asset holders can be assumed to ignore the extent to which their own action makes the hyperinflation or devaluation more likely. They expect something bad to happen anyway. A run on a bank does not have to be organized collectively, which is not to say that it is politically inconsequential. But the participants in a run on the central bank do not intend a devaluation; they fear one.

Historically, the most important class of political capital flows is the capital strike. This term could be applied to any shift of assets that seeks to win political or policy change, but it inherits a connotation of class conflict. Of this phenomenon, Albert Hirschman has noted that

> exit of capital often takes place in countries intending to introduce some taxation that would curb excessive privileges of the rich or some social reforms designed to distribute the fruits of economic growth more equitably. Under these conditions, capital flight and its threat are meant to parry, fight off, and perhaps veto such reforms; whatever the outcome, they are sure to make reforms more costly and difficult.[38]

As this suggests, "political" flight occurs when the asset decision is intended to change the relevant policies, maybe by bringing down the government. It is therefore much more likely to be both organized and accompanied by an "explanation" directed at policymakers. Clearly

38. *Essays in Trespassing: Economics to Politics and Beyond* (New York: Cambridge University Press, 1981), p. 257.

this includes all the cases where flight is only threatened, where asset holders stay put while attempting to change the policy environment.[39]

Further, it makes sense to define a capital strike, like a labor strike, in part based on its having significant short-term costs. These would include not only transaction costs but also the opportunity cost of asset transfer. The latter justifies calling the shift a political one. If a set of policies hurts profits, many wealth holders will shift out of domestic assets anyway, perhaps all at once, but without any coordination. Conversely, if policies do not threaten profitability, any shift will bear a cost equivalent to the expected profit from the abandoned asset, minus the expected return on the new one, plus transaction expenses. Capital flight therefore acts as a *deliberate* tool of pressure, as opposed to a method of increasing expected return, insofar as it costs something. This is not to deny that, in relatively small developing-country currency markets, a few big asset holders can destabilize things. It is to say that, unless some financial cabal truly "organizes" capital flight and forces a policy change favorable to itself immediately, as is sometimes alleged, agents either act in response to an economic incentive or they pay at least a short-term cost for their political protest.[40]

39. Notice that tax policies are better candidates for "political" flight (in this sense) than is the exchange rate. When faced with a speculative opportunity presented by expected devaluation, the movers of wealth are not trying to eliminate the perceived overvaluation. Why should they act politically to remove an incentive they apparently expect to profit from? They may, however, have reason to deny they are moving capital, avoiding the opprobrium of "speculation" or the chance of provoking exchange control.

40. Allegations of deliberate destabilization by a few agents have been quite common, especially in Mexico (see Chapter 3). For the most recent one to my knowledge, see the complaint of Rafael Caldera that "criminal hands" were at work in the rapid depreciation of the bolívar in the first week of May 1994 (Notiven Servicios por Día, on-line service, news of 9 May 1994). See also the remarks of Argentine Economy Minister Domingo Cavallo in late February 1991. Regarding the 1987 capital flight that took place as agents sold out of the Mexican stock market and bought dollars, Miguel Basáñez describes the small number of major brokerage houses that were "again capable of organizing capital flight on a large scale and provoking another devaluation of the currency." *El Pulso de los Sexenios: 20 Años de Crisis en México* (Mexico City: Siglo 21, 1990), p. 106. I would not deny that, by giving the same advice to their largest clients and trading on their own account, these agents could bring about a currency crisis in those months. The main point here is that if they produced a self-fulfilling prophecy of devaluation without an incentive implied in the peso's departure from a long-term equilibrium level, then the outflow reduced the profits of their clients—which in fact was probably the case after November 1987, given the huge real returns on Cetes (Mexican Treasury Certificates) over the following year as inflation declined, and the even greater dollar returns as the peso appreciated significantly in real terms (the last can be seen in Table 3.3). The brokers may well have come to similar but independent

Once out of the reach of the local authorities, the return of capital obeys similar considerations. Any shift has costs and benefits, but the prospect of capital return to a poor, indebted country constitutes a bargaining chip in the possession of its owner. The owner would rationally wait to invest domestically until he has been given some credible basis to expect a greater return on the repatriated capital than on its present form (the margin exceeding transaction cost plus risk premium). One might expect also that the likelihood of government compliance increases with the scale of the capital flight, for symmetrical reasons: a more decapitalized country needs overseas funds more badly; and as the stock of overseas resident capital is larger, so are the potential gains from regaining the confidence of its owners.

In these conditions a true negotiation is unlikely. While an organization of businessmen might claim to know the appropriate "lessons" of the capital flight and the policies necessary to get it back, it may err or even lie. If the question concerns only a reflow of capital into anonymous financial investments, the organization will not have the power to make good on a promise to reward certain policies because it does not control the portfolios of its members and cannot verify their disposition. Only if it commits its members to a certain level of fixed (and visible) investments can its promise be credible. Still, its guess on the necessary policy reforms is likely to be a good one and, of course, it *is* trying to influence policy by speaking for mobile capital.

Under these circumstances, the most likely pattern might be the following: *threat* of capital flight where domestic assets are relatively illiquid or profitable and "voice" is relatively cheap; *actual* capital flight when economic incentives such as those discussed above present themselves; and, finally, the *promise*—enforceable or not—of capital repatriation as a reward for good policies and revived profitability.

International capital mobility may be regarded as political in a third, fundamental sense, revolving around the issue of distribution. A basic premise of the political economy of finance has to be the following: asset markets are different. In this arena not only does the state have an abiding interest but the private sector is also present at its most unequal. Income distribution may tell us how, in relative

---

assessments of the market and, though proven wrong *ex post,* they were wrong because the government vigorously contradicted the conventional wisdom about election-year economic policy in 1988, undertaking a fiscal adjustment while holding labor and business to a pact. The move out of pesos looked pretty rational *ex ante.* For a brief summary of the 1987 episode, see *Unomásuno,* 18 April 1994, p. 18.

terms, everyone is getting along economically; but wealth distribution, everywhere more concentrated, gives us an essential datum for the measurement of power. Even in the United States, despite the undeniable prominence of pension funds, among households most stocks and bonds are held by a tiny minority. This is much more pronounced in Latin America, where income and property are even more concentrated, with some countries (Brazil, for example), on the former measure, among the least equitable in the world.[41] In Mexico, with income distribution in the middling-to-concentrated range for Latin America, a thousand families are said to hold most of the wealth.[42]

Late in the book I describe asset markets in Latin America as virtual senates, places where a narrow, internationally oriented elite of households and firms is "represented" and wields a veto over economic policy. I offer the metaphor in part to call attention to its limitations. While mobile money may win the kind of approval once extended to patricians or bodies of notables, its political power does not depend on conspiracy or even deliberation. Most important of all, it is based on the rule of one dollar equals one "vote." The latter deserves emphasis here because in one form or another the idea of representative money has deep and sturdy roots: it crops up, for example, whenever an economist or business reporter unself-consciously describes an event in the financial markets as reflecting "public" opinion about some government policy, even in a country as economically polarized as Mexico.[43] Here, then, is another sort of politics at work.

41. The U.S. income Gini coefficient (1980) is 0.33, that of Mexico (1984) 0.51, of Brazil (1979) 0.59. U.S., World Bank, *World Development Report 1988;* others: George Psacharopoulos et al., *Poverty and Income Distribution in Latin America: The Story of the 1980s,* Latin America and the Caribbean Technical Department Regional Studies Program, Report no. 27 (Washington, D.C.: World Bank, June 1993), p. 26. The U.S. net wealth Gini (1983) is 0.81, cited in Denis Kessler and Edward N. Wolff, "A Comparative Analysis of Household Wealth Patterns in France and the United States," *Review of Income and Wealth* 37, no. 3 (September 1991): 251. See also Vincent A. Mahler, "Income Distribution Within Nations: Problems of Cross-National Comparison," *Comparative Political Studies* 22, no. 1 (April 1989), table 1.

42. On wealth distribution in Mexico, see Luis Vega, cited in *Latin American Weekly Report,* 7 February 1991, p. 4.

43. Speaking of Mexico, William Cline said, "the financial crisis that forced a large devaluation after November was a message from the Mexican public that the rate was no longer credible and that the government has to reorder its priorities and make the control of inflation its primary objective" (Williamson, ed., *Latin American Adjustment,* p. 176).

Summary of the Book

The next chapter describes the context for capital mobility in Latin America. It has three sections. The first concerns changes in international finance since Bretton Woods, the second the regional pattern of industrialization during the same period, and the third, the Latin American pattern of financial integration, wealth distribution, and asset preference, described in contrast with that of East Asia. I argue, as others have, that the privatization of international balance-of-payments finance introduced two potential sources of instability, procyclicality and competition to lend. Abundant petrodollars prodded competing banks to dispose of loanable funds without much conditionality, while high commodity prices gave most Latin American countries an apparent creditworthiness. This was the case despite the fact that the model of inward-oriented industrialization was still largely in place in the region, a model in which exports had low priority and in which exchange policy had previously been used, in the long term unsuccessfully, to attract overseas capital. Within many borrowing countries in Latin America, a relative openness on capital account contrasted with the region's prevailing protectionism on trade, in a way that generally distinguished Latin American from East Asian industrializing countries. In Latin America the decisions of relatively few, internationally oriented asset holders could move the exchange markets significantly. These conditions, international and regional, tended to place a high premium on prudent economic policy.

Chapter 3 illustrates the last point, looking more closely at six countries, three of which had a lot of capital flight in 1980–83 and three, significantly less. Exchange policies account for much of the difference, and this chapter seeks to understand the structural and political origins of policy decisions in this area. It concludes that where exchange crises were small or absent during the 1950s and 1960s, they left undisturbed the old assumptions of import-substituting industrialization, which usually meant a fixed rate and, in Mexico and Venezuela, a free exchange market. In these countries policy continued to be determined by concerns for price stability and presidential prestige.

Crises were necessary but not sufficient to bring about policy change, however. Pro-export reforms became established best where the traditional export producers were both politically strong and vulnerable to international economic changes. This meant that they could support reform but were prepared to accept state intervention in the market in the name of export diversification. For Brazil and Colombia, world coffee problems meant that elites had less reason to fight for laissez-faire. Chilean rural elites depended on the state for protection and support and exported almost nothing, while the dominance of foreign mining companies in the export sector made any generalized pro-export policy unpopular. In Argentina, Pampa exporters suffered less than their counterparts in other countries from the international market; meanwhile, they had been traumatized by state intervention, especially under Perón. Export elites could reasonably argue that liberal policies would solve the country's balance-of-payments problems.

The survival of prudent exchange policies depended on the political results of success—the support of new export interests and state technocrats. By the late 1970s the newly permissive international lending environment tended to separate those countries in which the universal rhetoric of export promotion reflected established support from those in which it did not. Some governments revived an old strategy, using a combination of fixed exchange rates and open exchange markets as an invitation to international capital. Where states allowed other priorities—sometimes justified with reference to financial conditions—to lead them into gross currency overvaluation in a free exchange market, they suffered massive capital flight while borrowing abroad.

Chapter 4 examines the effect of mobile capital, and capital flight specifically, on the remarkable turn to economic liberalism in Latin America since about 1988. Did capital flight help "discipline" profligate governments, either by changing the preferences of the wealthy who held foreign assets or by quickening the lash of economic crisis? The chapter describes a rather strong correspondence between capital flight and subsequent liberal reform, and attributes this mainly to the contribution of flight to deepening and extending the debt crisis. This can be seen best in countries such as Argentina, Mexico, and Venezuela, which experienced recurrent capital outflows through the 1980s and later reformed a lot and quickly. Apart from these, ideas seem to have played a more important role in the reforms of Chile and Colombia, and in Brazilian resistance to change. Finally, the timing of the reforms had something to do with the fact that banks had begun to take losses in Latin America, thus toughening their stance in rescheduling negotiations, while the Brady Plan offered real rewards to reformers. It depended most of all, however, on the fact that governments had run out of options and, in some countries, hyperinflation made bold moves politically acceptable.

Chapter 5 considers the implications of mobile capital for political institutions. It first tries to pose clearly the political stake in the "discipline" of mobile money: it argues that Wriston and others appear to conceive of mobile capital as a kind of virtual senate, guarding property against arbitrary presidents and popular passions. Variants of this view also expect that governments, under market discipline, will build institutional safeguards for capital and people. Mobile capital would thus advance the rule of law. Noting instances in which this idea has been confirmed, I also argue that when property is held as narrowly as it is in much of Latin America, informal access to power may satisfy major players in the market without the advance of institutions of representation or those of law. While the market pressure of those with more capital than political access—chiefly foreign investors—may offer reasons for optimism in this regard, it is likely that most institutional reforms will still have to arise from political forces.

Chapter 6 summarizes the main themes and suggests some of the main implications of the previous arguments, in light of the Mexican crisis of 1994–95 and with reference to ideas about the political economy of development. It notes the reappearance of old patterns of exchange policy in contemporary Latin America, as the benefits of capital inflows force governments to choose between export promotion and accommodating overseas investors, with relatively few effective policy tools at hand. In considering the paradoxical fate of dependency writings at a time when developing countries are under greater international constraint in the choice of economic policies, the discussion turns to two important critiques of dependency views, relating to the East Asian experience and to the role of developing-country states in times of plenty. After noting the limitations of these critiques, I posit a partial model of international constraint, linking higher constraint to greater international asymmetry of financial market size and narrower distribution of domestic wealth. The chapter concludes with a consideration of the problem of the democratic legitimation of governments in economically stratified societies during an era of mobile capital.

Let me close my introduction with a few remarks about what kind of social science this is. Throughout this short book I return often to the theme of what I occasionally call structural influences on policy decisions. By "structures" I mean large patterns of economic specialization, income and wealth distribution, and economic culture, which do not change very quickly and which can be seen to vary meaningfully across regions. They are not just brute economic facts but durable patterns of material life and the institutions that regulate it.[44] The idea has some affinity with later dependency theory, but my use of it differs from dependency analysis on enough points that this resemblance may be misleading.

This work also intends to suggest certain causal relations by comparing a small number of instances. It boasts neither the apparent conclusiveness of a statistical inference nor the documentary and testimonial richness of close historical study. I hope that by combining a weak comparative inference with some focused, case-specific evidence, it manages to avoid falling between the two stools.[45] Breadth leaves one open to the charge of superficiality, of hiding an outsider's ignorance behind numbers or generalizations. I prefer to think that a broad and comparative view allows an observer to see unsuspected causal relations, to find common patterns in what others might have thought were local problems.

And of course this raises the issue of agency. Anyone who uses the word "structure" invites all the critiques brought to bear in the last decade against dependency theory: that of making it seem as if international forces controlled everything and domestic agents nothing; that of patronizing; or that of reinforcing Latin American "solitude."[46] I am temperamentally at odds with social science that makes excuses for bad actions. I agree that we ought to be offended by glib, poorly informed generalizations condemning other people to unrelieved misery at the mercy of big, blind historical forces.

The only problem, to my mind, is that there *are* big, blind historical forces out there. And just as understanding that there are circumstances beyond my own control need not lead me to despair or amorality, so indicating what may be "structural" about someone else's situation does not have to make us smug. When it comes to what we can and cannot change, as Reinhold Niebuhr's well-known prayer goes, wisdom lies in knowing the difference.

---

44. Thus I differ from the dominantly institutional connotation of Susan Strange's reference to "structural power" in "Finance, Information, and Power," *Review of International Studies* 16 (1990): 259–74.

45. By "case" here I do not mean a country but an event or pattern.

46. Tony Smith, "The Underdevelopment of Development Literature: The Case of Dependency Theory," *World Politics* 32 (1979): 257–58; the latter is a reference to García Márquez in Steve Stern, "Ever More Solitary," reply to Immanuel Wallerstein, *American Historical Review* 93 (1988): 897. See Stern's "Feudalism, Capitalism, and the World System in the Perspective of Latin America and the Caribbean" in the same issue, pp. 829–72.

2

International Capital and Latin American Development

The importance of international capital mobility to Latin American development did not arise suddenly in August 1982—or in December 1994. Nor are such moments rightly understood as the result of a few mistakes by presidents and finance ministers. In considering the role of international capital in Latin America's debt disaster of the last decade, it serves us well to distinguish between narrow, immediate causes and broader, structural ones. Mistakes by the debtors, yes, but the same mistakes in lots of countries; shortsightedness among bankers, too, yet nearly as short from one bank to the next; dismay and panic among the local wealthy in developing countries, but more crippling and acrimonious in Latin America than in many other regions.

In order to get at the broader causes, we may ask two fundamental questions. First, why did the lending market falter so dramatically in 1982? And second, why did its collapse begin in Latin America? In addressing the first question, I show (much as others have done) how the increasingly private character of international lending to middle-income developing countries created a potential for boom and bust. In responding to the second, I make two arguments. One of these looks at Latin America's postwar development strategy, noting the mismatch between increasingly complex economies and their continuing depen-dence, for their capacity to import, on a few primary commodities with volatile prices. The other compares Latin America, in very broad terms, with East Asian development after the late 1950s. Most an-swers to "Why Latin America?" stop at describing Latin American industrialization as overly closed to the world economy. But although Latin American economies were generally relatively closed on trade under the typical policy regime, they were nevertheless, on average, more open than their East Asian counterparts to capital flows. This, I will argue, relates to important and enduring structural features of the region: the early presence of multinational banks and other corporations, and the international orientation of an elite that pos-sessed an unusually high proportion of the region's wealth.

Before proceeding, let me again clarify the explanatory status of these propositions. Neither international nor regional characteristics explain variation across the six countries considered in the next two chapters. They cannot tell us why some experienced a great deal of capital flight while others did not, or why some later moved toward economic liberalism more decisively than others. However, considered together, such factors may help account for the immense scale of the panic outflows, the depth of the 1980s debt crisis, and, perhaps, the fact that it broke out in Latin America. They may also help us understand some of the challenges that will persist for many countries in the region, even if their marriages to free-market economic policies turn out to be both faithful and long-lasting—a topic to which I will return in the last two chapters.

The first section summarizes the evolution of the world financial regime in the postwar period, concentrating on the part of the story relating to the profile of international capital flows. The second describes the overall trend of exchange policies in the major countries of Latin America since the Depression, especially as they related to the strategy of deliberate, protected, import-substituting industrialization (henceforth ISI) that was pursued in the postwar period. The last section discusses Latin American development in comparative terms, emphasizing ele-ments of the contrast with East Asia that are rarely mentioned but that may be important to consider whenever we are asked to make the East Asian miracle into a model for developing countries.

The International Regime and Private Capital Flows

It is not news that international finance has changed immensely since 1944. Conceived in depression and war, the Bretton Woods monetary regime assumed that international regulation of exchange policies was a good thing. Coordination, it was thought, could avoid the competitive trade restrictions, beggar-thy-neighbor devaluations, and financial volatility that marked the 1930s. However, in the postwar period private international actors have eclipsed multilateral ones and financial volatility has gradually returned.[1] World foreign exchange transactions became increasingly divorced from international trade. Most important for our purposes, by the mid-1970s private actors came to dominate balance-of-payments lending to middle-income developing countries, displacing the IMF and creating the conditions for overlending, debt crisis, and massive capital flight. The situation placed a high premium on the borrowers' adoption of domestic policies adequate to deal with the new, more changeable financial environment.

In view of the debt crisis, the warnings of Depression-era observers may sound especially apt. Many thought that the 1930s proved the wisdom of insulating national monetary systems from all short-term international capital flows outside of normal trade. In a famous and gloomy article in 1933, Keynes said that "advisable domestic policies might often be easier to compass, if the phenomenon known as 'the flight of capital' could be ruled out."[2] H. W. Arndt, describing France of the mid-1930s, noted that falling tax revenue caused deficits that frightened orthodox-minded wealth holders into periodic runs on the franc, which in turn "completely offset the potential favorable effect of the budget deficit in maintaining consumer purchasing power."[3] In a similar vein, a 1944 League of Nations study concluded that "what may have to be prevented are the massive one-way movements, usually self-aggravating in character, which serve no useful social function and which may wreck any orderly system of international

1. The argument in this section is similar on many points to that of Stephany Griffith-Jones and Oswaldo Sunkel, *Debt and Development Crisis in Latin America* (New York: Oxford University Press, 1986), chaps. 4, 6.

2. John Maynard Keynes, "National Self-Sufficiency," *The Yale Review* 22, no. 4 (June 1933): 757. For a discussion, see James R. Crotty, "On Keynes and Capital Flight," *Journal of Economic Literature* 21 (March 1983): 59–65.

3. H. W. Arndt, *The Economic Lessons of the Nineteen-Thirties* (1944; reprint, London: Frank Cass and Co., 1972), pp. 140–43. See also Martin Wolfe, *The French Franc Between the Wars, 1919–1939* (New York: Columbia University Press, 1951), reprinted by AMS Press, 1968.

monetary relations."[4] The authors (Ragnar Nurkse preeminent among them) observed that international lending had also shown a perverse procyclical pattern, as "withdrawals of private credits from debtor countries are apt to occur at a time when foreign credits are most needed," and they noted the joke then current in southeastern Europe that compared foreign credit to an umbrella that a person may keep until it starts raining, at which time the lender demands its immediate return.[5]

Such qualms about procyclical flows and financial volatility would find only partial satisfaction in the IMF Articles of Agreement.[6] Compromise had to be reached among everyone's interest in postwar stability, the Europe-centered views noted above, and the interests of U.S. bankers and traders in maximizing the benefits they could derive from the country's overwhelming financial preeminence. The Articles showed a primary concern with protecting fixed rates and the IMF's resources, expressing a distrust of unfettered private capital only inasmuch as it affected these goals. They permitted controls on current transactions during a transition period of five years (Article XIV), after which members would have to consult with the Fund with a view toward eventual elimination of such restrictions (accepting the obligations of Article VIII). As for movements on capital account (Article VI), controls were expressly allowed: indeed, under some circumstances, such as a massive capital outflow, they could be "requested" as a condition of access to Fund resources.[7]

The effect of the war in fortifying norms of *raison d'état* at the expense of financial liberalism did not wear off immediately, even in the United States. As aid to Europe became an issue in the U.S. Congress in 1947–48, the Truman administration agreed to share information on some flight capital assets of Europeans in the United States. Although American bankers and the Treasury Secretary opposed the idea on grounds of private property rights and banker-client

4. League of Nations, Economic, Financial and Transit Department, *International Currency Experience: Lessons of the Interwar Period* (Geneva: League of Nations, 1944), p. 189.

5. Ibid., pp. 187, 187 n. 2.

6. Armand Van Dormael, *Bretton Woods: Birth of a Monetary System* (New York: Holmes and Meier, 1978).

7. J. Keith Horsefield, *The International Monetary Fund 1945–1965* (Washington, D.C.: IMF, 1969), 1:93–110; Fred L. Block, *The Origins of International Economic Disorder: A Study of United States International Monetary Policy from World War Two to the Present* (Berkeley and Los Angeles: University of California Press, 1977), p. 51; Kenneth A. Dam, *The Rules of the Game* (Chicago: University of Chicago Press, 1982), p. 100.

privilege, pressure to ease the tax burden of the Marshall Plan proved decisive. Important legislators in both parties defended the wallets of U.S. taxpayers against the interests of "bloated, selfish" European elites.[8] Much about the case marked it as exceptional, yet the U.S. government did act against the interests of private bankers in this instance.[9]

In the postwar period the multilateral Bretton Woods regime first yielded to the rules of private finance in the United States and later in Western Europe. The trend appeared earliest of all in the Fund's own handling of exchange control issues. United States bankers' opposition to capital controls, based on their fear of a loss of international financial discipline, passed through the reliably liberal U.S. Treasury Department and thus affected the operations of the Fund almost immediately: in 1946 a U.S. Treasury draft proposal of Fund regulations, according to critical directors from the U.K. and Canada, "betrayed a comprehensive suspicion of every form of exchange control."[10] After 1958, with European convertibility achieved, the trend away from capital controls continued. According to the IMF's official historian: "Although the Fund's Articles permitted controls on capital movements, liberalization was gradually extended even to these. A view that had been dominant before 1930 began to gain ground, namely, that freedom of capital movements was highly desirable in itself."[11] The Eurodollar lending market then accentuated the trend in the 1960s. Sophisticated and offshore, it lay beyond national or Fund regulation. The privatization of international finance pushed ahead rapidly. Ironically, as one observer has noted, "the very success of

8. Eric Helleiner, "Repatriating Flight Capital and the Role of the Receiving Country: Comparing U.S. Policy During the Marshall Plan and the Latin American Debit Crisis," Trent University, Peterborough, Ontario, 1993, photocopy, pp. 4–10; quote from *European Recovery Program*, Senate Committee on Foreign Relations, January 1948, p. 399, in ibid., p. 9.

9. Helleiner notes a strategic consideration, namely that an alternative policy, greater monetary orthodoxy in Western Europe, would have aided the Communist cause there (ibid., p. 11). It is also clear that war conditions were a factor—since the only assets ultimately to be mobilized were the ones already "blocked" in 1941, whose owners might be supposed to have been rich collaborators, especially in France, now discredited or in jail (see ibid., pp. 12–14).

10. Horsefield, *The International Monetary Fund*, 1:152–53 (emphasis added). On bankers see Block, *The Origin of International Economic Disorder*, p. 53. Cf. Jeffry A. Frieden, *Banking on the World: The Politics of American International Finance* (New York: Harper and Row, 1987), p. 76.

11. Margaret G. DeVries, *The IMF in a Changing World* (Washington, D.C.: International Monetary Fund, 1986), p. 35 (emphasis added); for a similar statement, see Horsefield, *The International Monetary Fund*, 1:504.

international banking eventually undermined the regime that had helped to get it started in the first place. . . . as capital mobility accelerated, the private sector began to play an ever greater role in determining both exchange rates and access to liquidity."[12]

Most important in the present context, in the 1970s the privatization trend widened to include many middle-income developing countries, relieving them of the need to face Fund discipline when borrowing internationally. While the IMF still possessed great potential influence on the foreign exchange policies of these countries, this potential was realized only insofar as they required its help in overcoming payments problems. Fewer and fewer of them did. Especially after the injection of petrodollars into the Euromarket after 1973, they found commercial financing plentiful. Meanwhile, despite the creation of the Compensatory Financing and Extended Funds Facilities, Fund quotas (upon which the amounts in the new facilities were based) were themselves left to lag behind the growth of the world economy. Measuring 16 percent of world trade in 1944, the quotas made up only 4 percent of it in 1980.[13] The result: in the 1974–79 period only about 3 percent of the financing for all developing countries was provided by the IMF.[14] In the words of one observer, "the Fund confronted a crisis of clientele" as these countries turned to the commercial banks, which offered more loan capital and on more favorable terms.[15]

Still, many resisted the notion that the privatization of international finance could mean a *loosening* of discipline. After all, it directly contradicted the main premise behind private bankers' criticism of the Bretton Woods institutions. Leading international bankers now expressed optimism about the conditionality that private banks could impose. One predicted that "if [banks] are reluctant to lend, they will often explain why. . . . if changes are desired by lenders, these changes will be inferred or stated explicitly."[16] One might guess that the very profitability of the new recycling practices meant that they would probably be defended vigorously from within the banks. Whatever

---

12. Benjamin J. Cohen, *In Whose Interest? International Banking and American Foreign Policy* (New Haven: Yale University Press, 1986), p. 69.

13. Griffith-Jones and Sunkel, *Debt and Development Crisis*, p. 104.

14. Dam, *The Rules of the Game*, pp. 296–97.

15. Tyrone Ferguson, *The Third World and Decision Making in the IMF: The Quest for Full and Effective Participation* (London: Pinter, 1988), p. 208.

16. Irving S. Friedman, "Private Bank Conditionality: Comparison with the IMF and the World Bank," chap. 6 in *IMF Conditionality*, ed. John Williamson (Washington, D.C.: Institute for International Economics, 1983), p. 119.

their motivation, the sanguine predictions proved catastrophically wrong.[17]

The problem was that by the end of the 1970s, international financial flows had become prone to two kinds of instability, both of which Bretton Woods had intended to abolish. Both also derived from the dominantly private character of international medium- to long-term lending. They gathered strength even as many countries kept regulating their exchange rates under some form of the old Bretton Woods rules. The first, procyclicality of flows, showed up most egregiously where private bankers competed to lend to countries with trade and current-account surpluses. Here the private market discarded the basic rationale of balance-of-payments financing—even as the defenders of private petrodollar recycling pronounced it efficient and socially productive. The procyclicality issue became especially relevant in countries whose exports remained (or became) highly concentrated in one or a few primary goods—which described much of Latin America, for reasons I will note in the next section. It led to the possibility that lending decisions might reinforce downturns in exports (and fiscal revenues), as in petroleum-exporting countries, denying the countries resources just when they most needed them (and helping to trigger capital flight on the bad news).[18]

The second, more widespread danger lay in the suddenly huge supply of loanable funds, which caused vigorous bank competition for borrowers. Combined with perverse tax incentives and poor information about total indebtedness, this meant that during the boom of the late 1970s, and despite the warnings of prominent regulators, banks granted commercial loans "with basically no economic policy conditions."[19] A German bank spokesman said in 1979 that "the apparently

17. Notable among the doubters was the journal *International Currency Review*, where one could find some of the most prescient and biting criticisms of contemporary lending practices (and of *Euromoney* for its uncritical boosterism). See vol. 12, no. 4 (1980), p. 141, on "the insatiable appetite for self-deception" among Brazil's creditors; vol. 12, no. 6 (1980), p. 146, on the perversity of Euromarket lending to Venezuela's public sector; and finally, vol. 14, no. 3 (1982), pp. 46–49, for the we-told-you-so "The *ICR* Warnings Bankers Ignored."

18. Griffith-Jones and Sunkel, *Debt and Development Crisis*, pp. 100–1.

19. On tax incentives, see Karin Lissakers, *Banks, Borrowers, and the Establishment: A Revisionist Account of the International Debt Crisis* (New York: Basic Books, 1991), chap. 5. The quote is from Margaret G. DeVries, *Balance of Payments Adjustment, 1945 to 1986: The IMF Experience* (Washington, D.C.: International Monetary Fund, 1987), p. 163. She adds that in the opinion of the fund management and staff, this abundance of commercial credit with few or no conditions was the reason for the decline in fund

inexhaustible supply of liquidity in the Euromarkets leads to temptation. . . . Instead of urging deficit countries to knock on the door of the IMF, the banks themselves continue to lend out money."[20] According to Robert Devlin, "the market . . . seems to have been capable of giving clear warnings and imposing discipline only when the borrower approached the credit limits of *the banking system as a whole*."[21] The loan market gave governments with large fiscal deficits or overvalued currencies little reason to adjust. Many of the countries whose "bad policies" were later held responsible for the debt crisis actually received easier terms than more "responsible" countries.[22]

As Chapter 3 notes, until mid-to-late 1981 bank enthusiasm often gave leaders of borrowing countries a reason, or an excuse, for what later would be seen as reckless borrowing and foreign exchange policies. Paul Volcker relates a story about how Mexican financial officials, alarmed in late 1980 at the rapid debt buildup, urged President López Portillo to cut back on borrowing. He asked his friends about it, who consulted bankers, who said they saw no problems. The president then rejected the advice of his worried subordinates.[23]

All of this took place as the transaction costs on international capital transfers declined. They did so, in part, because of obvious technological advances such as improved international telephone connections and the use of computers in foreign exchange trading. But there were other forces at work, too. Within developing countries, dollars became more widely available: in Argentina, for instance,

---

lending and the increased criticism of its conditionality provisions (which included management of foreign indebtedness). Had the fund been lending, its provisions would have regulated total debt and overall term structure. See also Cohen, *In Whose Interest?* pp. 209–10. One well-known warning came in mid-1978 from John Heimann, chief of the U.S. Office of the Comptroller of the Currency, who proposed that for the regulation limiting single-country bank exposure to 10 percent of capital, all state companies be considered as one entity. Under pressure from banks (who spoke of a loss of business to Japan and Western Europe), and with protests coming from big debtors, he dropped the proposal (*Latin America Economic Report*, 18 August 1978).

20. Wilfred Guth of Deutsche Bank, quoted in Otmar Emminger, "The International Debt Crisis and the Banks," *Intereconomics* 20 (May/June 1985): 109.

21. Robert Devlin, *Debt and Crisis in Latin America: The Supply Side of the Story* (Princeton: Princeton University Press, 1989), pp. 64, 106–7, 111, 121–23, quote is from p. 107, emphasis in original. See also David T. Llewellyn, "The International Capital Transfer Mechanism of the 1970s: A Critique," in *The International Financial Regime*, ed. Graham Bird (London: Surrey University, 1990), pp. 38–40.

22. Devlin, *Debt and Crisis in Latin America*, p. 111, showing the Euromoney rankings of February 1981 and February 1982.

23. Paul A. Volcker and Toyoo Gyohten, *Changing Fortunes: The World's Money and the Threat to American Leadership* (New York: Times Books, 1992), p. 197.

whereas one could buy dollars only in Buenos Aires in the 1950s, two decades later they could be found even in the tiniest provincial towns.[24] The international (and internationally oriented domestic) banks built more branches and sought foreign deposits more aggressively. And as one might expect, the leading banks in international lending also tended to have important international private banking departments. In New York the big banks created special departments for handling visitors and would meet their most privileged customers at the airport with a limousine.[25] Even in Mexico, where only Citibank had a full-fledged branch, in the early 1980s private bankers often visited wealthy businessmen at their offices, inviting them to open dollar accounts.[26] People also reduced their own transaction costs with experience. Perhaps initially motivated to shift assets by an earlier traumatic episode of populism, they soon learned the ropes and would thereafter find it less daunting and costly to place money abroad again, perhaps now in much larger amounts.

This was the international context that put a high premium on sound and pragmatic economic policies among the borrowing countries during the critical years of the borrowing boom. Though each of the six countries considered in the next chapter enjoyed record foreign exchange reserves because of high export prices and loans, some were more inclined to caution and resisted the temptation to double public spending or fight inflation with shortsighted foreign exchange policy. Meanwhile, the sheer size of the private balance-of-payments lending had raised the stakes. It made it possible for small differences in debtor countries' economic policies to have multibillion-dollar consequences.

As is well known, the explosion of the debt bomb in mid-1982 brought rapid changes in the organization of finance for developing countries. The banks ceased voluntary lending to Latin America while the IMF became the organizer of rescues and then the official approver of policies in debtor countries seeking to reschedule or obtain fresh funds. At the same time, as private capital continued to flow out of most of the region, the U.S. government enacted policies welcoming it. In July 1984 the Reagan administration, facing the need to finance a growing fiscal deficit and predisposed toward free capital, abolished

24. Interview, José María Dagnino Pastore, Buenos Aires, 13 July 1987.
25. *Foreign Broadcast Information Service Latin America*, 28 June 1989, p. 44; translated from *Veja*, 31 May 1989.
26. Interview, Jesús Silva Herzog, 11 February 1987. This aspect of the debt crisis has been well described by James S. Henry. See his "Where the Money Went," *New Republic*, 14 April 1986, and "Poor Man's Debt, Rich Man's Loot," *Washington Post* 11 December 1988, p. C1.

the 30 percent withholding tax on interest income accruing to nonresidents on U.S. debt securities, and in 1985 it made such securities available to foreigners in bearer form.[27] This placed indebted governments under additional pressure to grant tax holidays at a time when the weight of debt service claimed a rising portion of fiscal revenues. The international context had become even more difficult for governments trying to keep domestic capital at home.

The Shaping of Economic Policy in Postwar Latin America

For a decade it has been common to criticize the dominant postwar Latin American development strategy as too closed and too inward-oriented. A favorite target of this critique has been the overvaluation of exchange rates, especially where they are supported by exchange controls. This argument has substantial merit, but it also has its limits. International private banks did not shy away from Latin America on account of bad development policy, and their enthusiasm actually helped appreciate the region's currencies in the crucial years before August 1982. Foreign investors have always liked stable nominal currency values, and especially if looking to the short term, they have often benefited from real currency appreciation too.

Yet the critique of ISI is right in one regard: the typical ISI policies in postwar Latin America made the region especially vulnerable to financial disturbances. They did so because they failed to diversify and expand exports, leaving the fate of the balance of payments closely tied to the volatile prices of a few primary commodities. This problem became especially acute as international financial integration proceeded—a process that included not only newly attentive foreign lenders but also, among Latin America's wealthy, a more widely shared desire for (and access to) foreign assets. Hence the key point is not about "inwardness" or "outwardness" but the *character* and *mix* of each. To see this better, let us look back at the forces shaping Latin American development strategy since the Depression.

The Depression dealt a threefold blow to Latin American economies.

27. Helleiner, "Repatriating Flight Capital," p. 21; Charles E. McLure, Jr., "U.S. Tax Laws and Capital Flight from Latin America," *Interamerican Law Review* 20, no. 2 (1989); *Christian Science Monitor,* 27 March 1989, p. 9.

The region's terms of trade deteriorated; the volume of exports fell off sharply; and there was a severe cutback in new international lending. Governments first tried to balance the state budgets and maintain investor confidence, but especially after Britain went off gold in September 1931, they devalued and (except in Mexico) turned to some form of exchange control.[28] Exchange control helped direct available hard currency to foreign creditors. Currency depreciations in depressed economies led to rather durable shifts in relative prices, and import substitution accelerated.[29] Industry became a larger sector of the region's economy.

It should be noted in passing that the political changes of the decade, significant as they were, did not have much independent effect on the making of foreign exchange policy. To Díaz-Alejandro,

> the balance-of-payments crisis and the threat of financial collapse were of greater significance in the adoption of [devaluation and exchange control] than whether the new governments which came to power during the 1930's represented a shift to the right, as in Argentina, or toward more reformist positions as in Colombia and Mexico. . . . [Use of these policies] depended on the magnitude of the foreign-exchange and financial crisis, and on country-specific characteristics of the external sector.[30]

The three countries hit hardest by foreign exchange crisis in the 1930s were Brazil, Chile, and Colombia. Here, in Thorp's words, "a foreign exchange constraint clearly 'bit' and strongly influenced policy."[31] (Interestingly, although the story is much more complicated than this suggests, these three also experienced relatively little capital flight during 1980–82.)

World War II altered the picture. Exchange problems following the outbreak of hostilities had eased by 1941–42. European refugee capital, U.S. commodity agreements, the lack of imports from the belligerents, and some new industrial exports added up to a net inflow of funds to the region. By the end of the war, the major countries had

28. This discussion draws upon my "Capital Flight and the Politics of Exchange Policy in Six Latin American Countries, 1930–1983," Ph.D. dissertation, University of California at Berkeley, 1989, chap. 1 and to a lesser extent, chaps. 3–8.

29. Carlos Díaz-Alejandro, "Latin America in the 1930s," in *Latin America in the 1930s: The Role of the Periphery in World Crisis,* ed. Rosemary Thorp (London: Macmillan, 1984), p. 24.

30. Ibid., p. 47.

31. Ibid., p. 3.

record levels of foreign exchange reserves. But they had also postponed a lot of demand for imported investment and consumer goods, and the wages of their swelling industrial work forces had been held behind inflation during the war years. Moreover, in most major countries (except Argentina) price inflation outpaced that of the United States during the 1940–46 period, while exchange rates stayed fixed; hence the goods they had gone without now also seemed cheap in terms of appreciated domestic currencies.[32] By the end of the war, then, the stage was set for the outbreak of another series of foreign exchange crises.

Between the Depression and the end of World War II the forces shaping Latin American industrialization had changed fundamentally. During the 1930s the main spur to import substitution was a change in relative prices, brought on by a shortage of foreign exchange. By contrast, during most of the war years what was scarce was not hard currency but goods on which to spend it.

Governments now found that the path of least economic and political resistance led them to preserve artificially the import scarcity experienced during the war. Above all, devaluation was strenuously avoided. Economically, there were good reasons to expect this move to prove costly in the short to medium term: "elasticity pessimism" about the supply response of a country's existing primary-commodity exports; a similar problem on the demand side for the biggest producers (Brazil in coffee, for instance); and, where the export sector was in foreign hands (for example, Chile until 1971), the application of overvalued rates to the domestic expenditures of the foreign firms, which constituted an easy tax.[33] Politically, while the United States had some interest in pushing against devaluations in Latin America, the measure's most important opponents were generally urban consumers.[34]

32. Raymond Mikesell, on the U.S. staff at Bretton Woods, later wrote that then-overvalued exchange rates in much of Latin America were allowed to stand because the Fund "evidently believed that stability of exchange rates was more significant than an appropriate rate pattern." See "The International Monetary Fund," *Journal of Political Economy* 57, no. 5 (October 1949): 397.

33. The "elasticity pessimism" term refers to the expectation that an export commodity's total supply will not expand commensurate with the rise in domestic prices. More formally, devaluation will have a positive expenditure-switching effect on the trade balance if the Marshall-Lerner condition holds—the sum of import and export price elasticities (of demand and supply, respectively) exceeds unity. The crucial factor here is time: while the expectation of ISI advocates was usually correct in the short term, the longer-term stagnation of exports in the 1950s and 1960s also reflected a response to disadvantageous prices.

34. On the first point, C. Fred Bergsten notes that "in the previous days of dollar-

In contrast to the 1930s, two decades of industrial growth (and a decade and a half of reduced or interrupted trade) meant that policy was now influenced less by the traditional export and commercial elites and more by industrialists and urban labor. For labor the issue was clear-cut: since devaluations would accelerate inflation, they would also tend to depress real wages as nominal wage corrections inevitably lagged. Hence labor and the new industrialists favored exchange policies that overvalued the rate and penalized exporters.

This implied an import-substitution model whose chief instruments were protection and subsidy rather than a reliance on relative price effects.[35] Many governments instituted multiple exchange rate systems and exchange controls to make selected imports (industrial inputs) available and relatively cheap. The systems generally featured penalty rates for luxury consumer goods and traditional exports, with the latter carrying the main burden of supporting industry.[36]

However, under this regime one of the major drawbacks of the old export model—the dependence of a country's capacity to import on a narrow range of primary commodities—persisted or even worsened. Export revenue stagnated or declined in many countries in the second half of the 1950s and the early 1960s (see Table 3.2). Balance-of-payments crises became a regular problem, marked by capital flight, speculation in goods, denials of credit by foreign bankers, negotiations with the IMF, unpopular devaluations, and dismissals of finance ministers.[37]

---

based fixed exchange rates, the U.S.—to the extent that it concerned itself at all with the effect of Latin American monetary policies on the U.S. economy—wanted the Latins to avoid depreciations, which would both raise at least marginal doubt about the fixed-rate system and hurt U.S. trade competitiveness in the region." See *Toward a New International Economic Order: Selected Papers of C. Fred Bergsten, 1972–1974* (Lexington, Mass.: Lexington Books, 1975), p. 433. The second point is a common argument that draws upon Richard N. Cooper, *Currency Devaluation in Developing Countries,* Princeton Essays in International Finance no. 86 (Princeton: Princeton University Press, June 1971), and Albert O. Hirschman, "The Political Economy of Import-Substituting Industrialization in Latin America," *Quarterly Journal of Economics* 82, no. 1 (February 1968), and *A Bias for Hope* (New Haven: Yale University Press, 1971); it has recently been summarized by Jeffrey Sachs, "Social Conflict and Populist Policies in Latin America," NBER Working Paper 2897 (Cambridge, Mass.: National Bureau of Economic Research, March 1989).

35. A benchmark on this topic is Werner Baer, "Import Substitution and Industrialization in Latin America: Experiences and Interpretations," *Latin American Research Review* 7, no. 1 (Spring 1972).

36. Wolfgang König, "Multiple Exchange Rate Policies in Latin America," *Journal of Interamerican Studies* 10 (1968): 35–52.

37. Especially on the last point, see Cooper, *Currency Devaluation in Developing Countries,* p. 29.

Equally important to the present argument was the financial effect of export concentration. A narrow range of exports made it more likely that commodity price changes would be aggravated in the currency market by financial flows. Goods traded in New York and London had their prices posted daily. These were followed closely in financial circles not only in Europe and the United States, but also in the countries exporting the commodities.[38] Wherever one such commodity dominated a country's balance of payments, it facilitated speculation against the exchange rate. The resulting volatility further jeopardized export diversification, which demanded not only a depreciated real exchange rate but also a predictable one. Thus while dependence on one export created fertile ground for destabilizing currency speculation, the possibility of overcoming this situation depended to some extent on suppressing the speculation.[39]

Two strategies emerged as governments sought to deal with their repeated exchange crises. The first involved enhanced incentives for foreign finance and a prominent role for its local counterpart. An Argentine observer remarked bitterly that with the appearance of balance-of-payments problems, "the local [financial] intermediary sector turns itself into the axis of economic policy and the savior of the country."[40] The package typically was initiated with a large devaluation to a fixed rate and a full opening of the exchange market. Thus, as officials publicly embraced economic liberty, they could also promise price stabilization around the new rate anchor while winning plaudits internationally. Real currency appreciation would follow,

38. For example, Chile's leading daily newspaper, *El Mercurio,* always posted a graph showing the evolution of the London copper price, right next to one of equal size showing the path of its stock market index. Some U.S. observers have considered a similar reaction to technological change. When an inexpensive foreign substitute to a country's main export is discovered, domestic asset holders shift their capital abroad in response. Here the outflows do not result from "distortionary policies" and represent "an economically efficient response to an event that altered the profitability of investing domestically." See David B. Gordon and Ross Levine, "The 'Problem' of Capital Flight—A Cautionary Note," *World Economy* 12, no. 2 (June 1989): 245. The resulting rapid depreciation would be efficient in the sense of providing the surest signal to other potential producers of exports. In the case of cyclical fluctuations, governments saw less justification for weathering the political effects of periodically steep income decline and unpredictable inflation.

39. Only part of the problem would be solved by placing minor exports in a thin and volatile free market. Although the free rates would be much more favorable to exports, they would be more variable also, exposing prospective exporters to greater uncertainty.

40. Marcelo Diamand, *Doctrinas Económicas, Desarrollo e Independencia: Economía para las Estructuras Productivas Desequilibradas: Caso Argentino* (Buenos Aires: Paidós, 1973), p. 402.

pleasing consumers; and if foreigners could accelerate their returns before the currency was devalued again, they too could expect to reap large gains.[41] Fundamentally the feasibility of this strategy depended, as Albert Fishlow has observed, on the relative lack of price responsiveness among the dominantly raw-material exports of the region, allowing a "Latin American tendency to use the [exchange rate] for other purposes."[42]

The alternate, export-promotion strategy generally faced bigger political obstacles. Reorienting exchange policy to favor exports meant seeking real over nominal exchange-rate stability. Now it is true that export diversification nearly always figured in the list of goals recited by heads of state in their inaugural addresses. In addition, most governments in the region had taken some steps to favor minor exports through tax exemptions, tariff refunds, or direct subsidies. Yet apart from the fact that subsidies required officials to identify the likely new export possibilities beforehand, the more serious export orientation needed to combine such measures with a more fundamental revision of exchange-rate policy.[43] Here the cost of export promotion could not be entirely diffused through the fisc. A real rate target entailed more than lip service and called for a stronger commitment than would the common subsidies or tax breaks. Politicians had to stop defending the national currency and adopt a strategy that would hurt labor in the short run and whose greatest immediate beneficiaries would be the traditional export sector—the "oligarchy" or the "foreign mining trusts." Finally, many officials became convinced that exchange controls, especially on capital account, should be part of the pro-export package in order to keep relative prices for minor exporters more

41. This assumes that local interest rates would fall relatively slowly. It also implies that the investors were to buy into nontradeables, heavily protected industries, or financial assets with controlled prices. Elsewhere (in exports or import-competing industry), the real appreciation would tend to diminish profitability. The best discussion of this and its political context, specifically in relation to the Krieger Vasena reforms of March 1967 in Argentina, is Guillermo O'Donnell, *Bureaucratic Authoritarianism: Argentina, 1966–1973, in Comparative Perspective,* trans. James McGuire (Berkeley and Los Angeles: University of California Press, 1988), pp. 97–98, 109–10.

42. He continues, "if there was an automatic effect, positive and negative, then there would be greater discipline." See Albert Fishlow, "Some Reflections on Comparative Latin American Economic Performance and Policy," in *Economic Liberalization: No Panacea: The Experiences of Latin America and Asia,* ed. Tariq Banuri (Oxford: Clarendon Press, 1991), p. 163.

43. This can be seen for Mexico in Rafael Jiménez Ramos, "Promoción de las Exportaciones Manufactureras de México, 1970–1986," *Comercio Exterior* 37, no. 8 (August 1987): 666–73.

predictable. But if the external balance turned favorable, they would face pressure from commercial interests who declared the exchange emergency over and controls unjustified.

As the next chapter shows, pro-finance exchange policy was politically and economically easier than a pro-export strategy. The former option also more closely resembled the pattern of policies in countries that suffered a lot of capital flight as the crisis broke. It was the other, export-promotion strategy in exchange policy, initiated in the 1960s and confirmed in the 1970s, that would later help avoid the worst capital flight associated with the first years of the debt crisis. This is not too surprising, given the similarity of the earlier crises to the later one. In this way, policy changes that responded effectively to previous "rehearsals" proved their worth when the curtain rose on the big drama after 1979.

Comparing Latin America and East Asia

The previous discussion relates to an important contrast between Latin America and East Asia, one that is rarely mentioned when East Asia is held up as a model for developing countries. According to the prevailing critique of Latin America's postwar development, these countries persisted too long with protected ISI. Some of the political-economic reasons for this have been mentioned previously, and as I will discuss below, on these points Latin America and East Asia contrasted quite strongly. However, I will also emphasize several other factors that are more closely linked to the behavior of international capital flows: Latin America's earlier ties with multinational corporations (MNCs) in banking and manufacturing; its notably more cosmopolitan elite; and the related fact that the Latin American model of ISI was in important ways significantly more open to the world economy on capital account than on trade—a pattern opposite that of East Asia. Let us begin with issues of economic strategy and proceed to those relating to capital flows.

Many accounts of the interregional contrast begin with income distribution or, relatedly, with land tenure. On the former the difference with East Asia is pronounced and, given the results of the debt crisis in Latin America, generally increasing.[44] As for land, most of

44. A recent study found increases in Gini coefficients over the 1980s for all major countries except Colombia (from the latter's urban data). See George Psacharopoulos,

Latin America, as opposed to Taiwan or South Korea (or China), has had no sweeping, peasant-based land reforms in this century. It is fair to attribute this, in part, to a long and relatively successful period of primary-product export that strengthened landholders locally and nationally, the latter because in many countries they owned the key resources for earning foreign exchange.[45]

Some have also assigned great importance to land distribution in accounting for the interregional contrast in development strategies. Jeffrey Sachs suggests that the prevalence of smallholders in the countryside of Taiwan and South Korea created a broad political base for currency devaluation, since this would have favored import-competing and exporting sectors in rice and other primary goods. This contrasted with the pattern in Latin America, as already noted, where an export-oriented strategy centered on real depreciation would have delivered a windfall to rural elites or foreign mining companies. Under ISI, these groups had weakened politically, relative to urban groups, above all labor. The first step in a reorientation of policy toward export promotion would have hurt these important new interests and would have offended nationalists.[46] Thus, according to this view, it was hard for Latin American governments to make what proved to be the right choice for the next three or four decades, in part because of concentrated property-holding in the sector exporting primary goods.

Samuel Morley, Ariel Fiszbein, Haeduck Lee, and Bill Wood, "Poverty and Income Distribution in Latin America: The Story of the 1980s," Latin America and the Caribbean Technical Department Report no. 27 (Washington, D.C.: World Bank, June 1993). Another recent summary concludes, "all the evidence points to persistent, even growing inequality in the distribution of income" in Latin America. Eliana Cardoso and Ann Helwege, "Below the Line: Poverty in Latin America," *World Development* 20, no. 1 (January 1992): 26. An earlier study concluded that income concentration actually increased in Latin America over the 1950s and 1960s, as growth benefited the top decile disproportionately. See Adolfo Figueroa and Richard Weisskopf, "Viewing Social Pyramids: Income Distribution in Latin America," in *Consumption and Income Distribution in Latin America: Selected Topics,* ed. Robert Ferber (Washington, D.C.: Organization of American States, 1980). See also United Nations Economic Commission for Latin America (UN ECLA), *Income Distribution in Latin America* (New York: United Nations, 1971). On income and wealth distributions in East Asia, see Robert R. Kaufman and Barbara Stallings, "The Political Economy of Latin American Populism," in *The Macroeconomics of Populism in Latin America,* ed. Rudiger Dornbusch and Sebastian Edwards (Chicago: University of Chicago Press, 1991), pp. 19–20, and the works cited in Sachs, "Social Conflict and Populist Policies."

45. Peter Evans, "Class, State, and Dependence in East Asia: Lessons for Latin Americanists," in *The Political Economy of the New Asian Industrialism,* ed. Frederic Deyo (Ithaca, N.Y.: Cornell University Press, 1987), pp. 215–21; Kaufman and Stallings, "Political Economy," p. 19.

46. Sachs, "Social Conflict and Populist Policies."

Of course, not everything flowed from land tenure. Strategic imperatives and a legacy of activist Japanese colonialism added to state
power in Taiwan and South Korea; and the United States played a
more constructive role in spurring policy change there.[47] In addition,
Latin America's commodity-exporting past had a more subtle and
perhaps widely felt legacy. The region's comparative success as an
exporter meant that countries intending to pursue a strategy of export-
led industrial growth would have had to undertake a larger income
sacrifice, through devaluation of currencies to achieve competitiveness
internationally, than did the poorer East Asian countries when making the transition. In economic terms the region was touched by
"Dutch disease" early (and in some places repeatedly), relative to its
industrial development.[48] As a result, countries inheriting relatively
high productivity in primary export production would have had their
exchange rates relatively appreciated, thereby raising their costs of
producing labor-intensive industrial goods above those of countries
without this heritage (Venezuela stands out here, for obvious
reasons).[49]

There is another side to the interregional contrast. While the two
regions did differ in their degree of openness to the world economy,

47. Stephan Haggard and T. J. Cheng, "State and Foreign Capital in the East Asian
NICs," in *The Political Economy of the New Asian Industrialism,* ed. Frederic Deyo
(Ithaca, N.Y.: Cornell University Press, 1987). For a comprehensive comparative over-
view of the politics of public policy in East Asia and Latin America see James W.
McGuire, "Development Policy and Its Determinants in East Asia and Latin America,"
Journal of Public Policy 14, no. 2 (1994): 205–42.

48. On Dutch disease a short summary is W. M. Corden, "Booming Sector and Dutch
Disease Economics: Survey and Consolidation," *Oxford Economic Papers* 36 (1984):
359–80; a longer exploration is J. Peter Neary and Sweder Van Wijnbergen, *Natural
Resources and the Macroeconomy* (Cambridge, Mass.: MIT Press, 1986). My proposition
here differs somewhat from these treatments in considering the longer-term or structural implications of natural-resource-led growth: to stretch the metaphor, Dutch
disease as deformative if contracted "young."

49. I deal with this at greater length in "Was Latin America Too Rich to Prosper?
Structural and Political Obstacles to Export-Led Industrial Growth," *Journal of Develop-
ment Studies* 28, no. 2 (January 1992). I make the wage sacrifice case in detail with an
international comparison of wage rates deflated by parallel-market currency values.
The argument finds support in Richard M. Auty, "Industrial Policy Reform in Six Large
Newly Industrializing Countries: The Resource Curse Thesis," *World Development* 22,
no. 1 (January 1994): 11–26. An early version of the argument is Diamand, *Doctrinas
Económicas,* esp. pp. 56–61; and "Overcoming Argentina's Stop-and-Go Economic Cycles," in *Latin American Political Economy: Financial Crisis and Political Change,* ed.
Jonathan Hartlyn and Samuel Morley (Boulder, Colo.: Westview Press, 1986). In the
former volume Diamand presents an example perhaps erroneously assuming very
low Taiwanese productivity in manufacturing, based on GDP per capita as a proxy
for productivity.

they differed in a more complicated way than is often depicted. First, East Asian industrializing countries were in general more open on trade than those in Latin America but were generally (excepting Hong Kong and Singapore) less open on capital account.[50] Second, Latin American elites have long been notably cosmopolitan in terms of their consumption tastes and their asset preferences. Those in East Asia have not.

On the first point, international capital flows to Latin America have a longer history than those to Japan. And after World War II, as more subsidiaries of manufacturing MNCs entered protected markets in Latin America, the firms nevertheless often enjoyed free or specially facilitated repatriation of profits. Relatively few had entered the East Asian countries. This difference between regions persisted into the 1960s, despite a slump in international investment in Argentina in the first half of the decade. This can be seen in Table 2.1, where six Latin American countries are compared to South Korea, Malaysia, Taiwan (ROC), and Thailand. Using annual outward flows of investment income as a rough proxy for the extent of this investment, and comparing these numbers to annual exports (in order to assess relative capital versus trade openness), we see a strong regional contrast, especially notable for the four prototypical newly industrializing countries (NICs), Brazil, Mexico, South Korea, and Taiwan.

The difference extended to banking. British and North American banks found the Latin American markets early and the latter expanded rapidly in Latin America after 1914.[51] According to an early study, "in 1922 only eight of the 30 most important banks" in Argentina belonged to locals, and the foreign banks had about half of all bank deposits in the country. As foreign manufacturing firms came in, so did their bankers, forming relationships in the new market that began with trade finance and later blossomed into medium- and long-term lending to a variety of local borrowers.[52] Thus the major Latin

50. For an idea of capital account openness, see IMF, *Exchange Restrictions and Exchange Arrangements,* Annual Report 1977. The distinction between the two kinds of openness is often missed, as is well argued by Alan Hughes and Ajit Singh (pp. 75–89) and Albert Fishlow (p. 154) in *Economic Liberalization: No Panacea: The Experiences of Latin America and Asia,* ed. Tariq Banuri (Oxford: Clarendon Press, 1991).

51. U.S. banks consistently had over half of all overseas branches in Latin America after 1914, nearly always more than double their number in Asia (including Japan and China) at least until 1969. See the compilation by P. Henry Mueller in "A Conspectus for Offshore Lenders," in *Offshore Lending by U.S. Commercial Banks,* ed. F. John Mathis (Washington, D.C.: Bankers' Association for Foreign Trade/ Robert Morris, 1975).

52. Argentina: Clyde W. Phelps, *The Foreign Expansion of American Banks: American Branch Banking Abroad* (New York: Ronald Press, 1927), p. 190; subsidiaries: UN

Table 2.1 Exports and Outward Flows of Investment Income, Latin America and East Asia, 1961–1970

Year		Latin America						East Asia			
		Argentina	Brazil	Chile	Colombia	Mexico	Venezuela	Korea	Malaysia	ROC/Taiwan	Thailand
1961	X	964	1,403	442	462	826	2,453	41	1,048	196	473
	YI	166	187	82	51	204	597	0	119	3	13
1962	X	1,216	1,214	482	571	930	2,544	55	1,056	218	454
	YI	80	202	94	57	237	643	0	110	4	15
1963	X	1,365	1,406	491	590	985	2,464	87	1,077	332	460
	YI	71	147	90	81	266	627	1	116	5	15
1964	X	1,411	1,430	589	749	1,054	2,480	119	1,093	434	589
	YI	113	191	106	73	324	700	2	124	4	22
1965	X	1,493	1,596	688	708	1,146	2,436	175	1,226	451	609
	YI	59	268	118	79	339	747	2	134	6	26
1966	X	1,593	1,741	860	524	1,199	2,404	250	1,244	543	664
	YI	163	289	201	86	413	724	5	142	10	33
1967	X	1,464	1,654	883	549	1,152	2,533	335	1,202	654	664
	YI	133	314	198	106	497	693	12	109	16	37
1968	X	1,368	1,881	904	603	1,258	2,538	486	1,331	826	636
	YI	179	312	206	116	595	752	18	118	30	38

1969	X	1,612	2,311	1,168	667	1,454	2,662	658	1,629	1,081	686
	YI	199	366	219	154	664	840	42	171	40	51
1970	X	1,773	2,739	1,135	782	1,429	2,756	882	1,640	1,469	686
	YI	252	402	200	199	762	716	75	193	65	60
Avg.											
1961–70	YI/X	.099	.153	.196	.159	.361	.279	.028	.106	.023	.050
1964–66	YI/GNP	.016	.033	.073	.039	.054	.286	.003	.137	.007	.020

Weighted regional average of investment income as a proportion of exports (YI/X)

	Latin America
1965	.200
1970	.238

	East Asia
1965	.068
1970	.084

SOURCES: IMF, *Balance of Payments Yearbook* (Washington, D.C.: IMF, various issues); World Bank, *World Tables* (Washington, D.C.: various issues).

NOTES: Balance-of-payments data in millions of current U.S. dollars. X = exports FOB YI = debit on total foreign investment income. Mexican figures exclude border income. Chilean GNP converted at average of quarterly trade conversion factor exchange rates for the year 1965; all others use period average exchange rates.

American countries came to have a more prominent position than did East Asia in the global strategies of leading international banks well before the first oil shock. Even in 1975, after several years of rapid expansion by Japanese banks in East Asia, the region trailed Latin America in the number of foreign bank entities by a wide margin.[53]

The early role of foreign investors in Latin America had another distinguishing effect. From the perspective of nationalists in a country absorbing foreign investment, an appreciated exchange rate represented a breakwater against foreign domination, the defense of the currency a defense of the national patrimony. Where foreign finance is active, devaluation can imply not only delivering a windfall to oligarchs but also enhancing the power of foreigners to bribe officials, manipulate markets, and buy up the country. In contrast to most East Asian countries, many Latin Americans felt this possibility continuously since the late nineteenth century.

This brings us to the second, more qualitative difference noted above. Compared to their counterparts in East Asia, not only do Latin American elites command a much greater proportion of national income and wealth, they are also much more cosmopolitan culturally.[54] Together, these differences meant that a greater proportion of aggregate wealth would be prone to international movement. Let us look at this more closely.

David Felix has noted that in the eighteenth and nineteenth centuries Latin America stood out for its high import component of elite consumption: "[I]t is the budget choices of the urban middle and upper classes of Latin America compared to Asian NICs that mainly account for the greater import intensity of consumption and lower household savings rates."[55] This depressed the fortunes of the local artisan sector,

Center on Transnational Corporations, *Transnational Banks: Operations, Strategies, and Their Effects in Developing Countries* ST/CTC/16 (New York: United Nations, 1981), pp. 23–24.

53. 612 to 380. The latter number excludes "financial centers" (presumably Hong Kong and Singapore). UN Center on Transnational Corporations, *Transnational Banks,* tables 6 and 7, pp. 36–37.

54. Let me qualify this generalization by noting that Malaysia has both an income distribution like those of more moderate Latin American countries and an overseas Chinese portion of its business class that is in many ways quite cosmopolitan. The generalization is nevertheless defensible, especially with reference to the most famous NICs in East Asia and Latin America: Taiwan, Korea, Mexico, and Brazil.

55. David Felix, "Import Substitution and Late Industrialization: Latin America and East Asia Compared," *World Development* 17, no. 9 (1989): 1464. See also UN ECLA, *Income Distribution,* pp. 31–34. Elsewhere Felix records travelers' and historians' accounts of the taste for imported goods among the elite, contrasting this with India, China, and especially Japan in these countries' twentieth-century industrialization. See

in strong contrast to East Asia, and Felix links this difference to subsequent degree of industrial success.[56] While it is true that everywhere ISI aimed precisely to reduce imported consumer goods, this did not necessarily imply a cultural turn inward among the richest Latin Americans. Felix also argues that since the frontier of foreign-based consumer tastes moved continuously, this may have complicated the ISI process. He observes that "the main difference between the 'easy' and 'hard' phases of ISI was that in the latter, the consumer industries were no longer replacing competing artisan products and imports, but older import substitutes with new products." In Latin America, he continues, the new goods were "overwhelmingly of foreign design" and each was initially more import-intensive.[57] Sweder van Wijnbergen has suggested this simple model: liberalizations of trade increase the trade deficit in the short run because residents already know what goods they lack, whereas it takes much more effort to sell new products abroad.[58] While this applies well to Latin America, it should not be assumed that consumers everywhere are equally aware of what they lack. Their knowledge and preferences are variables of potentially great causal importance. As the desire for imports rises, so will the

---

"Interrelations Between Consumption, Economic Growth, and Income Distribution in Latin America Since 1800: A Comparative Perspective," in *Consumer Behavior and Economic Growth in the Modern Economy*, ed. Henri Baudet and Henk Van der Meulen (London: Croom Helm, 1982), pp. 152–58. This is of course an observation made many times by early critics of Latin American development—with the object of the criticism ranging from the shoppers' trains of turn-of-the-century Monterrey to the *afrancesado* cultural pretentions of the elite. A systematic critique was Francisco Encina's classic *Nuestra Inferioridad Económica* (1911): the author described how contact with Europe excited in the Chilean elite the desire to travel abroad and consume foreign clothing, furniture, and carriages. He concluded that a "habit of waste" and a "desire for ostentation" were "national characteristics" (4th ed., Colección Imagen de Chile [Santiago: Editorial Universitaria, 1978], pp. 116–18, 92). See also Anthony MacFarlane, "The Transition from Colonialism in Colombia," in *Latin America, Economic Imperialism, and the State: The Political Economy of the External Connection from Independence to the Present*, ed. Christopher Abel and Colin M. Lewis, University of London Institute of Latin American Studies Monograph 13 (London: Athlone Press, 1985). For a recent account of the culture of consumption see Jeffrey Needell, *A Tropical "Belle Epoque": Elite Culture and Society in Turn-of-the-Century Rio de Janeiro*, Cambridge Latin American Studies 62 (New York: Cambridge University Press, 1995), pp. 163–71.

56. Felix, "Import Substitution and Late Industrialization," pp. 1461–66.

57. Felix, "Interrelations Between Consumption, Economic Growth, and Income Distribution," p. 162.

58. Comments in John Williamson, ed., *Latin American Adjustment: How Much Has Happened?* (Washington, D.C.: Institute for International Economics, 1990), p. 194. The same reasoning might apply to rises in domestic income under the same trade regime, that is to say the marginal import intensity of consumption (net of export changes).

relative importance of the moving frontier of foreign-determined taste to the balance of payments.

Most relevant to our purposes are the implications of consumption for finance. How might culture, in this restricted economic sense, have affected asset holdings among the wealthy? Here there is little but impressionistic evidence. To begin, it is reasonable to suppose that goods preferences, even where stifled by the vagaries of ISI, might still inform asset preferences. Anyone who has observed rich Latin Americans shopping in New York or Miami would believe that the avid taste for foreign goods persisted under late ISI.[59] These habits persisted even after Mexico's entrance into the General Agreement on Tariffs and Trade (GATT), when such goods were available domestically (though at somewhat greater cost): in 1993 a business magazine cited a market analysis which found that about 75 percent of the people in Mexico City's richest neighborhoods bought their gifts and smaller items locally but traveled abroad for clothing and "other big-ticket items."[60] The money for such purchases would often come, naturally enough, from foreign accounts.

If we admit that taste and culture make sense as economic variables in tracking consumption patterns, we ought also to agree that such considerations may affect the degree to which asset holders consider foreign assets as part of the menu from which portfolios are constructed. It is reasonable to suppose that the Latin American elites who historically preferred North American machines and French poetry would have formed a stronger awareness of foreign asset options than more inward-oriented groups would have done.[61] A Brazilian journalist has commented that "taking money out of the country

59. Of course, the desire for foreign goods among the very rich has been a point of critique since before Encina (see n. 57 above). A more recent and relevant example, the product of an insider's perspective, is Irma Salinas Rocha, *Los Meros Meros de Monterrey: Manual de Conducta para Multimillonarios* (Mexico City: Claves Latinoamericanas, 1983), a pseudo-anthropological satire of the life-style of Monterrey's elite (on foreign asset holdings specifically see pp. 13–14).

60. *Business Latin America,* 8 March 1993, p. 2. Six weeks later the same magazine noted, "by and large, Latin Americans are avid consumers and look to the USA and Europe to set their consumption patterns," although it cautioned that "in most countries only the richest 10 percent have buying power equivalent to that of consumers in developed countries" (19 April 1993, p. 3).

61. This is a mild version of an old theme on the Latin American left, especially in Mexico. Abraham Nuncio states the position well in this acid description of the Monterrey Group: "[This] bourgeoisie maintains itself within national boundaries only as long as it lacks sufficient power to export its capital." See *El Grupo Monterrey* (Mexico City: Nueva Imagen, 1982), p. 53.

is a sport that has been pursued in Brazil ever since the time of Pedro Alvares Cabral."[62] People are not born comparing local interest rates to those on another continent. Arguably, this consideration will be made more widely, other things being equal, where history has formed more cosmopolitan tastes and culture among those who own most of the country.[63]

If this is right, it implies that even in years not marked by attention-getting bouts of capital flight, Latin Americans would have placed a relatively large proportion of assets abroad. In the aggregate, there seems to be some evidence for this, based on measures similar to those making up the capital outflow estimates of the previous chapter. An ECLA report includes short-term capital and errors and omissions from balance-of-payments data and aggregates them regionally. For the period 1946–62 (excluding Cuba), these show a net outflow in every year except three (in which inflows were very small), with a total net outflow for the period of an estimated 5.4 billion dollars. Viewing the rising trend of outflows after 1958, the report concluded that this reflected "the sharp increase in the open or concealed flight of private capital."[64] But there were other ways to put funds abroad. International Monetary Fund trade data yield discrepancies in trade figures, and if we impute them to deliberate misinvoicing (and hence capital flight), we more than double the estimate of flight during, for example, the late 1950s (Table 2.2). The preponderance of error on the Latin American export side of the ledger (implying export underinvoicing) may reflect export taxes in the region; the commonly overvalued currencies may also account for the impressive size of the estimate.

To understand more systematically the contrast across regions in this regard, we have to ask how income and wealth concentration would affect *aggregate* demand for foreign assets. We give no consideration to periodic opportunities for speculative capital outflows, since we seek to compare the regions' long-run, fundamental orientations toward foreign assets. To begin, we need not suppose that there exists a greater appetite for foreign assets among Latin Americans than

62. Aluizo Falcão Filho, cited in *Foreign Broadcast Information Service Latin America,* 21 June 1989, p. 26; from a story in *Exame* (São Paulo), 3 May 1989.

63. I do not mean to deny that insofar as inflation and negative real interest rates consumed savings in local currency and bank accounts, even a more equitably distributed pie of national savings would have ended up with a large proportion of foreign assets, probably mostly in the form of currency. The question is one of degree.

64. UN ECLA, *External Financing in Latin America,* Department of Economic and Social Affairs (New York: United Nations, 1965), pp. 92–93; p. 94.

Table 2.2 Discrepancies Between Regional Exports and Imports, 1948 and 1956–1959 (20 Latin American countries) (millions of U.S. dollars)

Year	LAm reptd M from world	World reptd X to LAm	World reptd M from LAm	LAm reptd X to world	Export discrep	Total discrep	Total discrep/ exports (6/4)
1948	5,996.7	5,419.6	6,703.9	6,493.0	210.9	788.0	0.120
1956	7,581.2	7,321.7	9,140.3	8,395.0	745.3	1,004.8	0.120
1957	8,949.8	8,709.6	9,915.5	8,480.4	1,435.1	1,675.3	0.197
1958	8,188.0	8,134.6	9,143.9	7,686.8	1,457.1	1,510.5	0.196
1959	7,638.2	7,492.5	9,272.2	8,073.3	1,198.9	1,344.6	0.167
	(1)	(2)	(3)	(4)	(5)	(6)	(7)

SOURCE: United Nations, *Direction of International Trade 1960*, Statistical Papers Series T, vol. 9, no. 9 (New York: UN/IMF/IBRD, 1960), tables II-2, IV-2, V-c-2.

NOTE: Import figures already corrected to FOB and for other factors.

(5) = (3) − (4); (6) = (1) − (2) + (3) − (4). Total 1956–59 = 5535.2

"Lam" = Latin America; "reptd" = reported; "M" = imports; "X" = exports; "discrep" = discrepancy.

among East Asians of equal wealth. Instead, we need only assume
that (anywhere) the richer one is, the greater the proportion of one's
wealth will be directed into foreign assets.[65] Then, given the disparity
in income and wealth concentrations known to exist between regions,
we could conclude that a greater proportion of aggregate wealth in
Latin America will take the form of foreign holdings.[66] Now of course
if we believe there *is* a difference in foreign-asset preference between
asset holders of equal wealth across regions, this would only fortify
the conclusion already reached.[67]

   With all the qualifications noted, I believe there are good reasons
for arguing that the difference between Latin America and East
Asia was more complicated than one region's ability to select the
appropriate development strategy, or to listen to the market. Despite
the common critique that Latin American industrialization after
World War II was too inward-oriented, two points must be remem-

65. In Chapter 6 I discuss a possible model for this in consumption preferences in
relation to the expected return of flight capital to Latin America.

66. Wealth distribution data are notoriously hard to obtain, and few surveys exist for
Latin America. Luis Vega has reported that one thousand families in Mexico own most
of the wealth (cited in *Latin American Weekly Report,* 7 February 1991, p. 4). Another
approach is to assume a similar relationship between income and wealth distributions
as obtains in industrial countries and to extrapolate from the best data on income.
Doing so yields estimates of a very high concentration of similar magnitude, as
Vega suggests.

67. The following anecdote may suggest some of the hidden contours of overseas
capital owned by Latin Americans. In mid-1964 the "Mexican miracle" was rolling
along and *The Economist* called Mexico a "money magnet" because of its attraction for
direct foreign investment. As evidence for the good times, the magazine also reported
that "Mexican capitalists, who according to one of the country's leading stockbrokers
used formerly to keep only about 20 percent of their wealth in Mexico and the rest
abroad, are now raising their home stake to around 30–40 percent." While we cannot
infer that these clients typified Mexican asset holders, the report is nevertheless an
interesting one. It bears repeating that this was not a time of political crisis, expected
devaluation, or pessimism. The country's GDP would grow about 11 percent that year
and inflation stayed below 2 percent. The article characterized Mexico as enjoying a
"happy combination of political stability and steady economic growth" (23 May 1964, p.
860). It was the last year in the *sexenio* of Adolfo López Mateos, who had in 1960 and
1961 alienated many in the prviate sector by, among other things, his remarks in favor
of the Cuban Revolution. But these conflicts really had reached their peak in late 1960;
after mid-1962 domestic investment rose again as relations returned to normal, despite
the government's independent stand on Cuba. See Juan M. Martínez Nava, *Conflicto
Estado Empresarios en los Gobiernos de Cárdenas, López Mateos, y Echeverría* (Mexico
City: Nueva Imagen, 1984), pp. 130–58. In fact, this is now a period Mexican businessmen view wtih nostalgia, when theirs was perhaps the region's most successful example
(especially in financial terms) of ISI—a model of industrialization whose major sin is
now supposed to have been its excessive inward orientation.

bered: first, that this industrialization process was heavily linked to firms with global financial strategies and connections, who often found the combination of closed trade and more open finance quite profitable; and second, that this "inward" model coexisted with, and enriched, a relatively narrow elite that was generally more cosmopolitan than its counterpart in East Asia. The "inward-developing" countries had elites who were much more "outward" culturally, a difference that was perhaps most consequential in its effect on consumption habits and asset preferences.

What does this imply for the subject of the next chapter, the political economy of foreign exchange policy? At the very least, Latin American policymakers trying to impose or manage exchange controls would have been more likely to encounter a powerful group with unmet demands for foreign assets, which would have led it to constitute a more vigorous opponent of exchange restrictions. (And, as noted above, if we exclude Hong Kong and Singapore, exchange control policies were stricter in Asian NICs than in Latin America during the 1960s and 1970s.) It is also why the often procyclical capital-account effects of export concentration had greater consequences in Latin America. Financial circles in the region were significant in size, relatively attentive to international price changes of a country's dominant export, and therefore capable of aggravating trade trends with capital movements. This mattered later on. During the critical years of the lending boom (1979–82), reforms aimed at export diversification proved beneficial to several countries not because they engineered export expansions but in large part because they reduced the incentives for procyclical swings of domestically held (but internationally oriented) private capital.

Conclusion

Let us pull together the threads. I have argued that international trends made many developing countries more vulnerable to financial instability by 1975 and that Latin America had two additional, structural sources of potential instability, especially visible when we compare it to East Asia. Among general trends, international finance to middle-income developing countries had become quite privatized, introducing two potential sources of volatility—procyclicality and competition to lend—into flows that until then had been dominated by multilateral lending institutions and direct investment. High commodity prices gave the impression of creditworthiness, while abundant oil-country deposits prodded competing banks to dispose of loanable funds without much conditionality.

As for Latin America's own structural features, I have pointed out the continued dependence on a relatively narrow range of commodity exports with volatile price histories—a problem left unsolved by the prevailing anti-export bias of the protected ISI policies of the postwar. Potentially aggravating this problem was the more pronounced international orientation of Latin American finance and elite savings. More concretely, openness on capital account was continuous in some countries in the region throughout the postwar period, while in others it represented the occasionally satisfied desire of liberal elites. This contrasted with the region's prevailing protectionism on trade in a way that generally distinguishes Latin American from East Asian industrializing countries. Because of the contrast between regions with regard to financial integration, wealth distribution, and elite culture, in Latin America the decisions of relatively few, internationally oriented asset holders could move the exchange markets significantly.

These conditions, international and regional, tended to place a high premium on prudent economic policy. A major part of the latter entailed keeping fiscal deficits manageable. On foreign exchange, policy succeeded best where it reflected an awareness of the potential instability of export proceeds, preserved incentives for minor exports through the exchange rate, and tried to control procyclical flows in the exchange market. This kind of policy did not arise everywhere, and in some places where it arose it did not catch on. The reasons for this had to do with politics and economic structure, and they are presented in the next chapter.

3

Exchange Policies and Capital Flight

Six Countries Compared

Why is it so hard to make exchange controls work in Argentina?
. . . the answer seems to be that they are not here felt to be
morally justified.
> —*Review of the River Plate,* April 1964

The President who devalues is devalued.
> —José López Portillo, 1982

While the Latin American debt crisis of the 1980s originated in large,
systemic problems, it did not break out in the same way in each
country. In particular, three of the largest debtors (Argentina, Mexico,
and Venezuela) had a lot of capital flight in the critical 1980–82
period, while three others (Brazil, Chile, and Colombia) had much
less. In this chapter I try to explain the difference.

Although in most countries capital flight worsened after 1980–82,
the episode deserves study for two reasons: first, because by rapidly
draining central bank reserves, especially in Mexico in 1982, capital
outflows served as midwife to the regional debt crisis; and second,
because the flight took place as foreigners were still sending funds to
Latin America rather freely, as they have done in the 1990s and will
surely do in the future. In turn, because many economic analyses have
linked the capital flight of this period to exchange policies, as I noted

in the opening chapter, the main but not exclusive focus of my political-economic analysis rests upon decisions about exchange rates and controls. Beyond this, foreign exchange policy in postwar Latin America deserves study because in doing so we encounter broader issues, introduced in the previous chapters, about the politics of economic strategy. As Jeffrey Sachs has observed, "exchange rate policy appears to reflect political conditions in Latin America as much as technical mistakes."[1]

So what accounts for the difference among the six countries considered here?[2] The short answer is: the presence of exchange policies that were originally designed to promote exports and to attenuate destabilizing capital flows. Import-substituting industrialization had a bias toward currency overvaluation that hurt exports and tended to keep them confined to those best established. Reforms of the ISI exchange regime were undertaken in several countries in the mid-1960s. Despite their moderate scope, they nevertheless entailed the particularly difficult decision to use a more depreciated and stable *real* (as opposed to nominal) exchange rate to encourage export diversification.[3] The favorite package included a crawling-peg system of minidevaluations to avoid dramatic overvaluation and some method of wage indexing to moderate the distributional struggle that typically followed depreciation. It also featured exchange control (especially on capital account), justified as a way to reduce market volatility and stabilize the incentives to new exporters.[4]

1. "Introduction" to Jeffrey D. Sachs, ed., *Developing Country Debt and the World Economy* (Chicago: University of Chicago Press, 1989), p. 15.

2. This draws upon my "Capital Flight and the Politics of Exchange Policy in Six Latin American Countries, 1930–1983," Ph.D. dissertation, University of California at Berkeley, 1989, chaps. 3–9.

3. Its moderate nature can be seen in figures for Brazil, as noted by J. Scott McClain and Benedict J. Clements, for which exports as a proportion of GDP rose only from 6.6 percent in 1964 to 7.8 percent in 1973. See "The Political Economy of Export Promotion in Brazil," in *The Political Economy of Brazil: Public Policies in an Era of Transition,* ed. Laurence S. Graham and Robert H. Wilson (Austin: University of Texas Press, 1990), p. 64. On the politics of policy reorientation, see Robert R. Kaufman, "How Societies Change Developmental Models or Keep Them: Reflections on the Latin American Experience in the 1930s and Postwar World," in *Manufacturing Miracles: Paths of Industrialization in Latin America and East Asia,* ed. Gary Gereffi and Donald Wyman (Princeton: Princeton University Press, 1990). Perhaps because of my primary focus on exchange policy, I diverge from Kaufman in finding more difference between Mexico and Colombia, in imputing less relevance to Hirschman's elasticity thesis, and on a few other points.

4. The "crawling peg" is a system of frequent (daily, weekly, or monthly) small devaluations of the exchange rate. Since most of these countries had high inflation rates

What determined whether such reforms would be undertaken, or would survive? Again, this question can be partly answered quite simply. Policymakers contemplated reform only where severe and recurrent foreign-exchange crises put it on the political agenda. In Mexico and Venezuela these conditions were largely absent. Especially in Venezuela, abundant oil exports engendered a nonchalance about foreign exchange that proved costly in 1981–83. In Mexico, expanding tourist income, along with adequate export performance prior to 1976, kept the topic of export promotion marginalized enough that it did not affect exchange-rate policy, which continued to be determined by concerns for price stability, the avoidance of labor conflict, and presidential prestige. And after 1976 an oil boom removed exchange reform from the agenda even after a serious crisis had placed it there.

In countries that did experience a host of exchange problems between 1946 and 1970—the other four included here—the picture is more complicated. Pro-export exchange reforms caught on best where traditional rural elites were politically strong but faced serious market problems internationally. The former meant that as a powerful organized interest, these producers could provide significant support to an exchange-rate policy reform of which they would be the immediate beneficiaries; the latter made the need for diversification obvious; and both made the rural elites less likely to join export merchants in opposing the *dirigisme* of exchange controls. For Brazil and Colombia, oversupply in the international coffee market was prolonged and unmistakable. Relatively unthreatened politically, growers welcomed state intervention in coffee and did not oppose exchange manipulation as strenuously as did their counterparts in Argentina. In the 1970s, the key policies mainly persisted, thanks in large part to the growth of new export interests that were sensitive to the real exchange rate.

Chile and Argentina represent two intermediate cases. In Chile, rural elites depended on state protection even more than did the coffee producers of Colombia, and they exported almost nothing. But a long heritage of export dominance by foreign-owned mineral firms made a generalized pro-export policy harder to sustain, at least while democracy lasted. By 1981 or so, exchange market behavior came to depend critically on the perceived policy orientation of a largely autonomous dictator. In Argentina, unlike the coffee countries, Pampa exports did

---

relative to their major trading partners, the crawl sought to correct for these differences in keeping the country's real exchange rate stable. I assume, I think realistically, that none of the countries concerned would have been willing to permit, for a significant period, an exchange market with one freely fluctuating rate and no central bank participation.

not face world glut. They owed their poor performance of the late 1940s to state intervention, and Pampa elites retained a conviction that liberal policies, including the total abolition of exchange control, could solve the country's balance-of-payments problems. The important thing is that (despite the beef cycle) they were often right, at least in the short term. In part because the country exported foodstuffs consumed by urban wage earners, a large devaluation to a fixed nominal rate often solved the problems immediately while promising price stability and (along with free exchange markets) serving to welcome foreign capital. Argentina policymakers could opt for price stability and foreign capital inflow while exploiting the short-term ease on the trade account.

As I noted above, in the late 1970s abundant international finance encouraged debt, free capital movements, and currency overvaluation (on the last, see Table 3.3, end of this chapter). It also enhanced the autonomy of governments, allowing them to satisfy conflicting claims or, depending on their ideology and situation, to wage an assault on inflation. As before, leaders also found that borrowing could finance an attack on inflation through the exchange rate; to this were now added new forays into financial deregulation, as in Argentina and Chile, that made trends of real appreciation into lucrative opportunities for short-term speculation. The financial abundance tended to separate those countries in which the (by now universal) rhetoric of export promotion reflected established support among price-sensitive producer groups from those in which it did not. Where states allowed other priorities to lead them into gross currency overvaluation in a free exchange market, they would lose billions of dollars through capital flight while they borrowed billions more abroad.

Moreover, in all three cases of massive flight, policymakers justified overvalued exchange rates (as they sometimes did fiscal deficits) with reference to market conditions, namely the still-plentiful supply of international bank loans.[5] Thus, whether they arose from a history of

5. During the borrowing spree, "all the actors embraced the idea that the available financing, the capacity to pay, and the level of indebtedness were almost unlimited, an idea that was supported by the most widely held rhetorical view of the time, which made no distinction between external transactions on current account and on the capital account of the balance of payments. There were few exceptions to this view, such as that of Colombia." See United Nations Economic Commission for Latin America and the Caribbean (UN ECLAC), *Postwar Transfer of Resources Abroad by Latin America,* Cuadernos de la CEPAL 67 (Santiago, 1992), p. 13. See also Eduardo Wiesner, "Latin American Debt: Lessons and Pending Issues," in *American Economic Review* 75, no. 2 (May 1985): 193. We will see the most egregious instances of this in the countries that experienced capital flight.

export abundance or from an inclination to favor capital inflows, the "bad policies" that led to capital flight in 1980–82 resulted as much from perceived accommodations to international market forces as they did from attempts to insulate the country from these forces.

Colombia and Brazil: Coffee and Policy Reform

Coffee-producing countries were relatively precocious in efforts to regulate commodity markets for two reasons. First, coffee production in Latin America rests overwhelmingly in local hands. Partly because of this, in both Brazil and Colombia the coffee sector enjoyed more political power than foreign-owned sectors elsewhere. Moreover, in neither country did coffee growers face serious land reform or any sustained, Perón-like scheme of surplus extraction. In Colombia, the relatively broad (in Latin American terms) size distribution of coffee land added another, "popular" aspect to the claims of the main export interest, one to which politicians proved very attentive.[6]

A second, structural feature is also important here. Coffee's low price elasticity of short-term supply leads to extreme price volatility and has contributed to world overproduction.[7] Unlike many other

6. See, for example, William P. McGreevey, *An Economic History of Colombia, 1845–1930* (New York and London: Cambridge University Press, 1971), pp. 196–97. One political effect was the easy identification of coffee with national interests, even by elected politicians. For example, in 1950 a Conservative minister of finance said "when the coffee market has been defended, it was not a defense of the people linked to the industry only, but of the total interests of the national economy." See *Memoria del Ministerio de Hacienda, 1950–1951*, cited in Federación Nacional de Cafeteros de Colombia, *Los Propósitos de la Industria Cafetera Colombiana, 1850–1986*, ed. Siverio Pérez Gómez (Bogotá: Federación Nacional de Cafeteros de Colombia, 1987), p. 278. On the unusual power of the National Federation of Coffee Growers, see UN ECLA, "The Economic Policy of Colombia in 1950–1966," *Economic Bulletin for Latin America* 12, no. 2 (October 1967): 91. On Federation-government relations, see Miguel Urrutia, *Gremios, Política Económica, y Democracia* (Bogotá: Fondo Cultural Cafetero, 1983), and Mariano Arango R., *El Café en Colombia, 1930–1958: Producción, Circulación y Política* (Bogotá: Carlos Valencia Editores, 1982). There were almost 303,000 farms with substantial coffee plantings in 1970. About half of the area planted in coffee occurred on farms of less than 20 hectares (1 ha = 2.4 a); still, one-third of the nation's coffee growers did not produce enough to belong to the federation. Data from FEDECAFE census, in Roberto Junguito Bonnet, ed., *Economía Cafetera Colombiana* (Bogotá: FEDESARROLLO and Fondo Cultural Cafetero, 1979), pp. 43, 49–51, 55.

7. To my knowledge this argument was made first by Albert O. Hirschman in *A Bias for Hope* (New Haven: Yale University Press, 1971), pp. 11–12. I take up his further suggestion, about politics and elasticities of short-term supply, in the summary at the end of the chapter.

commodities, chronic problems in the coffee market did not end after 1945 but reappeared a decade later. Thus, the world market drove otherwise conservative governments to face the challenge of export diversification early on.

These factors help us understand why Brazil and especially Colombia would have moved earlier and more decisively toward export promotion in the postwar period. They can also give us some insight into the politics of exchange control. Coffee interests took a relatively mild view of state intervention in the exchange market not only because of their dependence on state subsidy and price control for much of their income but also because they usually operated close enough to the center of political power to be able to trust its intentions. All in all, the result has been what, referring to Colombia, Rosemary Thorp has called a "tradition of pragmatic interventionism."[8]

As elsewhere in the region, in Colombia ISI policies dominated for two decades after the war. Exports took a back seat as long as there was hope that balance-of-payments stability could be attained without disturbing urban interests. This meant a presumption against devaluation—visible in the 1957 stabilization program, in Lleras Camargo's (1958–62) hesitations, and especially in the actions of president Valencia (1962–66), who paid a heavy political price for a muddled devaluation in 1962 and refused to contemplate another for the rest of his term.[9]

Yet coffee had enough power so that this anti-export bias remained moderate. Even the dictator Rojas Pinilla (1953–57), admirer of Perón, failed to defend a tax to fund industrial development, which he had imposed on coffee after a steep rise in its world price. When in 1954

8. *Economic Management and Economic Development in Peru and Colombia* (Pittsburgh: University of Pittsburgh Press, 1991), p. 157. In a statement that describes Brazil even better than Colombia, a historian of Colombian coffee said that the Depression bound the coffee interests to the state with the strength "of an old Catholic marriage." Marco Palacios, *El Café en Colombia: Una Interpretación Económica, Social, y Política,* 2d ed. (Mexico City and Bogotá: El Colegio de México and El Áncora, 1983), p. 501.

9. For detailed summaries, see Eduardo Wiesner D., "Devaluación y Mecanismo de Ajuste en Colombia," *Política Económica Externa de Colombia 1978,* ed. Eduardo Wiesner (Bogotá: Asociación Bancaria de Colombia, 1978), or Carlos F. Díaz-Alejandro, *Foreign Trade Regimes and Economic Development: Colombia,* NBER Conference Series, vol. 9 (New York: National Bureau for Economic Research, 1976). On Lleras and Valencia, see Carlos Sanz de Santamaría, *Devaluación 1962: Historia Documental* (Bogotá: Tercer Mundo, 1963), esp. pp. 57ff. On the political climate, see Jonathan Hartlyn, *The Politics of Coalition Rule in Colombia,* Cambridge Latin American Studies Series, no. 66 (New York: Cambridge University Press, 1988), pp. 121–26.

the National Federation of Coffee Growers (FEDECAFE) opposed him forcefully, Rojas backed down, and he modified the tax to direct its now-reduced revenue to the Federation-controlled National Coffee Fund.[10] Hence, there would be no Colombian equivalent of Perón's Instituto Argentino para la Promoción del Intercambio (IAPI), not primarily because of economic factors (for example, coffee's relatively low elasticity of supply), or the stable clientelism of the country's party system, but in large part because of the effective political opposition of coffee's interest organization.[11]

When Carlos Lleras Restrepo became president in 1966, the coffee sector had reason to expect favorable treatment. With his pro-coffee record as finance minister under Santos in the late 1930s, along with his service as delegate to the Interamerican Quota meetings in 1940 and to Bretton Woods in 1944, Lleras brought to the job a long friendship with coffee and an unusual astuteness on economic matters. Faced with a severe exchange crisis, he played on resentment against the IMF to get support for a comprehensive policy response, which after nearly four months of intense negotiation and planning under emergency powers, became Decree-Law 444.[12] This included enhanced powers for the Monetary Board, strict exchange control, and a "crawling peg" system of frequent minidevaluations, with a target date for unifying the two existing rates. Yet the law did not have the career the IMF had hoped for or that the Colombians had planned. The IMF disliked the exchange control and wanted the crawl to be temporary.[13]

10. Carlos Villaveces R., *Memoria de Hacienda 1954* (Bogotá: Imprenta Nacional, 1954), pp. 113, 123–25; Arango, *El Café en Colombia*, p. 257.

11. On the latter I here register a minor quibble with Miguel Urrutia's stimulating essay "On the Absence of Economic Populism in Colombia," in *The Macroeconomics of Populism in Latin America*, ed. Rudiger Dornbusch and Sebastian Edwards (Chicago: University of Chicago Press, 1991).

12. Lleras had favored coffee as finance minister under Santos, and in his 1966 campaign he expressed sympathy with its dislike of exchange-rate policy. See *Revista Cafetera de Colombia* 17, no. 141 (July–August 1966): 11–17; see also Bennett E. Koffman, "The National Federation of Coffee-Growers of Colombia," Ph.D. dissertation, University of Virginia, 1969, pp. 137–38. On the exchange crisis, see Abdón Espinosa Valderrama, *Memoria de Hacienda, 1966–1970* (Bogotá: Banco de la República, n.d.), pp. 5–10; Díaz-Alejandro, *Foreign Trade Regimes*, pp. 27–28; Miguel Urrutia, "The Experience with the Crawling Peg in Colombia," in *Exchange Rate Rules: The Theory, Performance, and Prospects of the Crawling Peg*, ed. John Williamson (New York: St. Martin's Press, 1981); Richard R. Nelson, T. Paul Schultz, and Robert L. Slighton, *Structural Change in a Developing Economy: Colombia's Problems and Prospects* (Princeton: Princeton University Press, 1971), p. 240.

13. The basic source on DL 444 is the commemorative *Colombia: Veinte Años del Régimen de Cambios y de Comercio Exterior*, 2 vols. (Bogotá: Banco de la República,

Thus on precisely the two points most important to the later avoidance of capital flight, the IMF was not heeded. Rather, the law reflected its framers' main concern, that of making sure the central bank did not fund private capital outflows.[14]

The law had a bonus for the coffee sector, too. While it required all foreign exchange holdings to be registered, it also allowed existing holdings to be traded for "Pro-Colombia Bonds" without official scrutiny. The sizeable foreign exchange proceeds from these sales went to the National Coffee Fund, an arm of the Federation of Coffee Growers. Minister Espinosa commented, using familiar terms, that "these bonds achieved a double and transcendental mission in favor of the national interests. For one, they facilitate the repatriation of capital kept abroad by our compatriots, and for another, their product in dollars is assigned to cancel debts of the FNC [Fondo Nacional de Café]."[15] Thus coffee interests would benefit from strict exchange control, a policy then regarded with loathing by agroexport sectors elsewhere on the continent. When Lleras stepped down, the Federation extolled "the highest services which were dedicated to the cause of stability of the [coffee] industry by the government of Carlos Lleras."[16]

Within a few years DL 444 had become a widely acclaimed success. The main exchange rate had depreciated 17 percent by the end of 1967 and was stable for seven years thereafter. It attracted long-term capital while reducing incentives for flight, and it oversaw a steady improvement in the trade balance.[17] Success lent the law prestige and created new exporters with an interest in its continuity.

1987). It obviously says something about Colombia that the country's mainstream (and North American-educated) economists would participate in a celebration of, among other things, exchange controls. For an account that attributes greater authorship of the law to the IMF, see Lauchlin Currie, *The Role of Economic Advisors in Developing Countries,* Contributions in Economics and Economic History no. 44 (Westport, Conn.: Greenwood Press, 1981), p. 99. Formally, DL 444 did not prescribe a crawling-peg system but rather a "dirty float." See also Thorp, *Economic Management,* p. 157.

14. The Lleras government had spent about $200 million in reserves stabilizing the old "free" rate to keep it from disrupting other markets. See Espinosa Valderrama, *Memoria de Hacienda,* pp. 18, 350. In a message to Congress after the introduction of the law Lleras argued for the indispensability of the exchange control. See *Colombia: Veinte Años,* 2:6–7; see also Thorp, *Economic Management,* pp. 157–58.

15. Espinosa Valderrama, *Memoria de Hacienda,* p. 349.

16. *Revista Cafetera de Colombia* 19, no. 148 (September–October 1970): 22–23.

17. Urrutia, "The Experience with the Crawling Peg," 42 n. 4; *Colombia: Economic Development and Policy Under Changing Conditions* (Washington, D.C.: World Bank, 1984), pp. xxx and 59–60; Alberto Carrasquilla B. and Rodrigo Suescun M., "El Estatuto Cambiario y la Balanza Comercial," in *Colombia: Veinte Años del Régimen de Cambios y de Comercio Exterior,* 2 vols. (Bogotá: Banco de la República, 1987), 1:254–57.

This emerged clearly in a national debate on exchange policy in the late 1970s. The post-1975 coffee boom had lasted longer than expected, and by 1979 the old assumption of a temporary bonanza, with the idea that reserves should be husbanded with care, came openly to be questioned. Yet Colombia did not follow Argentina in liberalizing access to foreign exchange or in trying to dampen inflationary expectations by lagging the exchange rate, despite strong arguments for such measures (plus their apparent success in Chile and, up to that time, Argentina). Asociación Nacional de Industriales (ANDI), the main industrial interest group, came out for maintaining DL 444 and exchange control as crucial to export diversification, since many of its members now exported and thus had a stake in the system.[18] Apart from this, banker opinion was divided and the coffee sector vacillated.[19] Finally, the policies were supported by the majority of Colombia's political class, which appreciated the work of the *técnicos* and did not lightly remove restrictions of any kind.[20]

In the 1980s, DL 444 helped moderate capital flight, although the country's deep black market contributed as well. The main advantage of the latter, as Thorp notes, was that surreptitious drug exports were less likely to excite in foreign bankers the perverse tendency to accentuate the bonanza through increased lending, even as the Turbay government was borrowing abroad more freely than its predecessor.[21]

18. Hernan Vallejo M., "Balanza de Divisas, Inflación, y Subdesarrollo," Proposiciones Aprobadas en la 35 Asamblea General de Afiliados ANDI, *Revista ANDI*, no. 46 (1979): 47. See also the editorial "En Defensa del Control de Cambios," in *Estrategia Económica y Financiera* (Bogotá), 23 June 1979.

19. For laying out the alternatives the best two sources are Carlos Caballero Argáez, "La Libertad Cambiaria: Solución al Problema Monetario?" (Comentario), *Coyuntura Económica* 9, no. 4 (1979): 117–24; and Mauricio Cabrera G. and Rodrigo Quintero M., "La Política Cambiaria y el Manejo del Superávit en la Balanza de Pagos," *Banca y Finanzas*, no. 165 (September 1979). For a banker view favoring liberalization, see Jorge Franco H., "Libre Cambio en Colombia," speech of 2 August 1979, *Revista del Centro de Estudios Colombianos*, no. 21 (July–August 1979): 41; for a banker in favor of DL 444, see José Alberto Pérez Toro (of ANIF, the National Association of Financial Institutions), in *Carta Financiera* (January–March 1979): 43–53. The Federation's short-lived endorsement of free exchange is in "Los Cafeteros y la Política Económica Nacional," *Revista Cafetera de Colombia*, no. 172 (May–August 1979): 29–30. This position was reversed soon afterward.

20. Interview with official of the Federation, November 1988.

21. Thorp, *Economic Management*, p. 170. Carlos Caballero Argáez, a member of the Monetary Board during this period, claimed that the narcotics trade yielded only about a billion dollars in foreign exchange, no more than coffee, and that the board gave no consideration to the trade in its deliberations. Interviewed in *Latin American Weekly Report*, 30 March 1989, pp. 6–7.

Exchange controls raised transaction costs and thus lent a greater degree of friction to markets whose volatility had been awakened by movements of commodity prices, public statements by creditors, or other financial news. Thus they gave the authorities more time to react. Controls on *inward* capital movements (in the form of foreign loans), beefed up in 1974, also proved instrumental in avoiding a buildup of credits that otherwise would have been offered by bankers impressed by the coffee boom.

The relative success of foreign exchange policy well represents the distinctiveness of the Colombian political economy. Thorp points to "the confidence in and the acceptance of the state" that contrasts sharply with the proclivity for capital flight present in Peru, Mexico, and Argentina.[22] In the ideological climate of the 1980s, Colombia was one of the only places where one could find foreign-educated *técnicos*, well-placed and respected in their country's private sector, arguing the virtues of strict exchange control. This reflected a political environment friendly to the traditional rural elite, in which one legacy of relatively uncontroversial economic management was the wide compass given to Colombian officials to act in pragmatic response to the problems of a dependent economy.

As in Colombia, Brazilian policy also came to reflect an attentiveness to exports and to the management of capital flows. A politically powerful rural elite, chronic coffee problems, and recurrent exchange crises shaped policy priorities. One side of this could be seen in a famous observation by one of the dictatorship's more orthodox finance ministers, Mario Henrique Simonsen: "inflation wounds, but the balance of payments kills." The emphasis on foreign exchange management over inflation fighting has characterized Brazilian policy under a variety of governments. The crawling peg and the controls reflected this and saw the country through the "miracle" years (1968–73), encouraging the growth of new price-sensitive export producers. In the critical years of the debt cycle (1979–82), as these priorities and most of the key policies endured, Brazil suffered relatively little capital flight.

For the Brazilian economic elite, government intervention never bore the stigma it did in Argentina after Perón. On exchange controls the reasons for the difference are obvious. Apart from the severe problems of the Brazilian foreign sector during the 1930s, in postwar Brazil the circumstances surrounding the reimposition of controls differed markedly from those in Argentina. President Eûrico Dutra

22. Thorp, *Economic Management*, p. 198.

(1946–50) led a conservative administration governed by short-term priorities, and he reacted to evident international forces. He had also removed most of the wartime economic regulations soon after taking office in early 1946. In June 1947, however, strong import demand and speculative dollar buying forced him to reverse his course. Fearing inflation and convinced that devaluation would help exports little, he opted to control foreign exchange.[23] Dutra was no developmentalist: he had rejected earlier appeals for industrial tariff protection, and his longest-serving finance minister said publicly that Brazil's proper place in the world order was that of a provider of primary goods.[24] Though the exchange control of 1947 turned out to be a peculiar kind of pro-industrial policy, this was not its main intention. Nor was it accompanied by statist or anti-oligarchic rhetoric, at least from anyone close to the center of power.[25] It did not, therefore, seem arbitrary or dangerous to those it affected. Far from it. The coffee sector, which feared that devaluation would depress world prices and had grown accustomed to following government signals, went along without fuss.[26]

23. Joseph Kershaw, "Postwar Brazilian Economic Problems," *American Economic Review* 38, no. 2 (May 1948): 333–34; Albert Fishlow, "Foreign Trade Regimes and Economic Development: Brazil," summary for National Bureau of Economic Research series, vol. 10 (1976), photocopy, pp. 17–18; Carlos Lessa, *Quinze Anos de Política Econômica*, Caderno no. 4, Instituto de Filosofia e Ciências Humanas, Universidade Estadual de Campinas (São Paulo: Editorial Brasiliense, 1975), p. 9.

24. Nathaniel Leff, *Economic Policy Making and Development in Brazil, 1947–1964* (New York: Wiley, 1968), p. 53; Thomas E. Skidmore, *Politics in Brazil, 1930–1964: An Experiment in Democracy* (New York: Oxford University Press, 1967), p. 70. Lourdes Solá calls 1945–47 a "neo-liberal experiment" and says that the 1946 constitution "enshrined the principle of laissez-faire." See "The Political and Ideological Constraints to Economic Management in Brazil, 1945–1964," D.Phil. thesis, Somerville College, Oxford, 1982, pp. 44, 47.

25. Dutra even accepted the offer of an alliance with the economically liberal UDN (União Democrática Nacional) in 1946, although this ended up splitting the party. See John W. F. Dulles, *Carlos Lacerda, Brazilian Crusader*, vol. 1, *The Years 1914–1960* (Austin: University of Texas Press, 1991), p. 85.

26. "Fifteen Years of Economic Policy in Brazil" [by Carlos Lessa], *Economic Bulletin for Latin America* 9, no. 2 (December 1964): 156. On this point Robert Wade criticizes Stephan Haggard for overstating the coffee growers' position as one of opposition to devaluation. See "East Asia's Economic Success: Conflicting Perspectives, Partial Insights, Shaky Evidence," *World Politics* 44 (January 1992): 305 n. 77. In Haggard's defense, one can still make the argument, as I do here, that coffee growers would have been less adamantly opposed to the typical mix of ISI policies than price-taking producers elsewhere. Two other factors are crucial to add: first, this was a time of rising world prices; and second, the growers could not assume, as Wade does, that the benefits from devaluation would reach them. They feared that the profits would all go to American merchant houses. See Salvio Pacheco de Almeida Prado, *Dez Anos na Política*

After 1954, with industrialization policies that had become more coherent and conscious, foreign exchange problems soon put export diversification on the agenda also.[27] It was not to be pursued at coffee's expense, however. Coffee growers wielded enough local and national power to improve their exchange treatment during the decade and to enjoy high profits helped by government protection from the volatile international market.[28] In the face of world coffee problems, the Kubitschek administration found itself with an alarming rise in the fiscal deficit, to which generous coffee support prices had contributed significantly.[29] Thus cushioned, politically unthreatened, dependent on government subsidy, and aware of the obvious problems for coffee internationally, coffee growers did not fear exchange controls or active government nearly as much as did the *estancieros* of the Argentine Pampa. Their congenial political environment was, for the most part, later secured and extended by the 1964 coup.

Despite familiar pro-export rhetoric, the military regime did not move decisively on export promotion until after the personnel changes of 1967. At that time speculative capital flows provided a key motivation for the shift, since they had upset exchange-rate management in 1967 and early 1968 when outflows anticipated major devaluations. As in Colombia, by stabilizing exchange-rate expectations the Brazilian exchange reform of August 1968 proved a boon to exports, while the political drama of devaluation practically disappeared.[30] It also made

do Café (1945–1955) (São Paulo: Jornal dos Livros, 1956), p. 167. On the politics of coffee and exchange policy in the 1950s, see Verena Stolcke, *Cafeicultura: Homens, Mulheres, e Capital (1850–1980)* (São Paulo: Editorial Brasiliense, 1986), pp. 131–78.

27. Kubitschek mentioned export diversification in 1957 speeches. Juscelino Kubitschek de Oliveira, *Discursos; Proferidos no Segundo Ano do Mandato Presidencial, 1957* (Rio de Janeiro: Departamento de Imprensa Nacional, 1958), pp. 85, 163; see also Steven H. Arnold, "The Politics of Export Promotion: Economic Problem-Solving in Brazil, 1956–1969," Ph.D. dissertation, Johns Hopkins University, 1972.

28. Solá, "Political and Ideological Constraints," pp. 154–72; Stolcke, *Cafeicultura*, pp. 170–77. The latter notes that in 1956 coffee growers objected strongly to a businessman's suggestion that their incomes be subject to market forces (p. 164). For a discussion, see Kathryn Sikkink, *Ideas and Institutions: Developmentalism in Brazil and Argentina* (Ithaca, N.Y.: Cornell University Press, 1991), pp. 161–65.

29. Solá, "Political and Ideological Constraints," pp. 149–50; ECLA, "Fifteen Years of Economic Policy in Brazil," p. 183.

30. Donald E. Syvrud, *Foundations of Brazilian Economic Growth* (Washington, D.C.: American Enterprise Institute/Hoover Institution, 1974), pp. 189–91, 195; Roberto Fendt, in *Exchange Rate Rules: The Theory, Performance, and Prospects of the Crawling Peg*, ed. John Williamson (New York: St. Martin's Press, 1981), p. 141; Thomas E. Skidmore, *The Politics of Military Rule in Brazil, 1964–1985* (New York: Oxford University Press, 1988), p. 91; Jürgen B. Donges, *Brazil's Trotting Peg: A New Approach to Greater Rate Flexibility in Less Developed Countries* (Washington, D.C.: American

foreign borrowing more manageable, and thus, combined with improving prices and expanding trade volume, the new crawling-peg system helped bring about the so-called "Brazilian miracle."[31]

Although the policy mix became more complicated over the next decade, an enduring commitment to exports did help moderate capital flight in the early 1980s. Coffee no longer reigned as king of the export economy, as it was eclipsed after 1973 by manufactures, which were more price-sensitive.[32] Despite the shift toward state-led ISI after the oil shock of 1973, officials remained responsive to export interests, as could be seen even in the adventure with a preannounced rate scheme in 1979–80.[33] Whereas in Argentina the *tablita* was emplaced after a period of substantial real appreciation, the brief Brazilian experiment began with a large devaluation, despite well-founded fears about the cost of this move to firms indebted abroad. As a result, in Brazil the exchange rate stayed more realistic during the last, critical years of the borrowing period (Table 3.3), and the country suffered relatively little capital flight until after the debt crisis had broken out across the region.

Enterprise Institute, 1970), p. 22. On the generally enthusiastic reception among the private sector, see *O Globo* (Rio de Janeiro), 22 August 1968, p. 14, 23 August 1968, p. 14; Arnold, "The Politics of Export Promotion," p. 329.

31. On the official optimism about debt management that was seemingly confirmed by the "miracle": for an overview, see Jeffry A. Frieden, "The Brazilian Borrowing Experience: From Miracle to Debacle and Back," *Latin American Research Review* 22, no. 1 (1987); for official justification, Banco Central do Brasil, *The External Sector and National Economic Development,* September 1973, summarized in P. A. Wellons, *Borrowing by Developing Countries on the Euro-Currency Market* (Paris: OECD Development Centre, 1977), pp. 103–6; for commentary, Paulo Renato Souza, *Quem Paga a Conta? Dívida, Déficit, e Inflação nos Anos 80* (São Paulo: Editorial Brasiliense, 1989), pp. 18ff., and Paulo Davidoff Cruz, *Dívida Externa e Política Econômica: A Experiência Brasileira nos Anos Setenta* (São Paulo: Editorial Brasiliense, 1984), pp. 28ff.

32. José Carvalho, "Commercial Policy in Brazil: An Overview," in *The Brazilian Economy in the Eighties,* ed. Jorge Salazar-Carrillo and Roberto Fendt, Jr. (Oxford: Pergamon, 1985), p. 87, table 1.

33. President Figueiredo's comments after the December 1979 "maxi" expressed concern for export competitiveness. See *O Globo* (Rio de Janeiro), 8 December 1979, p. 24. Earlier in the year, Delfim's support for an export drive was said to get "the best reception among private business." *Revista da Associação Comercial* (Rio de Janeiro), no. 1140 (June 1979), p. 52. In 1976 the Federação das Indústrias do Estado de São Paulo, still probably the best-connected industrial group, had applauded exchange-rate changes aimed at preserving international competitiveness. *Relatório das Diretórias 1976* (São Paulo: FIESP, 1977), p. 134. On the failure of stabilization during 1979–84 and the influence of actors such as FIESP, see Deepak Lal and Sylvia Maxfield, "The Political Economy of Stabilization in Brazil," in *Political and Economic Interactions in Economic Policy Reform: Evidence from Eight Countries,* ed. Robert H. Bates and Anne O. Krueger (New York: Blackwell, 1993), pp. 40–49.

Chile

Notwithstanding the obvious political differences, the Chilean experience with barbed-wire neoliberalism offers the most useful historical analogy to the capital-receiving countries of early 1990s Latin America. The country suffered a brutal slump in 1982–83 despite a prior public-sector surplus and dominantly private-sector borrowing, while its fixed exchange rate collapsed. Still, Chile avoided serious capital flight during this time, apart from a brief panic in mid-1982. The most important reason for this lay in the evident power of the dictator, which engendered the widely held belief that he could and would decree a massive cut in real wages rather than devalue the currency. His power in this regard exceeded that of his counterparts in Argentina because the Chilean armed forces were more unified, the national bourgeoisie weaker, and because Pinochet drew upon a deeper well of class fear.

As in Argentina, the experience with ISI in Chile was punctuated by repeated and severe exchange crises. However, the politics of Chilean foreign exchange policy differed greatly from that across the Andes. First, in Chile from the 1920s onward, shortages of foreign exchange were more common than in Argentina. Related to this, in Chile there was a much weaker correlation between the repression of domestic demand and the appearance of export surpluses, due to the practical absence of wage goods in Chilean exports. Finally, the Chilean rural elite participated only marginally in overseas trade during this period (until 1971 foreign mining firms dominated the export sector), and hence found less to dislike in the exchange rates and controls typical of ISI.[34] As in Argentina, in response to repeated crises a variety of exchange policies were tried, but reforms generally failed because of weak export response, inflation, or the intractability of demand for imports.[35]

---

34. Domestic support prices and restrictions had greater salience to them (as producers) than did the exchange rate or exchange controls. For example, in January 1963 the council of the Sociedad Nacional de Agricultura (SNA) argued against a strong devaluation, noting that since agriculture received government-fixed prices it preferred a slow devaluation reflecting the rise in its internal costs. See *El Campesino* 95, no. 1 (January 1963): 13.

35. Ricardo Ffrench-Davis, *Políticas Económicas en Chile, 1952–1970* (Santiago: Ediciones Nueva Universidad, 1973); Enrique Sierra, *Tres Ensayos de Estabilización en Chile: Las Políticas Aplicadas en el Decenio, 1956–1966* (Santiago: Editorial Universitaria, 1969); Jorge Marshall, "The Central Bank of Chile During the Period 1950–1970," *Estudios Monetarios* 8 (Banco Central de Chile, 1983).

In one notable instance, President Jorge Alessandri and his liberal finance minister, Roberto Vergara, turned to what in the previous chapter I called the pro-finance strategy. Beginning with a large devaluation in early 1959, they fixed the exchange rate again and opened the exchange market to financial flows. A former central bank official commented, "it was thought the liberalization would bring about a large influx of foreign capital in order to increase investment." "On the other hand," he added, "it was feared that an excessing [sic] trade liberalization could create unnecessary risks to the national industry."[36] Though it did succeed in drawing foreign MNC capital to a highly protected import-substituting industrial sector (notably in automobiles), the program collapsed in December 1961 under the burden of a trade deficit and capital flight. This shook the governing coalition and forced a return to familiar restrictions. The authorities did later achieve some success in favoring exports by devaluing periodically over the next two years, only returning to a fixed rate four months before the presidential election in 1964.[37]

This experience, and its context of exchange crises and foreign domination of the export sector, shaped the career of policy reform under Eduardo Frei (1964–70). After his party had fortified its apparent mandate with a majority in the lower house in March 1965, Frei undertook a comprehensive exchange policy reform, which included a more explicit crawling-peg exchange rate. The new exchange policy prevailed with difficulty at the central bank but, given the other issues in the air, met relatively little public resistance.[38] It sought to boost new exports but also kept controls on capital account, reflecting the failed experiment in 1959–61, as part of an effort to avoid speculative capital movements—and it was fairly successful.[39] But familiar politi-

36. Marshall, "The Central Bank of Chile," p. 39.

37. Ffrench-Davis, *Políticas Económicas en Chile,* pp. 82–83; Oscar Muñoz G., *Economía Política de la Industrialización Chilena, 1940–1970,* Apuntes CIEPLAN no. 37 (Santiago: Corporación de Investigaciones Económicas para Latinoamérica, 1982), p. 24; Marshall, "The Central Bank of Chile," p. 41.

38. Ffrench-Davis, *Políticas Económicas en Chile,* p. 98; Cristóstomo Pizarro, *Políticas Públicas y Grupos de Presión en Chile, 1965–1970: Un Análisis Exploratorio,* Estudios CIEPLAN 26 (Santiago: Corporación de Investigaciones Económicas para Latinoamérica, 1978), p. 25; Ffrench-Davis, personal communication.

39. The Alessandri experiment was one of those in which attachment to a fixed rate was meant to attract foreign investment, which it did. See Ffrench-Davis, *Políticas Económicas en Chile,* pp. 82–93; Muñoz, *Economía Política,* p. 24. On Frei, see Jere R. Behrman, *Foreign Trade Regimes and Economic Development: Chile* (New York: National Bureau of Economic Research and Columbia University Press, 1976), p. 75; Ffrench-Davis, personal communication; Jorge Cauas, "Short-Term Economic Theory and Policy, the Chilean Case, 1964–1972," Universidad Católica de Chile, April 1972,

cal pressures led the Christian Democrats to end the new system in the midst of the 1970 election campaign. According to Behrman, it succumbed to "the traditional claims raised by the opposition in the presidential election campaign—that it was inflationary and that it favored rich foreign and national exporters."[40] Besides, foreign exchange reserves stood at a record level. The virtues of the crawling peg seemed superfluous and its vices now made it a political liability.

While the Allende government (1970–73) revived an extreme version of the old ways of exchange management, in two key areas it wrought changes that would alter fundamental parameters of exchange policy. Each area tended to fortify state autonomy against domestic and international economic interests. First, the copper nationalization undermined one argument for defense of the currency. Devaluation would now benefit the state rather than the key "rich foreign exporters." The second, more important change involved class relations. Nationalization, class conflict, and capital flight under Allende left national business decapitalized and afraid. In the subsequent resale of assets the structure of Chilean productive property became more concentrated, and the specter of class warfare continued to drive the bourgeoisie into Pinochet's arms.[41] In this sense the situation differed from contemporary Argentina, even under Videla.

Exchange policies varied greatly in the dictatorship's first ten years.[42] Rate policies shifted several times (crawling peg to *tablita* to

---

mimeograph. Cauas was later "Superminister" under Pinochet. World Bank, *Chile: An Economy in Transition* (Washington, D.C.: World Bank, 1979), pp. 26–35 and table 3.2, p. 354.

40. Behrman, *Foreign Trade Regimes,* p. 76.

41. Patricio Meller, Ernesto Livacic, and Patricio Arrau, "Una Revisión del Milagro Económico Chileno (1976–1981)," *Colección Estudios CIEPLAN* 15 (Santiago: Corporación de Investigaciones Económicas para Latinoamérica, December 1984). The point about class fear is made by Alfred Stepan, "State Power and the Strength of Civil Society in the Southern Cone of Latin America," in *Bringing the State Back In,* ed. Peter Evans, Dietrich Rueschemeyer, and Theda Skocpol (New York: Cambridge University Press, 1985), p. 321. It is used adeptly in a comparative argument by Jeffry Frieden, *Debt, Development, and Democracy: Modern Political Economy and Latin America, 1965–1985* (Princeton: Princeton University Press, 1990), pp. 150–77. Similar arguments were that the radical line was facilitated because so much of domestic business had been taken over or disorganized by Allende and that the shock approach, by calling for huge but short-term sacrifices, made better use of the fresh memories of the Allende period among the Chilean business class. Both of the latter arguments were made by *Trading in Latin America,* Business International Research Report 123 (New York: Business International, 1976), p. 48.

42. Overviews include Gary M. Walton, ed., *The National Policies of Chile,* Contemporary Studies in Economic and Financial Analysis, vol. 51 (Greenwich, Conn.: JAI Press,

a fixed rate) as inflation declined and the country passed through copper price cycles, while controls gradually loosened as the central bank gained reserves and the trade balance improved after 1977. In the present context, what is most important is that from early 1979 to June 1982 the authorities deliberately fixed the exchange rate in the presence of moderate inflation, using the exchange rate to freeze inflationary expectations while using open trade and the "law of one price" in an attempt to squeeze out price increases in the goods markets.[43] This scheme attracted foreign capital, as was its intention (thus it resembled the Alessandri-Vergara experiment of 1959–61), and it resulted in a significant real appreciation of the exchange rate. But despite virtually free exchange markets by late 1981, Chilean capital flight did not approach the magnitude of Argentina or Mexico.[44]

Why not? It appears that the regime's proven ability to cut inflation, repress labor, and ignore domestic interests kept flight in check. While much speculation probably did take the form of imported goods instead of financial assets, the idea that this activity accounts for the relative lack of capital flight in Chile is contradicted by the steady decline in imports in late 1981 and early 1982.[45] Sergio de Castro and other members of the economic team had preferred to mandate a 15 to 20

1985); and Joseph Ramos, *Neoconservative Economics in the Southern Cone of Latin America, 1973–1983* (Baltimore: Johns Hopkins University Press, 1986).

43. Ricardo Ffrench-Davis, "Exchange Rate Policies in Chile: The Experience with the Crawling Peg," in *Exchange Rate Rules: The Theory, Performance, and Prospects of the Crawling Peg,* ed. John Williamson (New York: St. Martin's Press, 1981), pp. 162–169; speech of Alvaro Bardón, 21 January 1980, in *Estudios Monetarios* 7 (Banco Central de Chile, 1981), p. 10.

44. The argument for continued confidence on the basis of exchange-rate differentials is made by José Pablo Arellano and Joseph Ramos, "Chile," in *Capital Flight and Third World Debt,* ed. Donald R. Lessard and John Williamson (Washington, D.C.: Institute for International Economics, 1987), table 7.5, p. 161; it is made with reference to net outflows from monthly central bank data by Hernán Cortés Douglas, "Stabilization Policies in Chile: Inflation, Unemployment, and Depressions, 1975–1982," in *The National Economic Policies in Chile,* ed. Gary M. Walton, Contemporary Studies in Economic and Financial Analysis, vol. 51 (Greenwich, Conn.: JAI Press, 1985), table 6, p. 73. Figures from Banco Central de Chile, *Monetary Synthesis* (October 1982).

45. Dornbusch derives this from yearly trade volume figures. See "External Debt, Budget Deficits, and Disequilibrium Exchange Rates," in *International Debt and the Developing Countries,* ed. Gordon W. Smith and John T. Cuddington (Washington, D.C.: World Bank, 1985), pp. 221–22, 230. Monthly data (IMF, *International Financial Statistics,* series 22871.DZF, imports CIF) peak in August 1981, decline steeply after December 1981, then show unbroken low figures until a spike in May 1982, after the resignation of de Castro (and before the June devaluation). The May figures reflect speculation, the low figures in early 1982 show how confined it was.

percent reduction of real wages—and this preference had been reported publicly for over a year. Only after de Castro resigned did speculation surge, accelerating when Pinochet chose an 18 percent devaluation in June 1982.[46] Overall, only two of three key elements motivating speculative flight were truly present, since most agents did not think a devaluation imminent. A deflationary solution was seriously discussed and widely regarded as politically possible.[47]

Capital flight, which had really begun in April and gained strength in June, reached a climax in August when the authorities floated the peso and liberated the exchange market of all remaining controls. It was an expensive gesture. Because the central bank did not retire completely from the floating market, it funded a great part of the outflow by drawing down reserves (and in the same month the government also took over several failed banks). Reversing its course on 21 September, the regime restricted "general purpose" foreign exchange purchases to one-tenth the previous limit, and reinstated the crawling peg. This settled the exchange market, allowing it to weather the dramatic intervention of most of the remaining private banks, undertaken under pressure from foreign creditors, in February 1983.[48] In the meantime, the country had slipped into depression.

What did Chile have in common with other cases in which capital flight was mostly avoided in this period? Although Chile had earlier applied a crawling-peg system and exchange control under Frei (from 1965 to 1970), its subsequent political discontinuity clearly distinguished it from Brazil or Colombia. Still, the dictatorship did not make policy in a vacuum but with reference to rather widespread perceptions about the ills of the Chilean economy. These included the outstandingly acute problems of protected ISI in a small country, the clear need to diversify exports beyond copper, and the familiar obstacles to policy change. Many of Pinochet's senior economic officials had served in the Frei administration, too.

46. According to one account, memories of the 1931 Navy mutiny influenced Pinochet's decision not to decree a wage cut. See Arturo Fontaine Aldunate, *Los Economistas y el Presidente Pinochet* (Santiago: Zig-Zag, 1987), pp. 152, 159–60.

47. This is the view of Arellano and Ramos in *Capital Flight and Third World Debt*, ed. Lessard and Williamson, p. 160; see also Laurence Whitehead, "The Adjustment Process in Chile: A Comparative Perspective," in *Latin American Debt and the Adjustment Crisis*, ed. Rosemary Thorp and Laurence Whitehead (Pittsburgh: University of Pittsburgh Press, 1987), p. 143; and Luis Felipe Lagos and Fernando Colonia, "Expectativas de Devaluación, Credibilidad, y Sustitución de Moneda en Chile," Documento de Trabajo 108, Universidad Católica de Chile Instituto de Economía, March 1987.

48. A good description in English is *International Currency Review* 15, no. 1 (May 1983): 53–54.

Argentina

According to the most common critique of postwar Latin American development strategies, overvalued currencies and capital flight originated in the protectionist and fiscally irresponsible economic strategies of populist-inclined politicians. Yet by mid-1980, four years after a coup by a regime professedly committed to extirpating populism and ushering in the reign of the market, Argentina had both a grossly overvalued currency and massive capital flight. Why?

Argentina did not enjoy such continuous abundance in the postwar period as did Venezuela, but neither did its periodic exchange crises call forth the kind of durable policy reform eventually undertaken elsewhere. The most obvious explanation lies in the country's political instability; another relates to Perón's politicization of exchange policy. The former placed a high premium on the apparent stability of a fixed exchange rate, if only as a way of attracting wary foreign (or expatriate) capital. The latter fortified opposition to exchange controls among anti-Peronists, especially export elites, who associated controls with arbitrary and confiscatory policies.

I would like to argue that the politics tie in with a more subtle, structural explanation, too. Compared to its counterparts in Colombia or Brazil, Argentina's primary export sector had less trouble in the international marketplace. There was the remarkable export-led growth at the turn of the century, and in the 1930s the Argentine recovery came to an unusual degree from a revival of exports.[49] But the war, and later Perón, disturbed the connection to the international market. The country produced a greater volume of exports in the late 1920s and even during 1931–37 than in any similar periods before 1976. Hence there were good reasons for the Pampa export elites to be nostalgic and liberal. They blamed state interventionism for their decline, pointing to a relatively favorable world market and good results from brief experiments with liberal policies, such as the transitional Guido regime in 1962–63 (with Pinedo, Alsogaray, and then Martínez de Hoz at the Ministry of Economy), during which export volumes recovered quickly.[50] In part this was because the Pampa

49. This stemmed from the Roca-Runciman agreements and the drought in the North American plains. See Arturo O'Connell, "Argentina into the Depression: Problems of an Open Economy," in *Latin America in the 1930s: The Role of the Periphery in World Crisis,* ed. Rosemary Thorp (London: Macmillan, 1984), pp. 194–201.

50. A temperate but politically consequential version of this liberal nostalgia can be seen in José Alfredo Martínez de Hoz, *La Agricultura y la Ganadería Argentina en el Período 1930–1960* (Buenos Aires: Editorial Sudamericana, 1967), pp. 9–22. Here I

exported mainly foodstuffs eaten by wage earners: a sharp devaluation coupled with domestic price decontrol could substantially depress urban demand and turn exports (and the trade balance) around, depending on the stage in the beef cycle (Table 3.1).[51] Whenever foreign trade did respond to these incentives, it also made possible the "pendular" behavior of the large bourgeoisie, which allied with the Pampa during foreign exchange crises and, as the balance of payments eased, looked to its interest in economic expansion.[52]

For the Argentine elite and much of the urban middle class, Perón gave state intervention, including exchange control, the stamp of arbitrariness. As is well known, although he dared not greatly disturb rural property relations, he led a highly charged verbal and symbolic attack on the "oligarchy." He also enforced a state monopoly over agricultural trade through IAPI that took away the profits from the surge in agricultural prices immediately after the war. Thus, unlike the situation in Brazil under Dutra, the move to reimpose controls

---

should register my partial disagreement with William C. Smith's "politics in command" view on the stop-go cycles. My argument is that had the fortunes of the Argentine rural sector resembled those of Brazilian coffee, exchange control would not have ended up among those policies forever tainted by association with "totalitarianism" in the eyes of the traditional export sector. My support for this is mainly the relatively uncontroversial nature of even strict exchange control in other countries. Cf. William C. Smith, *Authoritarianism and the Crisis of the Argentine Political Economy* (Stanford: Stanford University Press, 1989), pp. 36–37.

51. The seminal treatment of the structural conflict is Carlos Díaz-Alejandro, *Exchange Rate Devaluation in a Semi-Industrialized Country: The Experience of Argentina* (Cambridge, Mass.: MIT Press, 1965). A close look at the results of devaluations shows the influence of climate and the beef cycle could dominate the supply effects of devaluation in the short run. After October 1949 trade volume recovered; after the October 1955 devaluation of the "Liberating Revolution" it rose slightly, despite plunging international prices; after Frondizi's depreciation of the first three quarters of 1959 it did not rise, colliding with the beef cycle. The large devaluation under Guido in the second quarter of 1962 had a large and rapid result. See IMF, *International Financial Statistics,* quarterly indices of total export volume, various issues. Total export indices for the IMF end in 1965. Using Argentine government Instituto Nacional de Estadística y Censos (INDEC) figures for exports in constant dollars deflated by Paasche indices, one can see that the March 1967 devaluation had a big effect in the second quarter of that year but had to overcome adverse climatic conditions and shows little effect afterward. (Thanks to Guillermo Escudé for providing me with a detailed series of INDEC numbers.) Although the beef cycle sometimes depressed exportable totals, ranchers would not consider it a kind of market trouble that called for government support, since they were trading income for capital.

52. See Guillermo O'Donnell, "State and Alliances in Argentina, 1956–1976," *Journal of Development Studies* 15, no. 1 (October 1978): 13–15.

Table 3.1 Argentina: Terms of Trade and Volume of Exports, 1928–1976
(1970 = 100; gains in index favor Argentina)

Year	Volume	Terms	Year	Volume	Terms
1928	104.7	124.5	1953	53.1	117.2
1929	105.2	113.2	1954	57.2	102.4
1930	72.8	109.7	1955ᵃ	50.4	102.2
1931	99.8	82.0	1956	56.2	91.7
1932	92.0	85.1	1957	59.8	88.5
1933	86.6	80.5	1958ᵃ	64.9	89.7
1934	90.2	98.7	1959	65.9	95.3
1935	95.1	98.7	1960	66.2	100.5
1936	85.8	120.5	1961	59.7	106.7
1937	100.1	138.2	1962ᵃ	83.0	99.4
1938	64.8	126.6	1963	82.9	117.9
1939	83.2	110.9	1964ᵇ	80.8	118.8
1940	70.2	114.3	1965ᵇ	89.4	109.2
1941	62.7	125.8	1966ᵇ	92.4	108.8
1942	61.1	119.6	1967ᵃ	86.6	111.1
1943	62.8	123.7	1968	83.1	105.9
1944	69.0	111.6	1969	93.5	108.4
1945	70.2	100.0	1970	100.0	100.0
1946	73.1	153.8	1971	86.1	109.0
1947	79.6	155.2	1972	83.1	123.2
1948	72.0	159.1	1973	98.6	146.7
1949	48.0	141.4	1974	92.8	127.7
1950	59.4	138.5	1975ᵃ	76.9	102.4
1951	47.0	131.3	1976ᵃ	106.1	95.4
1952ᵃ	32.7	102.2			

Source: Comisión Económica para América Latina, *América Latina: Relación de Precios de Intercambio, 1928–1976* E/CEPAL/1040 (New York: UN Economic and Social Council, 2 August 1977), p. 20.

ᵃYear of a major devaluation, post–1945. ᵇYear of many small devaluations, post–1945.

was not forced upon a reluctant conservative administration by an obvious crisis. While Perón saw controls as part of a scheme that would also reduce price fluctuations (and a few years later IAPI did offer above-market purchase prices), to the Pampa it seemed like a robbery whose malicious intent was confirmed by the tenor of Peronist discourse. Thus Perón left Argentine foreign exchange policy thoroughly politicized, as state intervention became the focus of intense opposition and engendered enduring distrust.[53] According to Mallon and Sourrouille, "many of the farmers most adversely affected by the new rules of the game [under Perón] steadfastly refused to accept anything short of a complete reversal of these rules."[54]

Still, after 1955 the rules were never completely reversed. First of all, it had long been the case that the export sector could not translate its economic power into electoral victories. Even within the military, liberal ideas had been in retreat since the 1920s; even as they repudiated Perón, most military men did not repudiate ISI or an active state. When in 1956 Generals Lonardi and Aramburu kept a 25 percent retention on Pampa exports instead of dissolving many state enterprises, the most important rural export organizations (SRA and CARBAP) denounced "greedy public officials" and retreated from active support of the military regime.[55] When in 1967 the Onganía dictatorship imposed exchange retentions of 16 to 25 percent along with a large devaluation, the Pampa again complained bitterly.[56]

Nevertheless, the liberal point of view won more often on the question of exchange control. One could see this in Frondizi's stabilization plan of 1958, in the Guido regime's plan of 1962–63, and in the reforms of Krieger Vasena in 1967. Although each included familiar IMF-recommended policies, they were marked by an unhesitating embrace of free currency markets.[57]

53. Dardo Cúneo, *Comportamiento y Crisis de la Clase Empresaria* (Buenos Aires: Editorial Pleamar, 1967), esp. pp. 163–65, 215–19; Gary Wynia, *Argentina in the Postwar Era: Politics and Economic Policy Making in a Divided Society* (Albuquerque: University of New Mexico Press, 1978), pp. 63–64. For more detailed examination of Perón's exchange policy, see Pablo Gerchunoff, "Peronist Economic Policies, 1946–55," in *The Political Economy of Argentina, 1946–1983,* ed. Guido DiTella and Rudiger Dornbusch (Pittsburgh: University of Pittsburgh Press, 1989); and Jorge Fodor, "Péron's Policies for Agricultural Exports 1946–1948: Dogmatism or Commonsense?" in *Argentina in the Twentieth Century,* ed. David Rock (Pittsburgh: University of Pittsburgh Press, 1975), pp. 155–58.

54. Richard D. Mallon in collaboration with Juan V. Sourrouille, *Economic Policymaking in a Conflict Society: The Argentine Case* (Cambridge, Mass.: Harvard University Press, 1975), p. 36.

55. Wynia, *Argentina in the Postwar Era,* p. 158, citing *Review of the River Plate,* 22 May 1956; Pablo Gerchunoff, "A Note on the Economic Policies of the 'Liberating Revolution,'" in *The Political Economy of Argentina, 1946–1983,* ed. Guido DiTella and Rudiger Dornbusch (Pittsburgh: University of Pittsburgh Press, 1989), p. 104.

56. CARBAP, *Memoria y Balance* [1967–68] (Buenos Aires: Confederación de Asociaciones Rurales de Buenos Aires y La Pampa, 1968), p. 9.

57. On Frondizi, see Díaz-Alejandro, *Exchange Rate Devaluation,* pp. 145–47; Alberto Petrecolla in collaboration with Graciela Simón, "Unbalanced Development, 1958–1962," in *The Political Economy of Argentina, 1946–1983,* ed. Guido DiTella and

While the motivations for this embrace were many, Perón's legacy of distrust emerged often in discussions of the issue. For example, when in April 1964 the Illia administration imposed exchange controls because it faced an impending bulge of foreign debt payments, large commercial and agricultural interests reacted with alarm.[58] *La Nación* noted that Federico Pinedo, having inherited controls as finance minister in 1933, had loosened them as circumstances warranted, seeking total freedom in the exchange market, "without suspecting that the dictatorship overthrown in 1955 would push the inherent evils of the system beyond limit." The editorial continued, referring to the Illia administration, "the fact that many of the current shapers of economic policy collaborated in the foreign exchange regimes before 1955, or share their principles, has transformed a measure that might otherwise be effective into a factor that disturbs the economic activity of the country."[59] While advocating export expansion, an influential private-sector spokesman warned that "[the controls] bring us closer to political and economic collectivism."[60] In this climate, it mattered less that Illia kept the exchange rate relatively favorable to exports by undertaking nine small devaluations over his last two years.[61] The combination of exchange control and real-rate targeting disappeared with his regime.

Consider how this differed from Brazil, Colombia, or even Chile. There, relatively broad agreement on a reorientation of exchange

---

Rudiger Dornbusch (Pittsburgh: University of Pittsburgh Press, 1989), pp. 111–12. On Guido, see Juan Carlos de Pablo, "Economic Policy Without Political Context: Guido, 1962–1963," in DiTella and Dornbusch, eds., pp. 133–35.

58. For Economy Minister Carlos García Tudero, the debt justified both the controls and periodic small devaluations. See Guido DiTella and Carlos Rodríguez, *Argentina, 1946–1983: The Economic Ministers Speak* (London: Macmillan, 1988), pp. 79–80.

59. (Buenos Aires), 20 April 1964, p. 6. Also alarmed was the liberal weekly *Economic Survey* (20, no. 432, 14 April 1964), which concluded that total exchange control was "the well-known objective of a certain group of central bank functionaries" who "have never forgotten the important posts they occupied within the Central Bank in the days of Perón" (p. 193). It added that Argentine officials may have been wrongly influenced by contemporary British practices but that these were "carried over from the war" and could offer "no comparison" to Argentina (p. 194). For a Perón-era argument that controls are justified only in rare emergencies, see Walter M. Beveraggi A., *El Servicio de Capital Extranjero y el Control de Cambios: La Experiencia Argentina de 1900 a 1943* (Mexico City: Fondo de Cultura Económica, 1954), esp. pp. 224–25.

60. *La Nación* (Buenos Aires), 17 April 1964, p. 5.

61. *Review of the River Plate,* April 30; *Memoria de la Bolsa de Comercio de Buenos Aires, 1964* (Buenos Aires: Bolsa de Comercio, 1965), pp. 9, 26, 28–31; Mallon and Sourrouille, *Economic Policymaking,* p. 28; García Tudero in DiTella and Rodríguez, *Argentina, 1946–1983,* p. 75.

policy emerged from an experience of destabilizing capital flows and export problems. These motivated Illia, too, but for the export elites, Argentine problems resulted from misguided, statist departures from liberal orthodoxy. The importance of structure lay in the fact that this view was sometimes vindicated, at least in the short term.

Thus, even the most stridently anti-Peronist forces in Argentina did not see a high priority on a long-term restructuring of the country's export sector. There was less urgency, and other problems always clamored for solution. Stabilization and liberalization were better than real-rate targeting. The preferred mix also opened the door to foreign or expatriate capital by promising the profitable combination of a fixed rate and an open exchange market. For example, the military coup in June 1966 did not take place during a notable balance-of-payments crisis, because exports had been expanding quickly since 1961 and the trade balance was in surplus. The main problem, in the eyes of the Onganía regime, lay in attracting investment to an uncertain environment. Armed force constituted one part of the solution, of course, but like the Alessandri experiment in Chile during 1959–61, Krieger Vasena's program of March 1967 also placed considerable weight upon exchange-rate fixity as a signal of economic stability and as an incentive to overseas funds. As the minister later wrote, since there was widespread confidence that the new rate would persist, he "did not hesitate" to remove controls on capital and current account.[62]

The Argentine pattern could be summed up as follows: an unstable political setting made fixed rates politically desirable and convenient for attracting overseas capital; the fixed nominal rate, which implied a currency appreciating in real terms, did not immediately compromise the expansion of exports; and since strict exchange controls might repel nervous capital and they bore the stigma of Peronism (in part because of their slim historical precedent in a country with a

62. On solicitousness toward foreign capital, see Smith, *Authoritarianism and Crisis*, pp. 81–84, 99. He adds, judging from Ministry of Economy data, that "foreign capital was reluctant to make long-term investments and preferred taking quick profits from currency speculation in 'hot money' until internal economic expansion was well under way and political stability was achieved" (p. 99). According to Krieger, the large 1967 devaluation was to make the new fixed rate "an anchor which would last for several years and achieve reasonable stability." See DiTella and Rodríguez, *Argentina, 1946–1983*, pp. 87–88. Guillermo O'Donnell, *Bureaucratic Authoritarianism: Argentina, 1966–1973, in Comparative Perspective*, trans. James McGuire (Berkeley: University of California Press, 1988), p. 86, notes Krieger Vasena's trip to Europe and the United States before announcing his program of 13 March; on crisis and the need for orthodoxy, see pp. 93–98. See also Ministerio de Economía y Trabajo, *Argentina: Building for the Future: Economic Program for 1968* (Buenos Aires, 1968), esp. p. 12.

relatively sound export sector), Argentine conservatives abolished them repeatedly.

This pattern helps us understand why, despite the extraordinary power of the military regime under General Jorge Rafael Videla, its economic program failed in a flurry of capital flight.[63] Although the economy grew moderately through 1977–80 and unemployment did not spike upward, the regime could not reduce inflation below 100 percent annually; and between 1976 and 1982 the net foreign debt rose by over $30 billion while the total current account deficit for the period amounted to only about $8.8 billion. Less than one-fifth of the debt could be explained by the need for foreign financing.[64] Much, perhaps most, of the rest ended up funding capital flight in 1980–82. In view of these facts, it is ironic that among the variety of ills that accompanied the agony of Peronism in 1975–76, the Videla regime declared itself loudly against financial speculation and in favor of an "economy of production."

What were its mistakes? A limited critique regarding the order of economic liberalization asserts that the authorities should have sought domestic fiscal and financial equilibrium first, then liberalized trade, and only then liberalized capital movements. The exchange rate should have been indexed "passively" to past inflation (the typical mode for a crawling peg), at least until trade liberalization was complete.[65] Instead, as we shall see, capital movements were freed before the fiscal deficit was low enough to make debt finance sustainable and before trade liberalization had passed its first stage. So even if we embrace the narrowest critique (itself disputed by economists), two relevant questions arise. Why the hurry to free the exchange

63. On the economic record of the regime, see World Bank, *Argentina: Economic Memorandum* (Washington, D.C.: World Bank, 1985), vol. 1. Acute analyses of political economy are Adolfo Canitrot, *Teoría y Práctica del Liberalismo: Política Antiinflacionaria y Apertura Económica en la Argentina, 1976–1981,* Estudios CEDES vol. 3, no. 10 (Buenos Aires: Centro de Estudios de Estado y Sociedad, 1980); and especially Jorge Schvarzer, *Martínez de Hoz: La Lógica Política de la Política Económica,* Ensayos y Tesis CISEA no. 4 (Buenos Aires: Centro de Investigaciones Sociales Sobre el Estado y la Administración, 1983).

64. Roberto Frenkel, José María Fanelli, and Juan Sommer, *El Proceso de Endeudamiento Externo Argentino,* Documentos CEDES no. 2 (Buenos Aires: Centro de Estudios de Estado y Sociedad, 1988), pp. 11–12.

65. Ronald T. McKinnon, "The Order of Economic Liberalization: Lessons from Chile and Argentina," in *Economic Policy in a World of Change,* ed. Karl Brunner and Allan H. Meltzer, Carnegie-Rochester Conference Series on Public Policy no. 17 (Amsterdam: North-Holland, 1982), pp. 159–86. See also the comments by Jacob Frenkel and Ricardo Arriazu in "Panel Discussion on the Southern Cone," *IMF Staff Papers* 30, no. 1 (March 1983).

market? And why did they let the currency become so obviously over-valued?

The answer lies in a combination of neoliberal economic ideology, political division, and economic opportunity. The first, as already noted, possessed deep historical roots among much of the Argentine economic elite. They saw in the military's self-styled "Process of National Reorganization" a vehicle not only for ending inflation but also for liberalizing the economy and shrinking the state. Within ten days of the coup, the central bank president promised the "total liberation of the exchange market," and then made good on the promise over the next year.[66] Here we find an Argentine liberal mindset, strongly colored by its revulsion toward Peronist arbitrariness. In 1960, Martínez de Hoz had derided the *"manipuleo cambiario"* by which the Pampa subsidized the rest of the economy; in 1975 Roberto Alemann, brother of Videla's finance secretary and later himself economy minister under Galtieri, characterized exchange control as an "emergency regime," a violation of the constitutional rights of free contract and responsible for capital flight (so that "the country goes into debt while its residents invest abroad").[67] In a book later written in response to his critics, Martínez de Hoz echoed this: "[W]e did not believe in the efficacy of exchange controls in our country, and we still do not. . . . by their mere existence they produce capital flight."[68] Standing behind Videla, Economy Minister Martínez de Hoz incarnated the complex Argentine economic elite so perfectly that it would have been, and was, easy to overestimate the coherence of the group now running the country.[69]

66. *Review of the River Plate*, 9 April 1976, p. 465. An indication of this freedom was the disappearance of the black-market exchange-rate premium by early 1977. See Rudiger Dornbusch and Juan Carlos de Pablo, "Debt and Macroeconomic Instability in Argentina," in *Developing Country Debt and the World Economy*, ed. Jeffrey D. Sachs (Chicago: University of Chicago Press, 1989), p. 42. On the role of ideology in the diagnosis of the economy, see Roberto Frenkel et al., *El Proceso de Endeudamiento Externo Argentino*, pp. 4–5. On liberal priorities, see Martínez de Hoz's reflections in a *Prensa Económica* interview, no. 153 (June 1987): 48.

67. Martínez de Hoz, *La Agricultura y la Ganadería Argentina*, p. 88; Roberto T. Alemann with the collaboration of Manuel Horacio Aramovich, *Curso de Política Económica Argentina*, 2d ed. (Buenos Aires: Alemann y Cía., 1975), 2:91–93.

68. *Quince Años Después* (Buenos Aires: Emecé, 1991), p. 97; he makes a similar statement in DiTella and Rodríguez, *Argentina, 1946–1983*, p. 153.

69. Of a family long prominent in the Rural Society, he was schooled at Eton, chaired the country's most modern private steel firm (Acindar), operated the family's sugar interests, and is a personal friend of David Rockefeller. A feeling for the battles and the necessary division of labor between paternalist nationalists and liberals can be obtained from O'Donnell, *Bureaucratic Authoritarianism*, chap. 3.

But economic liberals did not fully dominate the state. Most of the armed forces effectively opposed any policies that would have meant sustained recession or unemployment, and they represented a large and unpredictable burden on public finance.[70] The neoliberal technocrats found themselves fighting to transform a highly statist economy while operating from an isolated position, concentrated in the central bank. So they tried to turn the ship of state onto a neoliberal course by pulling extra hard on what rudders they held. These included ending central bank financing of fiscal deficits, instituting financial deregulation and other policies to attract foreign finance, using the exchange rate to slow inflation and force industry to be competitive, and freeing the exchange market.

The overvaluation of the currency emerged from these circumstances. In 1978, the rapid real appreciation stemmed from the regime's desire to fight inflation while taking advantage of a favorable trade balance and newly eager foreign lenders.[71] The trend in relative prices did not escape notice on the Pampa or among manufacturers of tradeables, and it led nearly all the export and commercial-sector representatives to resign from the cabinet in 1978.[72] But exports seemed less pressing as the country slid into recession and as the neoliberals came under military pressure to revive the economy and improve their disappointing record on inflation.[73]

70. Based on their fears of social explosion, the armed forces reportedly instructed Martínez de Hoz not to provoke unemployment above 5 percent. *International Currency Review* 13, no. 5 (November 1981): 136.

71. The jump in the real currency value appears in two separate time series constructed by Rudiger Dornbusch. In each case the inflection point marking the onset of real appreciation corresponds to the financial reform of June 1977. One series uses the ratio of import to domestic prices. See fig. 8.5, p. 228, in Dornbusch, "External Debt, Budget Deficits, and Disequilibrium Exchange Rates," in Smith and Cuddington, eds. The other appears as fig. 13.4 in "Argentina Under Martínez de Hoz, 1981–1983," in *The Political Economy of Argentina, 1946–1983,* ed. Guido Di Tella and Rudiger Dornbusch (Pittsburgh: University of Pittsburgh Press, 1989). See also *International Currency Review* 12, no. 1 (1980): 144. According to this journal, Martínez de Hoz "cleverly exploited his position as the darling of the world banking community, so that international banks have been falling all over themselves since early 1977 to lend money to Argentina." For contemporary reaction to deindexing, the decision to allow real appreciation, see *Clarín* (Buenos Aires), 12 May 1978, p. 13.

72. Schvarzer, *Martínez de Hoz,* p. 65; see also various issues of *Review of the River Plate,* May–September 1978, esp. 31 May, pp. 788–89.

73. Canitrot emphasizes the armed forces' paternalism and fear of unemployment. See *Teoría Práctica del Liberalismo,* p. 32; also Juan Alemann interview, Buenos Aires, 15 July 1987; also Martínez de Hoz in DiTella and Rodríguez, *Argentina, 1946–1983,* p. 169.

The result was a flawed imitation of Chilean policy, the *tablita* or preannounced schedule of exchange (and other) rates. While anticipating some price "lags" (since it was in projecting a rate of devaluation below the current inflation rate that the latter was to be dragged downward), the plan required great credibility in the markets to keep real appreciation and real interest rates down.[74] As in Chile, the plan deliberately promoted a huge inflow of foreign finance, most notoriously into short-term switching operations that became known as *"bicicletas."* The plan's demise began before its second birthday, when a doubtful market pushed up real interest rates and slowed the economy in late 1979. In 1980, overleveraged firms defaulted, banks failed, government outlays for deposit insurance soared, and capital flight accelerated. In March 1981, just before Viola was to take over from Videla, smaller investors joined what had become a frenzied flight of capital. As foreign banks continued to open new offices in Buenos Aires, exchange houses imposed a lower limit of U.S.$5,000 per transaction in order to keep out panic-stricken small savers.[75]

Only massive foreign borrowing had kept the scheme afloat through 1980 and nearly 1981. Most of this was undertaken through the public enterprises, whose central bank subsidies had been cut off. But it should also be noted that many private firms continued to borrow abroad even as the exchange markets turned massively to dollar buying. Probably a great deal of this was distress borrowing, as a World Bank study concluded. Yet the tripling of foreign debt-to-equity ratios among solvent Argentine private firms between 1979 and 1981, while the private sector was a large net *buyer* of dollars in the foreign exchange markets, suggests that for many the acquisition of foreign debt and foreign assets went on simultaneously. In the most infamous cases, this process took the form of *autopréstamos* or back-to-back loans, made with a 100 percent corresponding balance and the conniv-

---

74. Many summaries of the Martínez de Hoz period concentrate on this policy and its effects. A brief one is Dornbusch and de Pablo, "Debt and Macroeconomic Instability," pp. 41–44. While the exchange lag was the most obvious indicator of disequilibrium, monetarist arguments emphasized the link between lack of credibility and fiscal deficits. See, for example, Roque Fernández and Carlos A. Rodríguez, *Inflación y Estabilidad: El Tipo de Cambio como Instrumento de Estabilización* (Buenos Aires: Ediciones Macchi, 1982), secs. V and VII, especially pp. 175–79 and 255–63. For further elaboration, see Roque Fernández, "Réplica" (to Ernesto Feldman) in *Desarrollo Económico*, no. 91 (October–December 1983): 456–57.

75. *Extra,* April 1981, p. 36; see also Horacio García Belsunce, *Política y Economía en Años Críticos* (Buenos Aires: Editorial Troquel, 1982), p. 141; *Latin American Weekly Report,* 16 January 1981, p. 6; 20 February 1981, p. 1.

ance of a foreign bank. As the World Bank delicately put it, firms "managed to hedge their risks."[76]

Interestingly, in the face of currency misalignment the authorities' mind-set resembled that prevailing in other countries absorbing private international capital. Even before the *tablita* Martínez de Hoz spoke of currency appreciation as a benign response to market forces. In a September 1978 interview he repeated that the original program of the "Proceso" included the elimination of exchange controls and a freely determined exchange rate "and not parities artificially established by the government at overvalued levels for the peso." But he also noted that "the fight against inflation is first priority and we had no intention of *devaluing artificially*." In view of the trade surplus and financial inflows, he saw this inaction as consistent with a free market and with "what nearly every business sector was asking . . . less state intervention and greater economic freedom."[77] Vigilance over relative price levels was government meddling.

In this way, the Videla regime's policy mistakes were strongly conditioned by the country's foreign-sector position, as foreign finance flowed in on top of a current-account surplus. To the neoliberal team the surplus justified the real exchange rates, making it possible to reconcile the *tablita* scheme with long-term stability. But this argument persisted after the trade balance had slipped into deficit in late 1979, and after Buenos Aires had become one of the most expensive cities in the world. Since international bankers still lent freely, it was thought, the market could not be very far out of equilibrium. In defense of policies that had led to what most now estimate (as many did then) as at least 40 percent currency overvaluation in early 1981

76. Carlos Díaz-Alejandro argued that major actors anticipated a government bailout and so "domestic firms relied heavily on debt" and "entrepreneurs placed as little as possible of their own money into firms" "Latin American Debt: I Don't Think We Are in Kansas Anymore," *Brookings Papers on Economic Activity,* vol. 2 (1984), p. 378. World Bank, *Argentina: Economic Memorandum,* 214 n. 3 and p. 215. On distress borrowing, see World Bank, *Argentina: Economic Memorandum,* p. 218. The bank links the back-to-back loans to the foreign exchange insurance program introduced after the June 1981 devaluation (and reintroduced in July 1982), but the incentives to acquire dollar assets were very strong before then. On the loans, see *World Bank, Argentina: Economic Memorandum,* 17 n. 7, 67 n. 12. For accounts of this period, see Canitrot, *Teoría y Práctica del Liberalismo,* p. 46; Frenkel et al., *El Proceso de Endeudamiento Externo Argentino,* p. 12. DiTella and Rodríguez nevertheless assert that the rising military spending of 1978–81 was "largely responsible" for both the widening fiscal deficit and the increase in external debt (*Argentina, 1946–1983,* p. 24).

77. *Mercado,* 14 September 1978; emphasis added.

(Table 3.3), Martínez de Hoz concluded that the true equilibrium level was "not so clear."[78]

Although most of the Argentine capital flight actually followed the departure of Martínez de Hoz, its roots could be traced back to his times of *plata dulce*. The outgoing administration left its successors with rising debt, rapidly declining output, and a still overvalued currency. Devaluations did nothing to arrest the flight, however, as labor fought to maintain its real wage and firms that had borrowed in the cheap dollars of 1980 now found themselves overwhelmed. The authorities gave out generous exchange insurance; firms took advantage of the insurance as they continued to borrow, some in distress and others engaging in back-to-backs. After the South Atlantic War, in July 1982, the economic team of Dagnino Pastore and Cavallo sought to relieve recession by at once imposing interest-rate ceilings and deliberately accelerating inflation. The result was a rapid and massive transfer from creditors to debtors, a collapse in the government debt market, a hyperinflationary spiral, and another flight to the dollar. As the currency rapidly depreciated, the government's real costs for exchange insurance jumped. In November the central bank invited those who wished not to renew swaps to allow the state to take over their foreign obligations.[79]

Venezuela

The Venezuelan case offers the strongest contrast to those of Colombia and Brazil. Venezuela suffered from the most conspicuous "policy mistakes," in the sense used here, of any government in the region.

78. *Bases para una Argentina Moderna, 1976–80* (Buenos Aires: Emecé, 1981), pp. 97, 95.

79. On July 1982, see Rudiger Dornbusch, "Argentina After Martínez de Hoz," in *The Political Economy of Argentina, 1946–1983*, ed. Guido DiTella and Rudiger Dornbusch (Pittsburgh: University of Pittsburgh Press, 1989), pp. 297–301. See also Eric Calcagno, *Los Bancos Transnacionales y el Endeudamiento Externo en la Argentina*, Cuadernos de la CEPAL no. 56 (Santiago: UN ECLA, 1987), p. 36. For contemporary reactions see, for example, "Cavallo: Cierra el Esquema?" *Mercado* (Buenos Aires), 5 August 1982, pp. 14–18; "Un Plan Económico que Deja Graves Problemas sin Respuesta," *La Prensa* (Buenos Aires), 21 July 1982. Cavallo blamed his successor at the central bank, Julio González del Solar, for the bailout: see *Clarín*, 21 March and 28 March 1989, cited in Norberto Galasso, *De Martínez de Hoz a Cavallo: Gatos y Sardinas en la Economía Argentina* (Buenos Aires: Editorial Fraterna, 1992), p. 124. Estimates place the transfer of wealth at several percent of GDP.

During the 1980s its capital flight was commonly estimated as roughly equivalent to the country's foreign borrowing during the 1977–83 period (as I noted earlier, misinvoicing reduces this estimate significantly). But the mistakes stemmed as much from the ways policy conformed to international market signals as the ways it opposed them. Venezuela had such continuous abundance on external accounts that policymakers rarely faced the need to control panic outflows or target the exchange rate, which had stayed strong and stable for most of the previous five decades. Moreover, until the 1970s, postwar petroleum prices also followed a less volatile trend than did most other commodity prices. With less price variation, the country did not experience large and repeated procyclical swings of private credits. As Venezuelan finances unraveled after 1980, policymakers acted according to the same optimistic oil-price projections used by the international banking community, managing the debt and the fisc carelessly, and foreign exchange barely at all.[80]

From the first large-scale exploitation of oil in the early 1930s, plentiful foreign exchange and tax revenue buoyed the Venezuelan currency, profoundly shaping the country's economic structure.[81] Domestic returns from foreign-owned oil production depended on taxes and company spending on local inputs, and for the latter the exchange rate was the key variable. In 1942 an official calculated that a devaluation would reduce receipts from the petroleum companies

80. Ricardo Hausmann has argued that the real currency appreciation of 1976–82 was "the standard general-equilibrium result of an unsterilized oil boom" and that "if the exchange policy is blamed for the crisis, a devaluation in an oil-exporting economy will drastically reduce or eliminate the fiscal deficit in the short run, and the Congress will then attach little importance to tax reform. Instead, subsidies to those affected by the devaluation will tend to receive more attention." See John Williamson, ed., *Latin American Adjustment: How Much Has Happened?* (Washington, D.C.: Institute for International Economics, 1990), p. 239. By emphasizing exchange policy here I do not intend to promote it as the sole explanation for the crisis. Obviously, after February 1983 Venezuelan governments should have resisted pressure for subsidies, in which there was a great deal of fraud anyway, and used the fiscal windfall from the devaluation to bring public finances into line. But if private capital outflows are a result of anticipated fiscal deficits rather than of speculation against the currency, those engaging in flight must have calculated that the eventual devaluation would have its fiscal effect eaten up by subsidy claims coming from agents like themselves. Without this assumption, the effect translates to little or no expected tax liability. While the above scenario may well describe the extreme cynicism of some Venezuelan asset holders, I believe reaction to interest and expected exchange rates is a more parsimonious explanation in this case.

81. Carlos Miguel Lollett C., *El Dólar Petrolero*, Ediciones de la Bolsa de Comercio de Caracas, no. 7 (Caracas, 1971), pp. 35–40, 69–70.

much more, and more immediately, than it would spur gains in coffee and cocoa exports.[82] Oil had biased the economy against the production of tradeables and toward construction, petty commerce, and services, especially government (since it collected the hard currency). In 1957 Celso Furtado warned that this had created a "rentier class with an ever-greater social weight" that would enjoy the income from its mostly foreign investments as the country became a permanent capital exporter. Another critic noted that even from the Left there was "not a word against the exchange structure that transformed us into a nation of shopkeepers and bureaucrats."[83]

While three years of moderate capital outflows did follow the fall of the dictatorship in 1958, the crisis was a relatively mild one and the government overcame it by 1964 with a devaluation and appeals to investor confidence.[84] Recalling the crisis period, Alfredo Machado Gómez, president of the central bank from 1961 to 1968, noted that even in its worst years (1960–61) the situation "did not reach the extremes and the persistence of similar crises confronted by other countries." From this he argued that for countries like Venezuela with historically plentiful reserves, exchange control was "illegitimate."[85]

With the bonanzas of the 1970s, oil dominated Venezuelan economic policy even more fully. Corruption and cronyism hobbled much of the public administration (the state oil company was an honorable exception). Imports surged after 1973, the oil industry was national-ized in 1975, and the Pérez administration pushed public investment projects while taking on debt from eager bankers. When prices fell in

82. Javier Lope Bello, "El Control de Cambios en Venezuela," *El Trimestre Económico* 9, no. 3 (October–December 1942): 360–61; see also José Antonio Mayobre, "La Paridad del Bolívar" [1944], in *La Economía Contemporánea de Venezuela*, ed. Héctor Valecillos T. and Omar Bello Rodríguez (Caracas: Banco Central de Venezuela, 1990), 1:57–59.

83. Furtado, "El Desarrollo Reciente de la Economía Venezolana" [1957], in *La Economía Contemporánea de Venezuela*, ed. Héctor Valecillos and Omar Bello Rodríguez (Caracas: Banco Central de Venezuela, 1990), 1:186; Domingo Alberto Rangel, *El Proceso del Capitalismo Contemporáneo en Venezuela* (Caracas: UCV Colección Human-ismo y Ciencia, 1968), pp. 218–19.

84. On the crisis, see Franklin Tugwell, *The Politics of Oil in Venezuela* (Stanford: Stanford University, 1975), pp. 78–84; Sergio Aranda, *La Economía Venezolana: Una Interpretación de su Modo de Funcionamiento*, 2d ed. (Mexico City: Siglo 21, 1978), p. 196; John D. Powelson, "La Fuga de Capital en Venezuela, 1961–1962," *El Trimestre Económico* 31, no. 121 (January–March 1964).

85. Alfredo Machado Gómez, "La Problemática Monetaria y Cambiaria del País en 1960–1961," *Resumen* (Caracas), 6 March 1983, p. 14; Alfredo Machado Gómez, *Crisis y Recuperación: La Economía Monetaria Venezolana entre 1961 y 1968* (Caracas: Banco Central de Venezuela, 1972), p. 41.

real terms in 1977–78 as the investment projects entered their most expensive phase, borrowing, often on short term and unregistered, bridged the gap.[86] Debt and capital flight both soared in this period, yet the Venezuelan government did not have a net debtor position because of the large overseas balances it had accumulated in various state funds.[87] Soon after, the second oil shock rescued the oil-fueled debt machine. Although he decried the "mortgaged country" when he took over from Pérez in early 1979, Herrera Campins introduced his own public-sector borrowing proposal only three months later. His government and its international bankers placed their bets on continuously rising oil prices. He paid little attention to exports other than oil: as late as 1982 there was still no serious policy concerning them.[88]

In the Venezuelan case we face the difficult problem of assessing why people did *not* act as crisis approached. Between the beginning of January 1982 and the end of February 1983, central bank reserves declined by $8.78 billion.[89] Officials knew of the outflow of private funds, and the central bank president, Leopoldo Díaz Bruzual, later reflected thoughtfully upon the entire crisis and its root causes.[90]

Yet it remains the case that the Herrera Campins government showed astonishing complacency. For example, after once abolishing interest-rate controls, the authorities reimposed them in March 1981, at a level well below that in the United States. Díaz Bruzual publicly justified this, in large part, as a move that would "allow the drainage

86. Debt with maturities under two years did not require approval by the Congress, just the cabinet (though it later turned out that even this was often lacking). For a discussion, see *Número* (Caracas), 7 June 1981.

87. For a brief account using public-sector data, see Pedro Palma, *1974–1983: Una Década de Contrastes en la Economía Venezolana,* Academia Nacional de Ciencias Económicas, Cuaderno no. 11 (Caracas, November 1985); on the debt position, see Miguel A. Rodríguez, *La Política Económica del Crecimiento para Venezuela,* Academia Nacional de Ciencias Económicas, Cuaderno no. 13 (Caracas, 1986), pp. 29–35.

88. See complaints of the Venezuelan Association of Exporters in Fedecámaras, *38 Asamblea Anual: Informe Final* (Caracas: Federación Venezolana de Cámaras y Asociaciones de Comercio y Producción, 1982), 2:299–309.

89. Oscar A. Echevarría, *Deuda . . . Crisis Cambiaria: Causas y Correctivos,* 2d ed. (Caracas: Universidad Católica Andrés Bello, 1986), p. 49, citing figures of the Banco Central de Venezuela. This is a net figure, not counting loan disbursements that became private capital flight. According to the Venezuelan comptroller general, gross foreign exchange sales through the banking sector totaled $22.66 billion in this period, the bulk of it through commercial banks in Caracas. See Roseliano Ojeda, *Cómo Se Desangra un País! . . . Qué Hacer?* (Valencia, Venezuela: Vadell Hermanos, 1987), pp. 158–60.

90. *Crisis y Recuperación* (Caracas: Editorial Arte, 1984). His assessment of the effects of the oil boom (esp. p. 33) agrees with the above.

of liquidity to the exterior, and avoid probable inflationary pressures."[91] He considered foreign exchange outflows a suitable way to shrink the monetary base. The government also missed an opportunity to reschedule short-term debts in mid-1981 because it was convinced that borrowing costs would go down and that the oil market would stay firm. Incredibly, President Herrera's annual speech to the nation in March 1982 contained only one oblique reference (in three hours of discourse) to the decline in oil revenues. He made no allowance for changes in the oil price in the annual budget, nor did the document reflect higher interest costs on the short-term debt. In clarification, the Minister of Mines and Hydrocarbons called the petroleum slump "a temporary problem."[92] And in a subsequent speech to the National Association of Bankers, Finance Minister Luis Ugueto said nothing about the foreign debt, to the stunned disappointment of his listeners. In September the central bank "centralized" the foreign exchange assets of PDVSA, a move widely perceived as an act of desperation to build up reserves.[93] With this, capital flight accelerated.

The oil boom had distorted the judgment of both officials and bankers, and the former came to see their most important mission as one of calming the markets after the Mexican crisis. In late August, Díaz Bruzual had even tried to talk mortgage banks into lowering their interest rates in tandem with falling U.S. rates. In the midst of a financial panic that everyone felt but few would acknowledge, he argued that bankruptcies and recession in the United States should have meant a risk premium in the United States equal to that of Venezuela. Viewed in isolation, this notion seems unaccountably obtuse. Taken in the context of past Venezuelan exchange policy and misapprehensions about the oil boom, it becomes more understandable. As reserves dwindled, pessimistic forecasts of oil prices and advocacy of exchange control were dismissed vehemently as threats to increasingly precious confidence.[94] Only in February 1983, after sev-

91. Miguel Rodríguez F., "Auge Petrolero, Estancamiento y Políticas de Ajuste en Venezuela," *Coyuntura Económica* (Bogotá) 15, no. 4 (December 1985), p. 215; Banco Central de Venezuela, *Informe Económico 1981* (Caracas: BCV, 1982), p. 78; Héctor Malavé Mata, *Los Extravíos del Poder* (Caracas: UCV Ediciones de la Biblioteca, 1987), pp. 739–42.

92. *Número* (Caracas), 7 June, 14 June, 25 October 1981; 21 March 1982.

93. *Resumen* (Caracas), 25 April 1982, p. 29; 10 October 1982; Echevarría, *Deuda . . . Crisis Cambiaria*, p. 49.

94. Interview, Felipe Pazos, Banco Central de Venezuela, 20 October 1988; Díaz Bruzual, *Número* (Caracas), 5 September 1982; in mid-August 1982 a former planning minister's advocacy of exchange control had met an acid response in the mainstream

eral more months of heavy outflows and under pressure from foreign creditors, was a package of exchange controls and (mostly devalued) multiple rates imposed, protecting the remaining $8 billion of reserves.

Mexico

By speeding the country through its downward spiral of financial panic and political recrimination in 1982, Mexican capital flight helped bring on the Latin American debt crisis. Impressed by the conflict under Echeverría in 1976 and the highly charged political atmosphere of late 1982, many observers have come to regard Mexican capital flight as inherently political. In perhaps the most nuanced of these interpretations, Carlos Arriola has argued that a PRI-dominated Congress drives Mexican businessmen to attempt to influence government policy through extraparliamentary means—primarily by cutting back investment and sending capital abroad.[95]

However, if we consider the country comparatively, it appears that events in Mexico between mid-1981 and mid-1982 did not differ very much from countries such as Venezuela, where private-sector distrust was not the main issue. In this period a spiraling fiscal deficit and the president's aversion to devaluation collided with an unforeseen softening in the oil market and the new reluctance of lenders, within an exchange market where dollars were freely available. Until 1981 Mexico had not experienced the problems of dependence on a narrow range of primary commodities under postwar ISI. Having faced fewer and more tractable foreign-sector problems than Brazil or Colombia before then, Mexican governments had not been shocked into making exchange policy a means of export diversification. The 1975–76 crisis might have done so, had it not been for the subsequent petrolization that took exchange reform off the agenda.[96] But given the foreign lending and grandiose ambitions it encouraged, this petrolization also made reform more necessary.

---

press. See *Resumen* (Caracas), 22 August 1982. On the official disdain for bad news, see Malavé Mata, *Los Extravíos del Poder,* pp. 783–85.

95. *Los Empresarios y el Estado, 1970–1982,* 2d ed. (Mexico City: M.A. Porrúa, 1988), p. 47.

96. On this point, see Gabriel Székely, *La Economía Política del Petróleo en México, 1976–1982* (Mexico City: Colegio de México, 1983), pp. 35–47, 57–58, 143–44.

Private-sector distrust explains more about Mexican exchange policy before the oil boom and after the bank nationalizations. Before the oil boom, however, it operated mostly at one remove, by producing inertia on exchange policy. Especially after the period of Cárdenas's most intense reforms (1936–38), the ruling party made capitalists anxious, but it also badly wanted them to invest, especially in industry.[97] Hence the system required ways to soothe fears, in the face of constitutionally unchecked presidents and their occasional obligation to speechify in the name of the Revolution.[98] After 1938 this pursuit of confidence drove governments to keep taxes on capital low, the financial system liquid, cross-border capital flows free, and the peso stable.[99]

The last two proved critical. To many Mexican capitalists, the right to property ultimately rested on the implicit guarantee that they could take their capital abroad whenever they wanted.[100] Apart from this important function, in Mexico the very fact that such controls would bear an extremely high administrative cost created a basis for their interpretation as something other than pragmatic measures. Govern-

97. Sanford Mosk, *Industrial Revolution in Mexico* (Berkeley and Los Angeles: University of California Press, 1954), p. 60. Ramón Beteta (finance minister under Alemán) noted in 1951 the reluctance of private banks to fund industrial finance, saying that "the environment is influenced by psychologies of distrust . . . aspects which may perhaps define [our situation] permanently." *Tres Años (1947–1948–1949) de Política Hacendaria: Perspectiva y Acción* (Mexico City: Secretaría de Hacienda y Crédito Público, 1951), p. 64.

98. Miguel Basáñez has taken this to be the central contradiction of the Mexican state—a conflict between its popular origin, embodied in the one-party, presidentialist form, and its capitalist vocation. See *La Lucha por la Hegemonía en México, 1968–1980* (Mexico City: Siglo 21, 1981), pp. 46–47.

99. On taxes, see Beteta, *Tres Años,* p. 58; Finance Minister Carrillo Flores in 1953, in Esteban L. Mancilla and Olga Pellicer de Brody, "La Política Económica," in *Historia de la Revolución Mexicana* (Mexico City: Colegio de México, 1978), 23:156–57; and Raymond Vernon's comment about capital flight in *The Dilemma of Mexico's Development: The Roles of the Private and Public Sectors* (Cambridge, Mass.: Harvard University Press, 1963), p. 185. On the financial system, see David H. Shelton, "The Banking System: Money and the Goal of Growth," in *Public Policy and Private Enterprise in Mexico,* ed. Raymond Vernon (Cambridge, Mass.: Harvard University Press, 1964), esp. pp. 121–22; Guillermo Ortiz and Leopoldo Solís, "Financial Structure and Exchange Rate Experience: Mexico 1954–1977," *Journal of Development Economics* 6 (1979), esp. pp. 522–23; and Sylvia Maxfield, *Governing Capital: International Finance and Mexican Politics* (Ithaca, N.Y.: Cornell University Press, 1990).

100. Interview with a PRI economist, Mexico City, August 1988. Maxfield cites a 1984 statement of Alfredo Sandoval, president of COPARMEX, to the effect that free access to foreign exchange constituted "a form of protection and defense of savings," and a PRI candidate for mayor of Ciudad Juárez who for similar reasons called capital flight "legitimate" (*Governing Capital,* p. 75).

ments that dared to enact them would have placed themselves to the left of Cárdenas (who rejected controls as a remedy for capital flight in 1938), with all this would have implied to the Mexican bourgeoisie.[101]

The same need for stability led presidents to identify their prestige with the peso. Defense of the currency sealed a social pact: it assured urban and northern consumers who thought in terms of dollars that their peso savings would not be "confiscated" by devaluation; it told labor that it would not suffer from a sudden uncompensated rise in prices; and since control over labor underpinned PRI rule, a stable peso could calm the political fears of businessmen while stabilizing their price expectations. Hence postwar governments found it convenient to erect free exchange and the fixed dollar parity as tokens of the government's competence and trustworthiness, especially when the relationship of revolutionary state and nervous private sector came under stress. This role for the exchange rate may also explain why situations of clear currency overvaluation proved so politically corrosive. Those taking advantage of the obvious price disequilibria could be accused of betraying the president and, by extension, the Revolution and the country.

Although, like other countries in the region, Mexico faced postwar inflation problems and a foreign-exchange crisis in 1948–49, in these matters its path diverged after 1954. In that year a large devaluation took many by surprise (reserves were still adequate), disoriented business expectations, angered labor, and hence alarmed the political establishment.[102] The inflationary shock raised the issue of how to divide the cost of its attenuation between labor and capital. Especially because this shock came from the government, it tested the PRI's dominance over labor.

The authorities skirted this issue during the next decade and a half

101. Cárdenas argued that Mexico's long border and poorly developed bureaucracy would make the restriction of illegitimate transactions impracticable while penalizing legitimate ones. Cited by Manuel Cavasos Lerma, "50 Años de Política Monetaria," in *Cincuenta Años de Banca Central: Ensayos Conmemorativos, 1925–1975*, ed. Ernesto Fernández Hurtado (Mexico City: Banco de México/Fondo de Cultura Económica, 1976), p. 83. See also Maxfield, *Governing Capital*, p. 72. For a glimpse at the debate over exchange control in the postwar period, see Alberto Noriega H., in *Investigación Económica* 15, no. 1 (1955): 158.

102. On 1954 as a watershed, see Leopoldo Solís, *Economic Policy Reform in Mexico: A Case Study for Developing Countries* (New York: Pergamon Press, 1981), p. 1; Roberto Newell and Luis Rubio, *Mexico's Dilemma: The Political Origins of Economic Crisis* (Boulder, Colo.: Westview Press, 1984), p. 103. For a fuller account, see José Luis Reyna, "El Movimiento Obrero en 1952–1964," in *Historia de la Revolución Mexicana* (Mexico City: Colegio de México, 1978) 22:83–95.

of what came to be known as "Stabilizing Development." As most accounts of this period indicate, the strategy relied on the banking system to finance the government deficit without inflation, and called on foreign loans and direct investment to equilibrate external payments. But when compared to Brazil or Colombia, it is clear that Stabilizing Development also depended on diverse and relatively buoyant exports along with rising travel income (Table 3.2). Taken together, these helped prevent severe exchange crises, maintain rate stability, and thus encourage foreign lenders.[103] Therefore, if 1954 tested the PRI's dominance over labor, relatively favorable trends in the foreign sector helped preserve this dominance undisturbed.

Stabilizing Development may not have been irremediably doomed economically, but given the political pressures for rapid expansion and redistribution after 1968, Mexico's financial dependence on business confidence became perversely self-propagating.[104] Higher expenditures and failures at tax reform brought budget shortfalls; a currency appreciating in real terms brought increasing trade deficits.[105] Filling these gaps with foreign capital created a deeper dependence on its good graces, while domestic business often waited for foreigners to invest first.[106] This situation raised what was already a high premium on financial and exchange-rate stability.

103. On the period of "Stabilizing Development" (1958–70) see René Villareal, *Industrialización, Deuda, y Desequilibrio Externo en México: Un Enfoque Neoestructuralista*, 2d ed. (Mexico City: Fondo de Cultura Económica, 1988); Antonio Gómez Oliver, *Políticas Monetaria y Fiscal de México: La Experiencia de la Posguerra, 1946–76* (Mexico City: Fondo de Cultura Económica, 1981); Mancilla and Pellicer de Brody, "La Política Económica," in *Historia de la Revolución Mexicana* 21:133–38; Roger D. Hansen, *The Politics of Mexican Development* (Baltimore: Johns Hopkins University Press, 1971), esp. pp. 50–54. Enrique Cárdenas alludes to this argument in "Comment," in *The Macroeconomics of Populism in Latin America*, ed. Rudiger Dornbusch and Sebastian Edwards (Chicago: University of Chicago Press, 1990), p. 260.

104. A good argument for its sustainability is Edward F. Buffie with the assistance of A. Sangines Krause, "Mexico 1958–86: From Stabilizing Development to the Debt Crisis," in *Developing Country Debt and the World Economy*, ed. Jeffrey D. Sachs, NBER Research Project Report (Chicago: University of Chicago Press, 1989), pp. 141–45.

105. Solís, *Economic Policy Reform*, pp. 21–23; Gerardo Bueno Z., "La Paridad del Poder Adquisitivo y las Elasticidades de Importación y Exportación en México," *El Trimestre Económico* 42 (April–June 1974).

106. For example, in a speech to the Mexico City Lions Club, the director-general of NAFINSA urged businessmen to invest by arguing that foreign banks had lent to the country, showing their confidence in its prospects. See José Hernández Delgado, "Confidence as a Decisive Factor in the Growing Mexican Economy," January 17, 1963 (Nacional Financiera, S.A., 1963). For this period, see Juan M. Martínez Nava, *Conflicto Estado-Empresarios en los Gobiernos de Cárdenas, López Mateos, y Echeverría* (Mexico City: Nueva Imagen, 1984), pp. 130–44; Vernon, *The Dilemma of Mexico's Development,*

The contradictions within the Mexican state became most apparent in the *sexenio* of Luis Echeverría. Among his generous campaign promises was a pledge to preserve the stability and convertibility of the peso.[107] There were a host of reasons for him to cling to a stable peso, but the most ironic of these was that, having clashed with business over taxes and other issues early in his term, the peso had become a symbol of *his* continuity with the assumptions of Stabilizing Development. So the more business distrusted him, the more he needed to stick to traditional exchange policy. When Nixon floated the dollar, Echeverría declined to follow suit; instead he brought reporters to the central bank to show them the gold.[108] Two years later he reaffirmed his commitment to the fixed value of the peso and its free convertibility: "[T]his policy, inalterably maintained, is in the present circumstances a basic factor of confidence for the people's savings and businessmen's reinvestment."[109] Nor did he face a strong lobby from exporters attentive to the real exchange rate: in 1975, after an alarming trade deficit for the first quarter was announced, major business organizations faulted the government for inadequate export promotion, but they neither advocated not hinted at devaluation.[110]

Economic trends eventually overcame the president's determination to defend the peso and his own prestige. In 1976 he ignored financial advisors and used foreign loans to support the currency, even as he kept real interest rates negative and as the currency appreciated in real terms.[111] In the face of accelerating flight, he called dollar buyers

---

pp. 119–22. On the use of foreign debt, see Rosario Green, *El Endeudamiento Público Externo de México, 1940–1973* (Mexico City: Colegio de México, 1976).

107. Green, *El Endeudamiento Público*, pp. 169–70; Solís, *Economic Policy Reform*, p. 201.

108. On the tax reform proposal of 1971, see Carlos Tello M., *La Política Económica en México, 1970–1976*, 2d ed. (Mexico City: Siglo 21, 1979), pp. 45–46. Here the Arriola argument applies to the break in informal relations between state and private capital. See Luis Bravo Mena, "COPARMEX [Confederación Patronal Mexicana] and Mexican Politics," in *Government and Private Sector in Contemporary Mexico,* ed. Sylvia Maxfield and Ricardo Anzaldúa M., Center for U.S.-Mexico Studies, UCSD, Monograph Series 20 (La Jolla, Calif.: UCSD, 1987), p. 97. On threats of capital flight that convinced LEA to back down, see Luis Suárez, *Echeverría Rompe el Silencio: Vendaval del Sistema* (Mexico City: Editorial Grijalbo, 1979), p. 197. On the decision not to devalue, see Solís, *Economic Policy Reform,* p. 59; *Quarterly Economic Review,* September 1971, p. 4; interview, John Christman, Business International, Mexico City, March 1987.

109. Tello, *La Política Económica en México*, p. 72.

110. *Expansión,* 23 July 1975, p. 6.

111. A comparison using wholesale prices in Mexico and the United States is presented in Norris Clement and Louis Green, "The Political Economy of Devaluation in Mexico," *Journal of Interamerican Economic Affairs* 32, no. 3 (1978): 50. The authors give a good summary of the events of this period, pp. 47–55.

Table 3.2   Exports, Six Countries, and Mexican Travel Income

Year	Argentina	Brazil	Chile	Colombia	Mexico Exports	Mexico Travel	Venezuela
1950	1,361	1,359	296	396	521		1,164
1951	1,169	1,771	378	460	629		1,347
1952	688	1,416	462	473	656		1,452
1953	1,125	1,540	339	607	585		1,514
1954	1,027	1,558	406	657	656		1,673
1955	929	1,419	487		807		1,903
1956	944	1,482	486	654	838	280	2,219
1957	975	1,392	399	590	740	304	2,740
1958	994	1,243	362	527	752	304	2,516
1959	1,009	1,282	449	514	747	341	2,391
1960	1,079	1,269	478	480	778	259	2,384
1961	964	1,403	442	462	839	269	2,452
1962	1,216	1,214	482	462	941	275	2,543
1963	1,365	1,406	491	474	985	306	2,464
1964	1,410	1,430	589	623	1,054	327	2,480
1965	1,493	1,596	688	580	1,146	361	2,436
1966	1,593	1,741	865	524	1,228	396	2,342
1967	1,464	1,654	883	549	1,152	441	2,533
1968	1,368	1,881	904	603	1,258	501	2,538
1969	1,612	2,311	1,168	667	1,454	528	2,523
1970	1,773	2,739	1,124	782	1,439	416	2,658
1971	1,735	2,882	997	752	1,405	531	3,112
1972	1,788	3,630	784	902	1,581	574	2,904
1973	2,740	5,111	1,104	1,059	1,796	704	3,947
1974	3,268	6,497	1,866	1,243	2,494	750	9,224
1975	2,439	7,002	1,293	1,414	2,478	669	7,393
1976	3,396	8,634	1,817	1,943	3,011	651	8,092
1977	4,843	10,214	1,872	2,278	3,943		8,156
1978	5,118	9,944	1,965	2,520	4,973		7,256
1979	6,049	11,792	2,968	2,664	7,195		10,959
1980	6,162	15,474	3,615	3,063	12,347		14,637
1981	7,776	19,795	3,523	2,678	16,867		16,930
1982	6,881	18,287	3,357	2,820	19,281		14,793
1983	7,328	20,508	3,580	2,778	20,888		13,630
1984	7,875	26,390	3,561	4,205	23,455		15,464

SOURCE: IMF, *Balance of Payments Yearbook* (Washington, D.C.: IMF), various issues.

NOTES: Exports FOB, current U.S. dollars to 1966, SDRs thereafter. Mexico travel account balance, U.S. dollars.

"disloyal, unpatriotic, bad Mexicans."[112] When he was finally forced to float the peso, he thereby reopened capital-labor conflict over inflation, while his rhetoric and subsequent actions alarmed the markets further.[113] Although by holding down nominal interest rates he had given wealth holders a strong incentive to sell pesos, Echeverría came away convinced that the capital flight was organized bourgeois sabotage.[114]

In contrast, the presidency of José López Portillo began with strong support from Mexican and foreign capital. Since he disassociated himself from many of his predecessor's last actions, obtained an IMF agreement, and promised to pump more oil, international commercial banks renewed lending immediately.[115] The new government brought business and labor together in an "Alliance for Production" whose goal was to reinvigorate private investment and coax flight capital home, which it did.[116]

Yet it soon became clear that, despite his stated commitment to promote nonoil exports and to keep a floating exchange rate, López Portillo put a stable peso first, for familiar reasons.[117] He found it

112. Newell and Rubio, *Mexico's Dilemma*, pp. 149, 195; *Business Week*, 10 May 1976.

113. Near the end of his term exchange transactions had to be restricted. See Economist Intelligence Unit, *Quarterly Economic Review*, 29 November 1976, p. 6; Tello, *La Política Económica en México*, p. 155.

114. Interviewed in 1979, he said "it is evident that the peso was being devalued gradually through the years of so-called 'Stabilizing Development,' but it is even more evident that there was a whole conspiracy of big foreign interests with Mexican oligarchic interests to take a lot of capital out of Mexico, in reprisal for the worker- and peasant-orientation of my administration, and also in order to push us toward financial and commercial disequilibrium that could only be compensated by foreign exchange gained from greater oil exports." Quoted in Suárez, *Echeverría Rompe el Silencio*, p. 242. On the issue of foreign pressure, see Richard R. Fagen, "The Realities of U.S.-Mexican Relations," *Foreign Affairs*, July 1977.

115. Several observers have linked López Portillo's more aggressive oil strategy to the crisis of private-sector confidence that ended Echeverría's term. See George Philip, *Oil and Politics in Latin America* (Cambridge: Cambridge University Press, 1982), p. 358; Lorenzo Meyer and Isidro Morales, *Petróleo y Nación: La Política Petrolera en México (1900–1987)* (Mexico City: Fondo de Cultura Económica, 1990), p. 186.

116. The testimony of observers in 1977 contradicts the World Bank residual estimates of capital flight cited in Chapter 1. See *Quarterly Economic Review*, May 1977, p. 9; Leopoldo Solís and Ernesto Zedillo, "The Foreign Debt of Mexico," in *International Debt and the Developing Countries*, ed. G. W. Smith and J. T. Cuddington (Washington, D.C.: The World Bank, 1985), p. 259.

117. David Mares links the quick turn away from export diversification to the jump in oil prices in 1979, which allowed a return to older conceptions of how trade should serve the Mexican national interest. The new situation was expected to open doors in oil-short markets for other Mexican goods without compromising Mexican autonomy as much as a more liberal strategy would have done. See "Explaining Choice of Development Strategies: Suggestions from Mexico, 1970–1982," *International Organization* 39,

harder to inspire investor confidence after Echeverría, in part because the private sector had become wary and financially more independent. (Several business organizations now tried to condition new investment on the composition of the cabinet, settlement of the land questions in the northwest, price controls, and salaries.[118]) However, labor had already made big sacrifices under the Alliance. Since López Portillo had removed many price controls under business pressure, the exchange rate now looked like an obvious candidate for a price freeze. So when a growing trade deficit brought talk of a new devaluation in late 1979, the government stood firm. The president had been driven into another doomed embrace of the peso.[119]

He deepened the petrolization of the Mexican economy. In January 1980 PEMEX suddenly raised its self-imposed oil export ceilings by over 80 percent. This action, though later partially reversed, effectively told lenders that more oil could be pumped if needed, and pressure to devalue the peso abated through 1980.[120] But in 1981 the debt-oil growth strategy collided with higher interest rates and shorter maturities, and in June the oil market began to soften and the government's bungled response drew attention to the problem.[121] The fiscal deficit rose, much of this due to a large program of investments in oil extraction.

no. 4 (Autumn 1985): 683–89. As Mares makes clear in his discussion of López Portillo's policies for export promotion (subsidies, improved financing, sectoral bargaining with MNCs, etc.), these did not include the exchange rate.

118. Rogelio Hernández R., *Empresarios, Banca, y Estado: El Conflicto durante el Gobierno de José López Portillo, 1976–1982* (Mexico City: FLACSO/M.A. Porrúa, 1988), chap. 3.

119. "It is not so much the inflationary impact of devaluation that has inhibited the government from 'managing the float' downwards, but rather its fear of the psychological impact. The younger executives and officials in Mexico, unlike countries such as Brazil and Chile, are unaccustomed to a 'crawling-peg' devaluation—or indeed, any at all, apart from the trauma of 1976. Having missed the boat when it failed to introduce such a policy after it took office in December 1976, the López Portillo administration has found itself returning to the psychological attitudes prevailing before August 1976." *Latin America Regional Report*, 16 November 1973, p. 1. "Three years after the traumatic devaluations of 1976, the idea of the peso/dollar rate as simply a price, rather than a symbol of the nation's strength, has not penetrated deeply in Mexico. The slightest downward movement in the technically floating rate is still enough to touch off significant outflows of capital." See Thomas J. Trebat, "Coping with the Oil Boom," *Euromoney*, September 1979, p. 144.

120. Székely, *La Economía Política del Petróleo*, p. 59.

121. *Expansión*, 8 July, 22 July 1981; Rosa María Mirón and Germán Pérez, *López Portillo: Auge y Crisis de un Sexenio* (Mexico: Plaza y Valdés, 1988), pp. 113–25; Mares, "Explaining Choice," pp. 690–91.

One of López Portillo's key misjudgments corresponded to a view of the exchange rate much like that of two contemporaries, Martínez de Hoz in Argentina and Donald Regan in the United States. That is, he seemed to accept foreign lending as a normal market force, trusting it to act that way. Like most international experts, he also expected the oil boom to endure. When the peso came under pressure in the second half of 1981 (as the country ran a $12 billion current account deficit), he said that despite the desires of businessmen and the counsel of some advisors, "we prefer to stay attentive to the market, and slide [the rate] when demand indicates it."[122] This typifies the kind of policy error that many later blamed for the debt crisis. But López Portillo let the peso appreciate in real terms because the supply of bank loans permitted it. He spoke of the decisions of private lenders on the same plane as the trade balance when gauging the appropriateness of the exchange rate.

Now he had fallen into the same trap as had Echeverría. Supporting the peso by pumping more and taking on increasingly expensive debt, the president tried to cajole and shame Mexicans into believing that he could keep the currency stable, even though it was already overvalued when oil began to cheapen (Table 3.3). He denounced a conspiracy against the peso and swore on several occasions to "fight like a dog" to defend it. But he was overmatched, and had to let the peso float on 18 February 1982. It depreciated about 30 percent immediately and almost 80 percent within a few days. But this time no panic took hold in the immediate aftermath. Private-sector organizations reacted positively on the whole.[123] Labor expressed its solidarity while submitting proposals for wage increases.

While the large depreciation of February removed one motivation for capital flight, by creating the expectation of inflation it also helped undermine the political edifice. Though it was widely expected, unlike the 1954 devaluation, the 1982 devaluation raised the same question of who would bear the costs of fighting inflation, and it did so right in the middle of the presidential election campaign. At the same time it cost the president, the system's supreme arbiter of class relations, a

122. Press Conference, 10 July 1981; quoted in Oscar Franco López Portillo, "La Política Cambiaria en México, 1977–1982," Master's thesis, Centro de Estudios Económicos, Colegio de México, 1986, pp. 21–22.

123. Hernández, *Empresarios,* pp. 221–22; Carlos Tello M., *La Nacionalización de la Banca en México,* 2d ed. (Mexico City: Siglo 21, 1984), p. 86; Mirón and Pérez take a different view, seeing private-sector political pressures beginning in January 1982 and increasing after February 18 (*López Portillo,* pp. 147–53).

Table 3.3   Annual Real Effective Exchange Rate Indices, 1970–1990, and
Quarterly Indices for Mexico 1987–1988 and Brazil 1987–1990

Year	Argentina	Brazil	Chile	Colombia	Mexico	Venezuela
			(1970 = 100)			
1971	95.3	102.0	83.4	102.0	99.7	101.7
1972	108.3	111.0	74.8	103.0	102.5	102.8
1973	101.4	115.1	92.4	103.1	101.4	103.5
1974	89.2	115.4	135.5	97.4	98.7	104.1
1975	137.0	117.3	177.8	102.5	97.3	100.8
1976	90.0	113.9	150.0	97.1	102.4	98.5
1977	116.5	114.6	124.9	88.5	113.0	92.1
1978	105.6	120.8	141.5	89.4	106.8	91.8
1979	79.8	135.2	142.8	86.1	102.2	92.8
1980	71.2	150.6	124.7	86.7	93.6	86.1
1981	93.4	125.9	102.2	79.9	84.6	78.7
1982	114.0	114.8	117.0	74.8	123.4	73.2
1983	110.5	147.4	138.3	75.9	162.2	78.6
1984	110.5	136.3	138.1	80.1	134.2	88.6
1985	112.2	137.0	159.5	90.2	133.4	80.9

great deal of credibility—by his own public admission.[124] Moreover, perhaps because much of their capital had been placed abroad, making them feel they had less to lose from labor strife at home, leading Mexican businessmen now bristled against price controls and resisted compromise on wages. In the wake of the 70 percent depreciation, important business groups objected to proposed wage rises of 10–30 percent and suggested 8–10 percent instead.[125]

Capital flight resumed in June and the air was soon clouded with political recrimination. López Portillo waited until after the July elections to respond, and then blamed large Mexican private banks for the flight, calling for an official investigation of *"sacadólares."* The authorities split the exchange market, devalued twice more in August, suspended dollar trading, effectively blocked local dollar accounts, and suspended payments on the foreign debt. The debt crisis had begun, and an enormous financial shock wave spread across Latin America.

124. This was when he made the famous statement in the epigraph to this chapter. See also Miguel Angel Rivera Ríos, *Crisis y Reorganización del Capitalismo Mexicano,* Colección Problemas de México (Mexico City: Era, 1986), pp. 98–102.

125. *Excélsior* (Mexico City), 21 March 1982, pp. 1-A, 21-A; Hernández, *Empresarios,* pp. 222–23, 243.

1986	136.0	142.6	179.9	115.7	179.8	91.1
1987	170.7	148.4	189.0	129.2	183.2	114.2
1988	161.9	134.7	214.7	130.6	152.3	117.9
1989	156.4	109.6	203.4	130.0	123.4	119.0
1990						
1987: 1		147.4			195.5	
2		145.6			187.6	
3		152.2			174.0	
4		147.9			175.9	
1988: 1		142.7			162.1	
2		137.7			153.8	
3		128.5			146.5	
4		129.6			147.1	
1989: 1		125.5				
2		110.4				
3		104.5				
4		97.8				
1990: 1		80.3				
2		87.7				
3		92.5				
4		110.3				

SOURCE: UN ECLAC, *Economic Survey of Latin America* (New York: United Nations), 1981, 1985, 1989, 1991.

NOTES: Period averages. Decline in index denotes appreciation. Computed from wholesale price indices of countries and trading partners, weighted according to proportion in exports. Venezuela and Chile home prices deflated by domestic product subindex of wholesale price index. Mexico after 1982, regulated rate.

Conclusion

Let us begin with the immediate policy causes of flight and then trace the origins of the policies. I have argued that during the last phase of the borrowing boom in 1980–82 exchange policy was particularly important. Rapid capital flight took place where three factors were all present: a currency was widely thought overvalued; this "overvaluation" was seen as likely to be "corrected" soon; and the public enjoyed free access to foreign exchange in a market supported by the central bank. All three had distinct political stories behind them. Regarding the first factor, I have suggested that in Mexico and Argentina a preference for fixed exchange rates arose from anxieties about political stability, the wish to draw in overseas capital, and, more particularly for Mexico, concerns for the prestige of the president and his party's control over labor. Yet a more important antecedent of currency overvaluation around 1980 was, judging comparatively, a relative weakness of prior motivation to target the real exchange rate, motivation elsewhere provided by an experience of recurrent exchange crisis and export stagnation. On the second factor, the likelihood of a "correction," the Chilean case reminds us why an estimate of "overvaluation" may be an unreliable proxy for expected devaluation of a currency. Market perceptions on this subject involve general judgments about the intentions, capabilities, and stability of the executive.

Regarding the third factor, the career of exchange controls partly resembles that of exchange-rate reform, in that bouts of destabilizing capital flows led governments such as Lleras Restrepo's to condemn free exchange right along with overvaluation. For them, exchange control become part of a package of measures designed to give favorable and stable market signals to exporters. But this policy was harder to carry out in some countries. Respected Venezuelans found little legitimate reason for controls; Mexican asset holders considered the geographical obstacles so obvious that any attempt to enforce controls might have painted the offending government with a red brush; and Argentine export elites, more confident of their international competitiveness, hoping to woo overseas capital, and having judged Perón's use of controls dictatorial, resisted them under any conditions. In each case also, much of the political opposition to controls could be related back to histories of relative ease on external accounts: if controls were applied when those affected did not see their practical justification, they came to be seen as arbitrary, as illegitimate in themselves.

After the defense of the currency had been broken by major devaluations in the borrowing countries, capital flight did not cease. New motivations for it arose. Devaluation had two results: it raised the real cost of the foreign debt; and it set the stage for distributional conflict as governments sought to reduce the inflationary surge. The former put asset holders at risk of future taxes or government bond defaults, but it was greatly compensated in those countries (Venezuela above all; Chile, Mexico) in which the government was the main exporter. The latter was especially important in countries with politically powerful labor movements (Argentina, Mexico; also Venezuela—more on this below). On both counts—raising the real cost of foreign debt and setting the stage for distributional conflict—Chile was favored with factors helping to reduce incentives for continued flight; on the former,

Mexico and especially Venezuela benefited (although for Mexico the distributional conflict after February was crucial). Argentina was hurt by both effects, especially since not only did the government's debt get more expensive in real terms after the rapid depreciations of mid-1981 and mid-1982, but so did the private debts the state had assumed.

Let us now extract some other conclusions, relevant to current ideas about capital flight, that may have remained tangled in the rather dense comparative thicket above. To begin, the 1980–82 period teaches us that despite their obvious political salience, convulsive episodes of capital flight do not necessarily bespeak political dissatisfaction among the propertied class.[126] It is true that sometimes the pursuit of an obvious speculative opportunity carried the stigma of *entreguismo* or bourgeois sabotage, and here the shift of assets may have been labeled "political" precisely for being coldly and individualistically economic in its motivation. But in two of the three cases of massive flight examined here, relatively conservative regimes sat solidly in the saddle—Generals Videla and Viola in Argentina, and the COPEI government of Herrera Campins in Venezuela.[127] Granted, the onset of crisis did have consequences that would create anxieties about the government (here I mean to separate it from the distributional results of devaluation) among business—a rapid turnover of finance ministers, or, in Mexico, bank nationalization and a period of exchange control—and these could themselves provoke additional flight, as will be discussed in the next chapter.

Regarding decisions about exchange controls, several types of influence appear to have been important. To begin with, we should note that the widespread and continued use of rather strict controls contradicts the idea that a *librecambista* international bourgeoisie *always* gets its first preference on this issue. While on average Latin American countries were more open on capital account than Taiwan or South Korea, there was substantial variation in the laws of the region. What distinguished the Argentine or Mexican situation from its counterparts in Brazil or Colombia? Why did some governments use this policy to woo foreign capital and others did not? On the latter, I

126. Cf. Albert Hirschman, *Essays in Trespassing: Economics to Politics and Beyond* (New York: Cambridge University Press, 1981), pp. 257–58.
127. The fact that Viola represented a more nationalist faction within the Argentina military than did Videla does not vitiate the point. It is plausible to suppose that because the Argentina currency was so overvalued by March 1981, and the possibility of correcting this without devaluation was so meager, that even a team of, say, Galtieri and Roberto Alemann (or permanent tenure for Martínez de Hoz) would have faced a similar crisis as the bubble burst.

have suggested that in times of political turbulence or where an undercurrent of business distrust existed, some regimes found it convenient to compensate for these by seeking to attract foreign and expatriate capital with a promise of both exchange-rate stability (or predictability) and a free exchange market. Where investors could be expected to have doubts about the sustainability of the exchange rate, a free exchange market provided a necessary complement. This combination of policies usually did succeed in bringing in short-term funds from abroad while braking inflation. It would also win international approval and domestic popularity, at least until trade balance trends undermined confidence and reversed the capital flows, leading to a new devaluation.

To what degree were supply elasticities responsible for the difference in policy environments between Argentina and the coffee countries? Probably not much. In what remains a notable example of the discovery of unsuspected economic influence on political patterns, Albert Hirschman has suggested that coffee's lower price elasticity of short-run supply allowed states in Brazil and Colombia to have greater success in squeezing coffee incomes to subsidize industry, compared to the efforts of Perón and others to do the same to Argentine grain and meat producers.[128] I have argued that this is better understood differently. First of all, apart from the fact that the Hirschman hypothesis glosses over the beef cycle, for most purposes (including mine) the more relevant difference lies in export response—net of domestic consumption—rather than simple supply response. Moreover, while in the narrow sense of government "success" the elasticity thesis may indeed hold, it does not account for the acute and open distrust that was, from the standpoint of later Argentine governments, the most difficult result of Perón's policies. Seemingly, if a producer could withdraw resources from the state by switching crops or slaughtering fewer animals, this would have tended to alleviate, rather than sharpen, his resentment of extractive policies.

It may be plausible that capital flight resulted from a strong labor presence in the governing coalition, for two reasons. First, governments unusually attentive to labor may have postponed devaluation longer or in more dangerous conditions. Of the three countries with the largest capital outflows in 1980–82, Argentina had the Peronists, Mexico the link between the ruling party and the Confederación de Trabajadores de México, and Venezuela the alliance between the

128. *A Bias for Hope*, pp. 11–12.

strongest party, Acción Democrática, and most of organized labor.[129] Second, as I noted above, discrete devaluation would open a distributive conflict over how to share the cost of attenuating the inflationary surge, and strong labor could push much of this cost onto capital, or at least promise a long fight. In fact this happened in Mexico and Argentina and, as I have noted, it helps account for the fact that capital flight did not cease once the currency-market incentive for it was removed. To the extent that this battle could have been predicted, it provided another reason for the fear of devaluation.

Still, there are problems with this. During the capital flight in Argentina professed anti-Peronists ran the country; in Venezuela the opposition COPEI held power. The links, insofar as they existed, were complex. In Argentina, for example, one reason for the installation of the heterodox *tablita* was the generals' concern with unemployment. Though justified fundamentally on national security grounds, this preoccupation nevertheless represented a different vision of national security than Pinochet's, resembling more the paternalistic corporatism of Perón than a thoroughgoing laissez-faire. For another example, Mexico before 1976, we would have to add the idea that any test of the PRI's control of labor would have worried capital too. That is, devaluation was to be avoided because it presented not just a fight with labor over the costs of restabilization but a fight that could weaken the authority of the state generally.

Extending this to take account of broader societal pressures, many observers have alleged a connection between Latin American "policy errors" before the debt crisis and vested interests in the policies of ISI. In the most inclusive of these arguments, Jeffrey Sachs has suggested that, along with the influence of labor, property distribution in the rural tradeables sector helps explain the difference in dominant economic strategies between East Asia and Latin America. Apart from protected urban manufacturing's interest in a relatively appreciated exchange rate, in Latin America devaluation would have had as its most immediate beneficiaries the landed oligarchy or foreign mineral companies. Sachs argues that because Taiwan and South Korea differed on this score, with poor but broadly held rural sectors after the land reforms of the early 1950s, their governments found it easier to

129. The opposition COPEI had a significant presence among labor, too, but it was far outweighed, historically and organizationally in the Confederación de Trabajadores de Venezuela, by AD. For discussion, see Ruth Berins Collier and David Collier, *Shaping the Political Arena: Critical Junctures, the Labor Market, and Regime Dynamics in Latin America* (Princeton: Princeton University Press, 1991), pp. 617–24.

break with ISI, despite the fact that urban interests there also opposed such a break.[130]

Can this explain the pattern of exchange policy across the six countries? Colombia seems to provide some support for it, since, as noted above, its relatively broad coffee sector undeniably constituted part of FEDECAFE's power and provided a political base for two rural-oriented, elite-led traditional parties. As a result, DL 444 had more of a "national" character than the same policy would have had in Argentina or Brazil, since a large number of small rural proprietors were to gain from it (though even here we should not forget that 444 was a *decree*-law and shifted power to the Monetary Board). Devaluation was politically unpopular in Brazil during the 1950s and early 1960s. Pro-export exchange reforms by Kubitschek in 1959 and especially by Quadros in 1961 did not last; it was a military government that emplaced a package similar to Colombia's in 1968. In Chile, the effective political use of the charge that Frei's crawling peg favored "rich foreign and national exporters" seems to support the Sachs thesis as well. Finally, in Argentina, the Pampa oligarchy's gains from devaluation have constituted a very salient political issue throughout the postwar period.[131]

There are limits to this thesis, however. When the state controlled natural resource exports, devaluation could boost *its* profits (by reducing local costs in terms of its foreign exchange revenues), winning it all of the benefits that, before the big nationalizations, had flowed mainly to foreign mineral companies. If sentiment against "rich foreign exporters" made the Chilean Christian Democrats back down from a pro-export exchange policy in 1970, by the end of the next year the key rich foreigners had been taken out of the loop, but exchange policy did not immediately move in the direction the Sachs thesis would have predicted. Mexico and Venezuela (after 1975), with large state-owned oil monopolies and a tendency to slide into overvaluation, also point to the following refinement: the positive side of the Sachs thesis, the presence of a well-organized and broadly held export sector, seems to have been more important than the unpopularity of delivering windfall benefits to an export oligarchy or foreign firms, since ending the latter seems to have had little effect.

I have argued above that a seemingly necessary condition for dura-

130. "Social Conflict and Populist Policies in Latin America," NBER Working Paper 2897 (Cambridge, Mass.: National Bureau of Economic Research, March 1989).

131. For example, Mallon and Sourrouille note the popular idea of agroexport interests and "the common good" as antagonistic (*Economic Policymaking*, p. 66).

ble policy reform, and thus of the later avoidance of large speculative outflows in 1980–82, was the prior experience of export stagnation and recurrent exchange crisis. In particular, by the mid-1960s the ongoing market problems of coffee had contributed to repeated, conflictual devaluations in Brazil and Colombia, in which the familiar concerns of the ISI coalition had usually won the day, but only temporarily; the situation obviously demanded that coffee-dependent countries find some way of expanding other exports. Had Mexico's ISI coalition been subjected to this kind of disruption, or had Argentina's traditional exports faced coffee's dismal market prospects, I believe the results would have differed.

This implies that much of the explanation remains structural, independent of the character of the political regime. On this I agree with the proposition advanced by Carlos Díaz-Alejandro about policy changes in the 1930s, noted in Chapter 2, and with some of the argument advanced by Haggard in contrasting Latin America and East Asia.[132] I do not think this exhausts the list of explanatory factors, and in every case I have indicated how others might have intervened between crisis and effective long-term response. But I do not have evidence to support a more sweeping claim about the political power of export producers. Government solicitude toward the export sector may have arisen largely from a long history of structural export problems that policymakers disliked because they periodically restricted their decision-making power. Moreover, when the countries are considered comparatively, the condition of the foreign sector helps explain several characteristics that many have ascribed to local causes: the relatively greater compatibility of coffee elites with broad developmentalist conditions; the lack of controversy around exchange controls in Brazil, Colombia, or Chile, as opposed to Argentina; the relatively short period of Argentine economic cycles; the durability of the PRI's promise of no devaluation after 1954, and thus its undisturbed dominance over labor; and, of course, the effect of a Venezuela-style oil boom on Mexico after 1976.

I do not wish to imply that structure itself had nothing to do with politics. Politics mediated in a subtle way. Traditional rural and commercial elites approved of economic pragmatism, and crises called forth pragmatic responses that often became more or less efficient

132. "Latin America in the 1930s," in *Latin America in the 1930s: The Role of the Periphery in World Crisis,* ed. Rosemary Thorp (London: Macmillan, 1984), p. 24; Stephan Haggard, *Pathways from the Periphery: The Politics of Growth in the Newly Industrializing Countries* (Ithaca: N.Y.: Cornell University Press, 1990), p. 28.

institutions. But in the absence of some obvious shock or market stagnation, to these elites state activism in exchange management would appear adventurous at best, totalitarian at worst. Perón gave exchange control a bad name that endured even after the really serious offender, IAPI, was long deceased. To rich Venezuelans, exchange control meant abridging property rights without good reason— and if the moment seemed to provide a good reason, the widely shared assumption of oil-based abundance led people to conclude that this moment had arrived only because of government mismanagement. Finally, to Mexican capitalists, only dangerous people advocated exchange control, a measure that even Cárdenas had judged futile. Thus each country's economic and social inheritance determined, within the sphere of exchange policy, what a large part of the traditional elite considered the line between the pragmatic and the arbitrary, between the acceptable and the alarming.

4

Capital Flight
and the
Triumph of Neoliberal
Economics

Not only are governments losing control over money, but this
newly free money in its own way is asserting its control over
them, disciplining irresponsible policies and taking away free
lunches everywhere.
—Walter Wriston, *The Twilight of Sovereignty,* 1992[1]

Just as 1929 began the rapid advance of state activism in Latin
American economies, so did 1982 start a broad if uneven retreat.[2]

1. Walter B. Wriston, *The Twilight of Sovereignty: How the Information Standard
Is Transforming Our World* (New York: Scribner's, 1992), p. 66. The fact that Wriston
meant such statements to apply to capital flight from Latin America can be inferred
from his references to the region in, for example, "Economic Freedom Receives a Boost,"
New York Times, 15 April 1986, Op-Ed page, where he makes an identical argument to
that which appears in the book.
2. Some would object to this generalization and mark the coming of the free-market
wave with the date of a military coup: 1964, 1966, or especially 1973. I would argue
that we should give more weight to events in more populous countries (e.g., Mexico) in
depicting the overall trend, keeping in mind also the substantial divergence among
authoritarian regimes—with Brazil under Geisel moving in a direction quite different
from Chile under Pinochet, and Argentina "regressing" toward the old pattern under
Viola and again with the outbreak of the South Atlantic conflict. My point is to highlight

Within a decade the Party of the Institutional Revolution had sold back the banks and abandoned land reform; and the Peronist president of Argentina had tied himself publicly to some of the most egregious figures in the country's old liberal economic establishment. Something clearly was afoot.

What was it? To many, the broad sweep of the changes seemed to point toward global, impersonal phenomena. These, as the statement in the epigraph attests, could impress even a man who has spent much of his life making consequential decisions. Yet Wriston's image of capital mobility as something like a force of nature, shorn of ideology and institutional context, seems odd. And in fact it has been more common to find people (especially in the business press) describing Latin America's turn to free markets less as a prudent navigation of unforgiving financial waters than as a religious conversion, part of a movement sweeping the planet.[3] Another common but contrary answer points to more concrete and visible (but no less global) agents of reform—for example, charging that the IMF, World Bank, and the United States "forced poor countries to accept 'structural adjustment plans' which open their resources to foreign corporate exploitation."[4]

What is at stake in this dispute? Above all, the woolly but crucial issue concerning the degree to which governments have chosen their

---

a common influence upon policymaking that pushed the rest of Latin America toward the Chilean model, when before 1982 it had shown no consistent trend in that direction. Here I agree with Marcelo Cavarozzi, "Beyond Transitions to Democracy in Latin America," *Journal of Latin American Studies* 24, no. 2 (1992).

3. For example, Bruce Babbitt, "The New and Improved South America," *World Monitor,* February 1991. He comments on García Márquez's *The General in His Labyrinth:* "[T]o the reader, it is as if a fictional Bolívar is now returning to liberate South America from itself by using history to smash Marxist dependency theories that assign external causes for those very political and economic failures" (pp. 33–34).

4. Jeremy Brecher, "The Hierarchs' New World Order—And Ours," in *Global Visions: Beyond the New World Order,* ed. Jeremy Brecher, John Brown Childs, and Jill Cutler (Boston: South End Press, 1993), p. 6; see also Tony Killick, "The Sound of Cautious Pessimism: Developing Country Adjustment in the 1980s and 1990s," in *The International Financial Regime,* ed. Graham Bird (London: Surrey University, 1990), p. 206. The global shift toward liberal policies obviously challenges the idea that "developing countries have consistently endorsed principles and norms that would legitimate more authoritative as opposed to more market-oriented modes of allocation" because the latter "can provide more stable and predictable transaction flows." See Stephen Krasner, *Structural Conflict: The Third World Against Global Liberalism* (Berkeley and Los Angeles: University of California Press, 1985), p. 5. Of course, this assertion could be an argument that today structurally determined domestic ideological preferences are being overridden by an extreme international constraint. More likely it may be that whenever transaction flows turn persistently negative, the existing basis for allocation will be discredited, whatever it is.

economic strategies under duress. In more practical terms, if global ideology propels the policy changes in Latin America, its winds might blow in a different direction within a generation, perhaps much less; but if technological advances and institutional change have made the global character of capital a newly decisive factor in every government's economic policy deliberations, we are in the presence of a more enduring constraint.

This chapter tries to assess the impact of internationally mobile private capital, especially but not exclusively in the form of capital flight, in spurring liberal reforms of economic policy in Latin America. I argue the plausibility of a path, above all in two notable reformers (Argentina, Mexico), running from the amount of capital flight to the depth of fiscal and financial crisis during the 1980s, and thence to the extent of policy reform. Typically, major reforms followed closely on the heels of the exhaustion of alternatives (in the form of domestic debt, commercial credits, and arrears) to medium- to long-term foreign finance. By adding to what was already an unprecedented transfer of wealth from public to private hands, capital flight hastened this day of reckoning—indeed, often making its arrival quite dramatic. However, reforms were also undertaken in countries that had little or no net flight, and here the connection between mobile capital and policy reform is harder to make. We cannot rule out an independent role for ideology—or perhaps merely "learning" about the prudence of neoliberal economics in a world of mobile capital.

Two qualifications. First, I do not seek to usurp the priority of detailed studies and memoirs of reform experiences, or of the existing works that compare a wide variety of such experiences in order to derive lessons that improve the chances of future reform efforts.[5] However, the most outstanding examples of the latter intentionally deemphasize international forces in order to focus upon the political requisites of liberal reform. I intend here to ask about such forces. Second, I also want to supplement, not supersede, works about the

5. Of the former we have Moisés Naim, *Paper Tigers and Minotaurs: Economic Policy Reform in Venezuela* (Washington, D.C.: Carnegie Endowment, 1992); of the latter, the outstanding contribution is John Williamson, ed., *The Political Economy of Policy Reform* (Washington, D.C.: Institute for International Economics, 1994). A multicausal assessment similar to the present chapter is David E. Hojman, "The Political Economy of Recent Conversion to Market Economics in Latin America," *Journal of Latin American Studies* 26, no. 1 (February 1994): 191–219. Hojman argues that there are six major explanatory factors: lessons from the debt crisis; more highly qualified technocrats; development of an entrepreneurial middle class; exhaustion of ISI; a combination of tax reform, financial modernization, and export diversification; and favorable public opinion (p. 191).

relationship between reform and regime type.[6] I am not trying to imply that politics and regimes do not matter; I would argue only that on this terrain they appear to have mattered less. Even those who vigorously champion the importance of political choice admit that "virtually all Latin American countries, regardless of regime, eventually have been obliged to implement similar strategies."[7]

The analysis begins with a broad comparative overview of economic trends, including estimates of capital flight and a summary of liberal policy reform. It first discusses what "the discipline of international capital" may denote, in terms of interest rates, capital outflows, and economic crisis. It then shows the moderate correspondence, in the six-country sample of major Latin American debtor countries, between net accumulated capital outflows and the degree of liberal reform later undertaken. This, I believe, provides weak support for the main hypothesis. The challenge here lies in distinguishing the role of mobile capital from other, related causes, such as the conditions imposed by international financial institutions (here I mean the IMF, World Bank, and the Interamerican Development Bank) and the effects of ideological changes. I consider these other hypotheses about liberal reform, discussing to what degree they explain away the coincidence of net accumulated capital outflow and policy reform and to what extent they account for instances in which these do not coincide. I then explore the possible ways in which the coincidence may have been a causal one, whether through the obvious contribution of capital flight to reform-inducing crises, or via a more subtle route that involved the political and ideological influence of resident holders of foreign assets. Finally, the chapter explores the politics of capital flight and crisis with regard to the public acceptance of sweeping neoliberal reforms.

6. A good example is Robert Kaufman and Barbara Stallings, "Debt and Democracy in the 1980s: The Latin American Experience," in *Debt and Democracy in Latin America,* ed. Barbara Stallings and Robert Kaufman (Boulder, Colo.: Westview Press, 1989), pp. 201–33. Their analysis assumes that liberal reform dominated the agenda of Latin American economic policy after 1982, and therefore that it would be useful to rank countries, as they did, according to their pursuit of this reform. I examine one aspect of the "need to reform," assuming that it may also have varied meaningfully.

7. Carlos Acuña and William C. Smith, "The Political Economy of Structural Adjustment: The Logic of Support and Opposition to Neoliberal Reform," in *Latin American Political Economy in the Age of Neoliberal Reform: Theoretical and Comparative Perspectives for the 1990s,* ed. William C. Smith, Carlos Acuña, and Eduardo A. Gamarra (New Brunswick, N.J.: Transaction Publishers/University of Miami North-South Center, 1994), p. 28. The authors' protest against determinism mostly asserts the variety of political significances and outcomes to be derived as similar policies are adopted in various countries (p. 20). This is probably true and it is quite important for assessing the future of reform programs, but it begs the main question addressed here.

Patterns of Capital Flight and Reform

As sweeping as the Wriston proposition may seem, Latin America's experience appears to support it. In the 1980s, presidents and ministers spent a lot of breath castigating "speculators" or, at other times, appealing for the return of flight capital. In Mexico, as I have already noted, overseas capital has long been commonly seen, rightly or wrongly, as a bargaining chip that the private sector deliberately plays against the state. Whether we follow this interpretation or not, the danger of rapid capital flight has long narrowed policy choices in Latin America. The principal difference between Wriston's argument and most other Latin American discussions of capital mobility lies in the positive valence he places upon it.

What might the discipline of mobile capital look like in practice? The Wriston thesis describes a world that has undergone a sea change. Dollars circulate everywhere, telecommunications links offer new avenues for asset transfers, people learn complicated accounting tricks, and exchange controls generally become more porous. Interest rates (corrected for expected exchange-rate movements and risk) may also be expected to converge toward international ones, more quickly insofar as the assets are more liquid. Governments are forced to adopt liberal policies, upon pain of rising borrowing costs, shrinking tax bases, disinvestment, and economic collapse. In this form the idea has been widely articulated by political analysts.[8]

8. The idea that a capital shortage is the main agent for reform is also quite widely held, most notably by U.S. Treasury Secretary Nicholas Brady. The general theme has an old literature, for which fixed investment, deindustrialization, and whipsawing are the main concerns, with a more recent one more focused upon financial flows. On the latter Jorge Schvarzer has noted (referring mostly to Argentina) the "erosion of the regulatory action of the State" derived from greater international capital mobility, which he saw as offering a powerful mode of action to large conglomerates and holders of highly concentrated wealth. See "Restricciones a la Política Económica en la Década del Ochenta en la Argentina," *El Bimestre Político y Económico* 2, no. 32 (1987): 6. See also Aldo C. Vacs, "Convergence and Dissension: Democracy, Markets, and Structural Reform in World Perspective," in *Latin American Political Economy in the Age of Neoliberal Reform: Theoretical and Comparative Perspectives for the 1990s*, ed. William C. Smith, Carlos Acuña, and Eduardo A. Gamarra (New Brunswick, N.J.: Transaction Publishers/University of Miami North-South Center, 1994). Among those who share Wriston's free-market optimism, some argue that international capital mobility has "forced world governments to become competitors for the globe's expanding capital base—by cutting tax rates, curbing unnecessary expenditures, eliminating inefficient regulations, and renouncing all the trappings of central state planning." See Richard B. McKenzie and Dwight R. Lee, *Quicksilver Capital: How the Rapid Movement of Wealth Has Changed the World* (New York: The Free Press, 1991), p. 9. In effect, their

With this in mind, let us now examine the pattern of reform in more detail.[9] We first create an index that aggregates observations of policy change in each specific area. Here I borrow from the work of John Williamson, who created a reform "scorecard" for ten countries (including all six considered here) in presenting the results of a large project on reform and adjustment.[10] Data from Williamson's summary appear in Table 4.1. They pertain to six countries and six (of nine) areas of policy reform as he has defined them: fiscal discipline, financial liberalization, tax reform, foreign direct investment, privatization, and trade liberalization. Exchange liberalization, though not one of his categories (he considers "realistic exchange rates," a criterion that now seems equivocal, as noted below), is also included.[11] The last column in the table sums the scores in the other columns, with the exception of those "+" symbols that represent policy reform undertaken before the 1980s. These mainly affect the score for Chile, but they also reflect the survival of Colombia's financial liberalization of the 1970s. Most of the 1980s liberal reforms took place in the years 1988–89.

Table 4.2 uses a variety of sources to update the Williamson scorecard after four years (1990–93). It shows the rapid advance of liberal policy reform in Argentina, some continuation of the process in Venezuela, new initiatives in Colombia, and relatively little change elsewhere.[12] The last column of this table adds all the other columns to

---

argument is that the sort of competition for investment typical among U.S. states and municipalities will be reproduced internationally. Cf. Paul E. Peterson, *City Limits* (Chicago: University of Chicago Press, 1981).

9. I do not use the word "test" to describe this exercise. With N = 6 (six countries each assumed to experience one period of reform beginning in the late 1980s, related somehow to capital flight in an earlier period), correlation is vague and causal inference very risky.

10. The summary scorecard appears as table 10 in his *The Progress of Policy Reform in Latin America,* Institute for International Economics Policy Analyses in International Economics, no. 28 (Washington, D.C.: IIE, January 1990), p. 64. This table summarizes nine others on each policy area. The same information is gathered by country in the text, and all of this is elaborated in the longer conference papers appearing in John Williamson, ed., *Latin American Adjustment: How Much Has Happened?* (Washington, D.C.: Institute for International Economics, 1990).

11. I could find no consistent data on public spending priorities and deregulation.

12. Argentina has seen major tax reforms in 1990 and 1993, sales of stock in many state companies, including the huge deal for the state oil company (Yacimientos Petrolíferos Fiscales), a financial liberalization in January 1993, and greater fiscal discipline. Venezuela's government has undertaken a reform of direct investment rules and in the summer of 1993 finally won enabling legislation for tax reform. Colombian direct investment laws have been liberalized somewhat, as has its foreign exchange

the last one of Table 4.1. The result for each country is a summary indicator of policy reform in four areas between around 1980 and the end of 1993. Argentina and Mexico traveled the farthest down the liberal path, followed by Venezuela (despite later reversals), Colombia, and then Chile and Brazil. Although in absolute terms Chile would have to count as among the most liberal, the index refers to reforms since 1980 only.[13]

Before measuring the significance of mobile capital, we first must decide between two ways to define it for our purposes. If we construe it broadly, we might take mobile capital to be a fact of life that is about equally salient for all governments—or at least its importance does not depend on the past history of net capital outflows from a country. It is true that international asset acquisitions by residents, even if done in ways whose balance-of-payments accounting leads them to be regarded as capital flight, could rise quickly without a detectable net outflow, provided there are flows of a similar magnitude in the opposite direction under the same rubric. If, for example, we look at figures for deposits held in U.S. banks by residents of the six countries considered here, we find substantial rises for countries with negative net capital flight: between 1977 and 1991, for example, Argentine deposits rose 423 percent, those of Brazilians 428 percent, Chileans 723 percent, Colombians 165 percent, Mexican deposits rose by 484 percent, and Venezuelan deposits added 245 percent. Even when deflated by figures for total trade, the rise in U.S. bank deposits during the 1980s is remarkable (Figures 4.1A–B). We might use this measure as a proxy for asset globalization, provided we assume that the relative preference for U.S. bank deposits remains stable over time. But the magni-

---

regulations. As for the other changes, Mexican finance is now more liberal and Brazil's tax system has been modified. For sources, see Table 4.2.

13. One might argue, following Wriston, that all countries inevitably must adopt neoliberal policies. If so, the extensiveness of economic reform would correlate best with the degree of illiberality at the outset. The problem with this idea is its unspecified time frame; apart from this, and the absence of an explanatory mechanism, it is not too different from the sense of the capital mobility hypothesis investigated here. To test it over the period in question, we score the pre-1980 reforms in Chile and Colombia as if they had taken place during the 1980s. This adds six to the former (scores of "+ +" for fiscal discipline, tax reform, and foreign direct investment liberalization) and two for the latter (a score of "+" for financial liberalization and an additional "+" for privatization to reflect the fact that Colombia had less to privatize). By this reckoning Argentina and Chile are most liberal with scores of 13, Mexico with 11, Colombia with 10, Venezuela with 9, and Brazil with 5. Given that this variant of the hypothesis expects convergence to liberalism, the main anomaly is, unsurprisingly, Brazil.

Table 4.1 Liberalization of Economic Policies in the 1980s

	Fiscal Discipline	Financial Liberalization	Tax Reform	FDI	Privatization	Trade Liberalization	Exchange Liberalization	Total (1980s)
ARG	+	0	0	+	+	0	0	3
BRA	0	0	+	−	+	0	0	1
CHI	+	++	+	+	++	+	+	7
COL	++	+	+	0	++	+	0	5
MEX	++	0	++	++	++	++	+	11
VEN	0	+	0	+	+	++	++	7

SOURCES: For all but exchange liberalization see John Williamson, *The Progress of Policy Reform in Latin America*, Institute for International Economics Policy Analyses in International Economics, no. 28 (Washington, D.C., January 1990), table 10. For exchange liberalization, see IMF, *Exchange Arrangements and Exchange Restrictions: Annual Report* (Washington, D.C.: IMF), to 1990.

NOTES: + +, substantial liberalization; +, some change (even if a reversion to liberal policy) or regime liberal through the period; 0, no change or mixed trend; −, diminished liberalism. FDI = regulations on foreign direct investment.

Table 4.2 Liberalization of Economic Policies, 1990–1993 and 1980–1993

	Fiscal Discipline	Financial Liberalization	Tax Reform	FDI	Privatization	Trade Liberalization	Exchange Liberalization	Total (1980–1993)
ARG	+1	+1	+2	+1	+1	+2	+2	13
BRA	0	0	+1	+1	+1	+1	0	5
CHI	0	0	0	0	0	0	0	7
COL	0	+1	0	+1	0	+1	+1	8
MEX	0	+1	0	0	0	0	+1	11
VEN	+1	+1	+1	+1	0	0	0	9

SOURCES: *Latin American Weekly Report*, various issues, 1992–93; Richard M. Bird, "Tax Reform in Latin America: A Review of Some Recent Experiences," *Latin American Research Review* 27, no. 1 (1992): 7–36; *Privatization in Latin America*, supplement to *Latin Finance*, March 1993; U.S. Trade Representative, *1993 National Trade Estimate Report on Foreign Trade Barriers* (Washington, D.C., 1993); IMF, *Government Finance Statistics Yearbook* (Washington, D.C.: IMF), 1992; IMF, *Exchange Arrangements and Exchange Restrictions: Annual Report*, 1991–93 (covers to end of 1992 only); *Wall Street Journal*, various issues, 1994.

NOTES: Scores for 1990–93 judged in terms of effect on whole 1980–93 period score, thus 0 = no change in trend noted in Table 4.1, +1 = new reforms, etc.

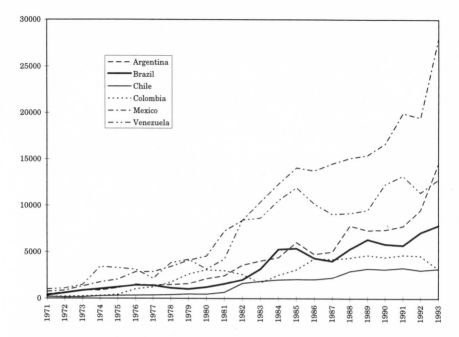

Fig. 4.1A.   Assets of nationals, by country, in U.S. banks, 1971–1993 (U.S. $ millions, year end). Federal Reserve, *Statistical Digest,* various issues.

tudes cannot be used to compare countries because of the bias in favor of countries close to the United States.[14]

A narrower view would take the policy significance of mobile capital to depend on the magnitude of net capital outflows, before and perhaps during deliberations on policy. Mainly because it is more manageable and avoids the bias noted above, this is the definition I use in most of what follows. The next step would then be to measure the relative magnitude of capital flight across countries in a way that captures its supposed effect on policy.

Table 4.3, below, shows estimates of capital flight (year-on-year) for periods that begin in 1976 and end with the year prior to the major reform initiative (the numerators in columns 1a and 1b). Except for Chile in 1984 and Mexico in 1988, the year reform begins (y) is either 1989 or 1990. In the Mexican and Chilean cases this date is less clear-cut than in the other three. For Mexico the fiscal adjustment and trade

14. Figures from Board of Governors of the Federal Reserve System, *Annual Statistical Digest,* 1970/79 and 1991 (Washington, D.C.: Federal Reserve). The assumption of constant asset preference may be further questioned based on the huge numbers for banks in haven countries, chiefly the British West Indies and the Bahamas.

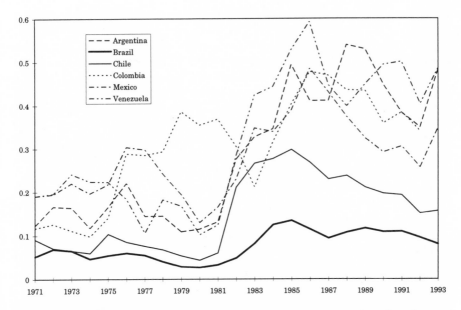

Fig. 4.1B.   Assets of nationals in U.S. banks, as a proportion of total trade, 1971–1993. *Statistical Digest* and IMF, *International Financial Statistics,* various issues.

liberalization efforts under de la Madrid are passed over; marking reform from 1988 captures the Pacto de Solidaridad Económica (beginning in mid-December 1987) and the major initiatives begun under Salinas from December 1988 forward. For Chile the fact that we are dealing with a limited reliberalization in the wake of the debt crisis means that a date has to be set rather arbitrarily, in this case upon the 1984 tax reform and sale of intervened bank assets, leaving aside the draconian and politically conflictual recessionary adjustments of 1982–83.

The capital flight estimates for the period 1976 to y-1 are then divided by the figure for exports in the year of reform. This corrects the estimates for the size of a country's foreign sector when gauging the importance of flight to the economy. Also in Table 4.3 is an average of investment as a proportion of GDP for the four years prior to the reforms.

Table 4.3 shows a moderate correspondence between the magnitude of capital flight in six countries after 1976 and the extent of the liberal policy reforms undertaken, usually beginning around 1989, in each. The pattern seems to imply some connection between capital outflow

(1976 to y-1) and the extent of subsequent (mostly 1989–93) policy reform. The fact that significant reforms were undertaken in Mexico and Argentina, both countries having suffered large waves of capital flight in previous years, supports the hypothesis best. Venezuela, also afflicted by flight, saw major reforms too. Chile, with no net flight, saw significantly more extensive liberal reform during the period than its amount of capital flight would predict, Colombia also reformed a bit more than would be predicted, and Brazil did a bit less.

Before we explore the correspondence between mobile capital and reform, let us first entertain rival explanations. We consider the two alternative views, mentioned in the introduction, of the impetus behind liberal reforms—those implicating international pressure and ideology (see also Table 4.5). Let us examine the relationship of these factors to mobile capital, along with their ability to account for instances in which policy reform does not seem to follow capital flight very closely.[15]

Ideology

There can be little doubt that ideological change weakened the socialist and nationalist positions in Latin America over the decade. The collapse of the USSR spoke volumes about the hopelessness of state socialism; recovery and rapid growth in Chile in the second half of the 1980s impressed many; and the ideas of *El Otro Sendero* stirred hopes for the revolutionary potential of economic liberalism.[16] Meanwhile, the organized Left lost its own sense that it could offer a credible alternative.

Yet it is notoriously hard to assess the independent effect of ideas, especially where they concern a subject, economic policy, that lies so close to obvious foreign and domestic interests. In many instances it is reasonable to suspect that convenience exceeded conviction. As has been widely observed, although Latin American neoliberal reforms

15. Here I am obviously passing over many other possible explanations. The most important of these involve political realignments within each country. I would not dismiss, say, the increasingly prominent role of technocrats in the PRI or the political opportunism of provincial Peronists, but I am seeking to understand the broader forces that pointed many countries in the same direction.

16. Hernando de Soto in collaboration with the Instituto Libertad y Democracia, *The Other Path: The Invisible Revolution in the Third World,* trans. June Abbott (New York: Harper and Row, 1989).

mostly came from freely elected governments, relatively few of these had actually been elected *as* neoliberals—a pattern most spectacularly exemplified in the postelection "pirouettes" of Carlos Andrés Pérez, Carlos Menem, and Alberto Fujimori.[17]

Certainly, many important minds were changed by the financial chaos of the 1980s. An exasperated Guido DiTella asserted in 1984 that capital would not return to Argentina unless a "total change" were made "in the next ten to twenty years."[18] Jorge Born, head of the Bunge y Born conglomerate and Menem's alliance partner, remarked that "perhaps the greatest merit of this president is his having opted for realism as a political philosophy."[19] But to Jorge Castañeda, "the strongest arguments heard in favor of the free-market radicalism . . . consisted precisely in the importance of the foreign constraint."[20] If Castañeda is right, how do we draw the line between assent to "strong arguments" (such as "realism" or the need for "total change") and the absence of choice? Even policymakers not buffeted by severe crises may well have become convinced of the constraints posed by international capital mobility. One does not need a change of heart to see which way the wind is blowing.

Where we find a coincidence of clear external constraints and a liberal ruling ideology, a familiar argument suggests itself: in Latin America, ideological currents enter through the social channels cre-

17. The present point concerning these about-faces is not that they represent a Machiavellian element of statecraft, a "voodoo politics" necessary to bring about reform, as John Williamson and Stephan Haggard discuss them. See "The Political Conditions for Economic Reform," in *The Political Economy of Policy Reform*, ed. John Williamson (Washington, D.C.: Institute for International Economics, 1994), pp. 584–86. They argue correctly that deception is not necessary or, above all, to be recommended in a reforming politician. The episodes nevertheless illustrate that the *conditions of governance* were such that leaders previously identified as populists or near-populists had to change direction. At least in these cases the ideology of the leaders or of those who voted for them was not what prompted the reforms.

18. *Mercado* (Buenos Aires), 9 August 1984, p. 25. DiTella was later Menem's first ambassador to Washington and then foreign minister; with Domingo Cavallo he was a leading liberal in Peronist ranks.

19. *La Prensa* (Buenos Aires), 18 February 1993, p. 6. In a valuable summary of Argentine stabilization efforts, Roberto Bouzas calls Menem's shift "paradoxical and probably illustrative." See "¿Más Allá de la Estabilización y la Reforma? Un Ensayo Sobre la Economía Argentina a Comienzos de los '90," *Desarrollo Económico* 33, no. 129 (April–June 1993): 10.

20. *Utopia Unarmed: The Latin American Left After the Cold War* (New York: Knopf, 1993), p. 422. For a similar comment, see Alan García, *El Nuevo Totalitarismo: Poder Sin Contrapeso* (Lima: Instituto de la Deuda Latinoamericana, 1992). García laments that "everything that is done today, supposedly in the name of 'pragmatism' and 'modernity' is only resignation" (pp. 9–10).

Table 4.3 Liberalization and the Incentive to Attract Overseas Capital

| Country and Year (y) Reform Begins | K Flight / Exports (1976 to y-1 / (y) | | Inv/GDP (avg, y-4 to y-1) (2) | Liberalization Index (Table 4.2) (3) | Ranks in Indices (Rank in 1a, 1b; 3) |
	Using World Bank Estimate (1a)	Using "Hot Money" Estimate (1b)			
ARG (1990)[a]	(31685/ 15089) = **2.1**	(16176/ 15089) = **1.1**	0.138	13	1,2; 1
BRA (1990)	(37050/ 35551) = **1.0**	(8368/ 35551) = **0.2**	0.199	5	4,4; 6
CHI (1984)[b]	(−3795/ 4636) = **−0.8**	(−2312/ 4636) = **−0.5**	0.146	7	6,6; 5

COL (1990)	(1447/ 9623) = **0.2**	(3316/ 9623) = **0.3**	0.198	8	5,3; 4
MEX (1988)[c]	(77631/ 37713) = **2.1**	(46963/ 37713) = **1.2**	0.205	11	1,1; 2
VEN (1989)	(25570/ 15610) = **1.6**	(4672/ 15610) = **0.3**	0.202	9	3,3; 3

SOURCES: Capital flight: Tables 1.1a–b (World Bank IECDI data base); Exports and GDP: World Bank, *World Debt Tables* (Washington, D.C.: World Bank); Investment: IMF, *IFS Yearbook* (Washington, D.C.: IMF), except 1988–89 Mexico and 1989 Chile from World Bank, *World Tables* (Baltimore: Johns Hopkins University Press, 1992).

NOTES: [a]Argentine year uses 1990, because of capital flight to July 1989; [b]already liberal, date marks sale of intervened assets and tax reform; [c]new stage of reform with PSE (see text) begins Dec. 1987.

ated by historically close relations with the international economy. Even as *Business Week* praised the "continental network of Harvard, Chicago, and Stanford grads" who were "back home atop businesses and government ministries spreading the new market mind-set," it admitted that, with the debt crisis, "Latin governments needed economists to balance their books and coax credits from international lenders." It added, "who better for the job than the English-speaking economists, many with classmates in the banks and the International Monetary Fund? With that foot in the door, the whiz kids rose to the top."[21] Whenever external forces strongly affect the game, the argument goes, a cosmopolitan and technocratic elite (perhaps connected with transnational corporations) holds the high cards.[22]

Against this argument, it must be noted that there are times and places where a wider range of choices does exist, and ideology here may play an important role. Where a country with a moderate debt load and healthy growth rates adopts liberal reforms, the imputation of an independent role for ideas can be more defensible. This describes Colombia upon the election of the Liberals in 1990. The free-market convictions of Gaviria and (Finance Minister) Hommes appear to have been quite important to the liberalization of trade, foreign exchange, and investment after August 1990.[23] And, of course, privatization and the liberalization of finance in Chile, after the deep recession and financial crisis of 1982–83, represented a return to the old pattern by a dictator whose faith in neoliberal economics had been only slightly shaken, in a country in which public opinion turned clearly in favor of economic liberalism during the second half of the 1980s.[24] Chile also reminds us that ideologically-motivated leaders might deliberately

21. "Latin America: The Big Move to Free Markets," 15 June 1992, pp. 51, 54.
22. The broader contention of international influence through this elite is common in dependency writings. In a more nuanced view, Sylvia Maxfield argues that, historically, a reduced strategic importance of international financial links (whether because of financial collapse, as in the 1930s, or due to the relative abundance of foreign financing, as in the 1970s) enhanced the influence of the more economically nationalist coalition over economic policy. At other times (the 1950s and the 1980s), relatively scarce foreign and domestic financing, the latter symptomized by capital flight, favored the ascendancy of the more orthodox "banker's coalition." See *Governing Capital: International Finance and Mexican Politics* (Ithaca, N.Y.: Cornell University Press, 1990).
23. One can read Rudolf Hommes's contribution in Williamson, ed., *Latin American Adjustment,* as a manifesto for his subsequent tenure as finance minister. Liberal conviction and some of the reasons for it are laid out in Miguel Urrutia, "Colombia," in *The Political Economy of Policy Reform,* ed. John Williamson (Washington, D.C.: Institute for International Economics, 1994), pp. 285–315.
24. Hojman, "The Political Economy of Recent Conversion," is especially persuasive on Chilean opinion, pp. 210–13.

embrace international market discipline as a remedy for economic and spiritual "decadence."

All in all, ideas may have played an independent role in bringing about liberal reform in many places, but where economic necessities were clear and binding—generally in the most sudden and surprising reformers—the argument for their causal importance is much harder to justify.[25]

International Influence

The U.S. government, international financial institutions (IFIs), and private creditors have obviously favored the liberal orientation of policy reform in Latin America, and they have used strong conditionality to promote it. Suspensions of payments, open support for shock programs, and long negotiations testify to the power of IFIs within the international system. Moreover, not only did commercial banks follow the policy-conditionality cues of the International Monetary Fund and World Bank, most of them also became less disposed to commit new money to Latin America as the decade progressed, and especially after the write-downs of 1987–88.[26] Hence, while the fact of a "Washington consensus" may not have implied that Washington absolutely determined reform outcomes, the breadth and assertiveness of international conditionality after 1982 cannot be ignored. With regard to the previous discussion, we can take this to argue against an independent role for ideas, at least in some places: the very fact that the Brady Plan required strong free-market reforms, well beyond those hitherto typical of the IMF, suggests that even the evangelists did not trust entirely to the zeal of the newly converted.[27]

25. Moisés Naim relates Pérez's ideological change to his contact with European socialists, especially his ability to compare the results achieved by two personal friends, Alan García and Felipe González. But he also documents the deep crisis of the Venezuelan economy quite completely, stating at one point that the Venezuelan reforms were like those of many other countries in which crisis was "forcing them to seek out alternatives to their traditional economic policies." See *Paper Tigers and Minotaurs*, pp. 45–47, 17.

26. Vinod Aggarwal, personal communication; Stephen Fidler, "Debt Fatigue in Latin America," *Financial Times*, 31 August 1988, p. 12. Fidler notes that while in 1982 Brazil had over seven hundred creditors, in 1988 fewer than half of these remained.

27. David Felix, "Reflections on Privatization in Latin America," Washington University Department of Economics Working Paper no. 151 (St. Louis: Washington University, March 1991), pp. 1–6; on the Brady Plan's effect see, for example, Peter Accolla,

The extent of international influence over a country mostly depends on how serious its economic difficulties are. The IMF and the World Bank have less occasion to shape a country's policies until it has serious problems, especially on the balance of payments. However, even without the exhaustion of reserves or an open crisis, good relations with IFIs are likely to make international finance cheaper and easier to get. Even in Colombia, Miguel Urrutia notes the key role of World Bank pressure—especially after commercial banks became more reluctant to lend in the late 1980s—in persuading policymakers that trade liberalization was "inevitable."[28]

It appears that where crisis preceded reforms, IMF influence worked in tandem with the prod of crisis. Just before Mexico and Venezuela began deepening or initiating liberal reforms in a dramatic way in 1988–89, things were bad enough to provoke tough new talk on debt repayment and to provide strong independent motivations for new reform initiatives aimed at arresting financial collapse.[29] The Brady Plan facilitated and supported liberalization because it promised to break the payments logjam (which had encouraged controls and .protection in the first years of the crisis) while linking this incentive to structural reform.[30] However, while it clearly helped make reform sustainable, it did not induce the first reform moves in Mexico or Venezuela; it *followed* the riots in Caracas. It offered less to Colombia, with that country's lighter debt load. And of course it did not budge Brazil very quickly, even after so many letters of intent signed by Brazilian governments.

While crisis provided the occasion for their authoritative application, international financial norms clearly shaped the dominantly liberal response to crisis. International financial institution personnel have stood quite close to the Latin American economic policymaking

---

Privatization in Latin America: 1988–1989, U.S. Department of Labor, Bureau of International Labor Affairs, Foreign Labor Trends Series FLT 89-20 (1989), pp. 10–11. I do not mean to imply that all recipients of Brady reductions could have been expected to avoid liberal reforms without a strong material incentive: from the U.S. Treasury standpoint, rules had to be made for the hard cases.

28. Urrutia, "Colombia," pp. 291–92, 302–3. In summarizing the Colombian case, Williamson and Haggard state flatly that since Colombia's crisis had passed, "there was no external pressure for reform" (Williamson and Haggard, "The Political Conditions for Economic Reform," pp. 539–40).

29. For example, see remarks on the debt reported in *Latin American Weekly Report*, 19 January 1989, p. 10.

30. John H. Welch, "The New Face of Latin America: Financial Flows, Markets, and Institutions in the 1990s," *Journal of Latin American Studies* 25, no. 1 (February 1993): 2.

process since 1982, and they generally became more liberal in their own ideas by the end of the decade. Even without this proximity, local decisionmakers usually knew what they would recommend. Above all, in situations of crisis the attractiveness of a liberal *salida* depended significantly on the promise that liberalism would win tangible rewards from the IFIs and commercial banks.[31] These rewards would also be expected to include nonbank capital flows, since it was clear that adherence to liberal norms would please other market participants, too. In sum, while a country's exposure to international pressure was in large part a function of broader financial problems, the IFIs shaped the perception of these problems and the ways governments sought to solve them.

Before continuing, we may note that the imputed role of international pressure complements that attributed to ideology. Pressure might be taken to explain reform in those cases in which crisis drives a government into the arms of the IMF, just as ideas are likely to have had their greatest independent importance where no such calamity took place. As will be noted below, this means that international pressure offers the main alternative explanation for those instances of reform seemingly motivated by the need to evoke the return of flight capital, and that ideology presents the main alternative for cases in which net capital flight is negative or of minor importance.

Causal Connections Between Mobile Capital and Policy Reform

Let us now explore the proposed causal relationship between mobile capital and reform. The first question we need to ask is, what tells us that capital flight, rather than a general desire to attract investment from any source, was the driving force?

Clearly, in the late 1980s the return of flight capital *was* an important concern for policymakers and a common topic of public discussion

---

31. Here I dissent somewhat from the dominant presumption of the contributions to *The Political Economy of Policy Reform* as articulated by Williamson, ed. (pp. 24–25). I agree with the idea that strings on external finance help reformers win "internal arguments," but it is misleading to characterize one of the competing hypotheses about this subject as saying "international agencies compel national governments to do things that the latter do not perceive to be in their national interest" (25 n. 13). I return to this topic in Chapter 6.

in Venezuela, Argentina, and especially in Mexico.[32] In 1989 *The Wall Street Journal* described many of Salinas's key policies as efforts to attract expatriate capital, noting the need to "make ever more dramatic reforms . . . and thus lure capital back the free-market way." The article mentioned an instance of military repression of labor (at Cananea) that "drew cheers from the sacadólares" but alienated labor even further. It concluded, quoting a Mexican lawyer close to holders of foreign assets, "how much money comes back, and how soon, all depends on whether Salinas continues to play this very dangerous game with the same skill he's shown so far."[33] Lots of policy moves spoke clearly to Mexicans: the saga of the banks; the fairly common practice in mid-decade of negotiating unneeded loans in order to demonstrate cooperativeness; the selection of Carlos Salinas and his public emphasis on continuity with his predecessor's project of "modernization"; and the symbolic, contentious privatization of Cananea.[34] The actions would have been much more meaningful to local capital, with its still-vivid memories of Echeverría's rhetoric or the events of 1 September 1982, than to the IMF or foreign investors.[35]

Still, some evidence on the motivations for policy change is equivocal on this question. Personnel choices were meant to impress both foreign and domestic capital. Argentina in 1989 had built up arrears with foreign private banks and suffered a World Bank credit suspen-

32. Interviews: Jesús Silva Herzog, 11 February 1987; Felipe Pazos, Banco Central de Venezuela, 20 October 1988; Julio Rodríguez M., *El Economista* (Buenos Aires), 10 July 1987. I recall one attention-grabbing headline in a Mexico City tabloid, "Regresa La Lana" ("The Money Is Coming Back"), a bit overblown and premature as it turned out (it was mid–1988), but indicating the level of consciousness about flight capital that the editors assumed to exist among the public.

33. Matt Moffett, "Mexico's Capital Flight Still Racks Economy, Despite the Brady Plan," *Wall Street Journal*, 25 September 1989, p. A10.

34. On the first, for example, noting the government's sales of firms acquired along with the banks in 1982, a business magazine commented, "evidently the concessions to the private sector are aimed at re-establishing confidence." See *Expansión*, 20 March 1985, p. 19; on borrowing, a point made by Víctor Urquidi, personal communication, 16 November 1987; on Salinas, for example, Fernando Ortega Pizarro, "Los Empresarios Esperan un Sucesor Que Trabaje para Ellos," *Proceso* 537 (16 February 1987); the point that Salinas's acceptance of de la Madrid's progress on state modernization was much more relevant to Mexican than foreign eyes was made by Víctor A. Espinoza in his remarks on the modernization of the Mexican state at the Congress of the Latin American Studies Association, Atlanta, 10 March 1994; on the first and last points, see John Waterbury, "The Heart of the Matter?" in *The Politics of Economic Adjustment: International Constraints, Distributive Conflicts, and the State*, ed. Stephan Haggard and Robert Kaufman (Princeton: Princeton University Press, 1992), pp. 213–14.

35. The priority on domestic confidence could be argued wherever privatization rules reserve majority stakes to nationals.

sion, so an emphasis on winning foreign confidence seems understandable. Menem hired Jeffrey Sachs as economic advisor and initially named internationally known economists as foreign minister (Domingo Cavallo) and ambassador to the United States (Guido DiTella). Yet Menem also played to a domestic audience. Among other moves, he appointed as economy minister, in succession, two officers of Bunge y Born (Jorge Born's company, one of Argentina's oldest and most prestigious private conglomerates). He also publicly tied himself to Alvaro Alsogaray and his daughter María Julia, both famous in the country for the diehard advocacy of free-market policies.[36] Colombian presidents also faced similar imperatives.[37]

To what extent do other policies reflect a dominant preoccupation with expatriate funds? Consider tax policy. It seems reasonable to say that a key indicator of a government's desire to attract capital is its tax treatment of wealth, interest, and capital gains. Here the pattern is an interesting one. Tax holidays, aimed at coaxing back expatriate capital, appeared soon after the crisis broke and again later. Viewing the Mexican government's 1989 decision not to tax individual capital gains from the stock market, one analyst concluded that "the threat of capital flight (or reduced capital repatriation) remained a powerful constraint on the government's taxing powers."[38] Still, after 1988

36. Soon after taking office Menem said that "no alternative remained" to the policies he chose. *La Prensa* (Buenos Aires), 11 July 1989, p. 4. See also *International Currency Review* 20, no. 1 (August/September 1989): 169. Others suspect the big economic groups of undermining Alfonsín's presidency in the first place. See Luis Majul, *Por Qué Cayó Alfonsín: El Nuevo Terrorismo Económico* (Buenos Aires: Editorial Sudamerica, 1990), p. 32.

37. Like Mexico and Argentina, Colombia in 1989–90 had problems: violence, a growing fiscal deficit, and an incipient investment slump. Yet these were economically benign compared to those of the other two countries, and Colombia had experienced less capital flight. The need to attract nervous *foreign* investors figured prominently among the justifications for reform there. Rudolf Hommes, "Colombia," in *Latin American Adjustment: How Much Has Happened?* ed. John Williamson (Washington, D.C.: Institute for International Economics, 1990); Sarita Kendall, "Bogotá Plans to Doff Economic Straitjacket," *Financial Times,* 12 September 1990, p. 7, in which she notes that FDI fell by a third in the first half of 1990; however, *Latin American Weekly Report* also noted that surveys of all local business showed a sharp downturn of planned investment in the second half of 1989 (14 June 1990, p. 3).

38. In Argentina the Alfonsín government agonized and debated before backing a tax "whitewash" *(blanqueo)* on repatriated assets. The measure had formidable political liabilities: some expressed worries that it would benefit torturers who appropriated the assets of their victims; the foreign minister and the head of the tax authority came out publicly against it; and the ruling party had always opposed similar policies in the past. The overriding consideration proved to be the need to attract flight capital back to the country. See the discussion in *Clarín* (Buenos Aires), 13 August 1986, pp. 2–3. The law

the governments of Mexico and Argentina, energized by crisis, also effectively broadened and rationalized their tax systems to achieve fiscal balance.[39] The Mexican government won cooperation from the United States in prosecuting a few nationals for tax evasion, and it even abolished the bearer bond (a proposal that had caused alarm when Echeverría made it in 1970).[40] It seems that there was enough administrative slack in both systems to improve collections while reducing rates substantially. An improvement in public finances was expected to do more to inspire private-sector confidence than a tax increase would do to dampen it, especially if most of the bite could be directed away from capital.[41]

With regard to exchange policy, countries with substantial net

---

was designed with a two-year time limit, testifying to both the fear of moral hazard and the immediate need for capital investment. Funds could be brought back into dollar accounts paying the London interbank offer rate during this period. Approved investments included privatized state companies. For a critical view from the Leninist Left, see Andrés Cammarota, "Blanqueos y Bancos: Cara y Cruz de la Misma Moneda," *Problemas de Economía* 24 (October 1986): 9–12. Another whitewash plan was implemented in 1990, and in 1993 the felt need to raise the national savings rate moved the economy minister to introduce exemptions for capital gains taxes and for personal income taxes on interest and dividends. *Foreign Broadcast Information Service Latin America,* 16 April 1990, p. 31, cited from *Buenos Aires Herald,* 15 April 1990, p. 4; *Latin American Weekly Report,* 30 September 1993, p. 449. Eduardo Conesa concludes: "[I]n our country it is probable that capital that went will not return if, from the mere fact of its return, the fisc considers it as a profit subject to tax." See *La Crisis del 93: Una Agenda de los Riesgos que Enfrentará la Economía Argentina* (Buenos Aires: Planeta, 1992), p. 217. In 1987–89 in Venezuela attempts to tax capital flight failed. See *Latin American Weekly Report,* 3 May 1990, p. 11; 30 May 1991, p. 4. Finally, in Mexico Salinas instituted a tax amnesty for repatriated capital in late July 1989. *Latin American Weekly Report,* 17 August 1989, p. 11; Moffett, "Mexico's Capital Flight Still Racks Economy, Despite the Brady Plan," p. A10. On stock market gains: Carlos Elizondo, "In Search of Revenue: Tax Reform in Mexico Under the Administrations of Echeverría and Salinas," *Journal of Latin American Studies* 26, no. 1 (February 1994): 179.

39. Richard Bird, "Tax Reform in Latin America: A Review of Some Recent Experiences," *Latin American Research Review* 27, no. 1 (1992): 18–28. Bird also notes that "major changes in tax structure and administration are usually possible only when times are bad, during a crisis of some sort." The extreme crisis point, at which no option but major reform remains, in Latin America "has too often meant only when the International Monetary Fund really puts on the pressure" (pp. 31, 23 n. 26).

40. Interview, Secretaría de Hacienda y Crédito Público, 29 July 1988; Elizondo, "In Search of Revenue," p. 175.

41. Richard Bird observes that along with Latin America's traditional problem of the "political impossibility" of levying direct taxes on "rich and powerful taxpayers" there had now been added "limits imposed by international capital markets on income taxation" (Bird, "Tax Reform," pp. 28, 31).

accumulated capital outflow also later embraced the greatest degree of exchange-market deregulation, returning to old patterns traced in Chapter 3. Mexico ended all exchange control in November 1991; Argentina removed restrictions in several steps (December 1989, March–April 1991, January 1993), ending with a system that permitted local dollar checking accounts to be used as legal tender domestically; and Venezuela abolished virtually all its remaining controls in March 1989. For Argentina, in particular, the conditions surrounding the adoption of the Convertibility Plan—massive dollarization, a continuing investment slump, recurrent inflation—spoke plainly of the need to meet the conditions necessary to attract dollar assets at home and abroad. Among the other three countries, the historical reluctance to free the exchange market generally prevailed: in Colombia the liberalizations of June 1991 and January 1992 left a system with export surrender requirements, a reduced but still dominant role for the Banco de la República, and controls on inflows; Chile's system remained moderately restrictive; and Brazil's stayed even more so.[42]

There seem to have been familiar reasons behind this reversion to old habits. As noted above, a major impetus for reform in Argentina and Mexico was an acceleration of inflation. It is not surprising, then, that these governments decided to keep the currency nominally stable. Nevertheless, the use of the nominal exchange rate as an anchor of stabilization suggests other motives, especially when it was combined with a dramatic liberalization of the exchange market. The previous chapter suggested that the combination of a fixed nominal rate and free exchange markets often reflected policymakers' desires to attract overseas funds by creating a reassuring and highly profitable arena of stability in an environment that such investors might not have trusted otherwise.[43] This would have pleased holders of flight capital. For

42. IMF, *Exchange Arrangements and Exchange Restrictions* (Washington, D.C.: International Monetary Fund), 1990–93 annual issues.

43. When combined with high real interest rates and domestic inflation in excess of the world rate, nominal exchange stability makes short- to medium-term financial assets extremely attractive. The currency appreciates in real terms, and so do the assets; and values may get another upward push as inward flows bid up asset prices over the interval, netting a large capital gain for the early bids. Furthermore, the real currency appreciation can mean that less of the necessarily large incentive for inward flows comes from domestic interest rates: as long as the market believes that the policy can be sustained, rates can be kept at levels that do not endanger growth. For a formal treatment, see Lance Taylor, "Economic Openness: Problems to the Century's End," in *Economic Liberalization: No Panacea: The Experiences of Latin America and Asia*, ed. Tariq Banuri (Oxford: Clarendon Press, 1991), pp. 127–30, or Roberto Frenkel, "Mercado Financiero, Expectativas Cambiarias, y Movimientos de Capital," *El Trimestre Económico* 50 (1983): 2041–76.

example, the stable peso fetish persisted during the 1980s and early 1990s among wealthy Mexican exiles: as a few told an interviewer, funds would return to Mexico if the government sold off state enterprises, made concessions to private business, and above all stabilized the peso.[44]

It is obviously hard to assess the relative weight of concerns for foreign capital, versus resident overseas capital, in such a wide range of policy decisions. However, we can reconstruct the economic basis for policy decisions from estimates of foreign direct investment and resident foreign assets. First, we *cannot* assume that Salinas or Menem could have anticipated the size of the eventual inflows their countries later received, especially insofar as the impetus to foreign portfolio investment was provided by the large decline in world (especially U.S.) interest rates. But we can assume that the importance of resident overseas capital, relative to other kinds of foreign investment, corresponded to the relative magnitude of inward flows that policymakers could have expected from these sources. Positing a target period of 1988–89, drawing on then-available estimates as well as the World Bank data cited in Chapter 1, and compounding each year's new stock (composed of the old stock plus new flows) by the U.S. T-bill interest rate for that year, we obtain impressive figures for imputed stocks of flight capital (Table 4.4). For Argentina, Venezuela, and Brazil (but only by the World Bank residual measure for the last two), stocks of overseas capital in the hands of residents are in the tens of billions of dollars, while for Mexico the World Bank method yields estimates well over a hundred billion.

Now, even if we take only the *interest* on this imputed foreign stock (as of 1988–89), it greatly exceeds the average annual flow of direct foreign investment for the preceding 1980–87 period for these countries. Even if we further confine ourselves to bank deposits in the United States (Figure 4.1, above, and Table 4.4, below), the imputed interest is of a comparable magnitude to foreign direct investment (FDI) for all countries except Brazil.[45] Whatever the measure, it is

44. Valdemar De Murguía, *Capital Flight and Economic Crisis: Mexican Post-Devaluation Exiles in a California Community,* Center for U.S.-Mexican Studies Research Report no. 44 (San Diego: UCSD, 1986), p. 23.

45. This assumes that all the direct investment is foreign and that the return of flight capital itself does not appear on the balance of payments as an inward flow of direct investment, an assumption that clearly exaggerates the real extent of true foreign investment. The repatriation of capital from overseas subsidiaries (perhaps in Panama or another financial haven) of transnational conglomerates may appear as FDI. For an estimate of grossed-up stocks and implicit interest income for Mexico (also using U.S. 1-

clear that especially in the countries that had large amounts of net capital flight, leaders seeking to attract capital inflows would have been well advised to worry mainly about the confidence of the *local* holders of overseas assets.[46]

This calculation seems to agree with the reasoning of at least one important player. In Argentina, Carlos Menem's key business ally, Jorge Born, circulated a memo in late October 1989 arguing, "it is a fallacy to think that great sums of foreign capital are waiting for the chance to be invested in Argentina. There are other areas of the world as or more interesting. This capital will only come after the tens of millions of Argentine dollars return from the foreign bank accounts."[47] Born and Menem sought to persuade this money to come back.

Political Influence or Economic Crisis?

Even if we believe that flight capital influenced policymaking in several Latin American economies, we need to ask a further question. How do we suppose that this economic fact came to have political implications? Here there are two kinds of causal mechanisms that appear plausible: the first, what might be called a political economy of globalization, points to changes in the economic interests of civil society, or in the balance of economic power between the private sector and the state; the second suggests that policy changes were made in response to learning, market signals, or (at the extreme) financial crises—imputing a more direct connection between economic trends and policy responses. These are arrayed in the middle columns of Table 4.5. Let us describe each of these in more detail before assessing their plausibility in the cases at hand.

The first includes the political-economic effects of economic globalization broadly construed, from the changes in interests that accompany international financial ties, to changes in asset liquidity. It sees a link based on political influence (a policy's political base), one that

---

year T-bill rates), see Collin Roche, "Capital Flight and Repatriation in the Mexican Context," Honors Thesis in Political Economy, Williams College, 1993.

46. The size of these figures is also the best answer to those who would argue that capital flight represented *merely* an effect of bad policies rather than also a consequential net loss for the economy (and here, mainly the fisc).

47. Quoted in Joaquín Morales Solá, *Asalto a la Ilusión: Historia Secreta del Poder en la Argentina desde 1983* (Buenos Aires: Planeta, 1990), p. 281.

Table 4.4 Imputed Net or Actual Foreign Assets, Interest, and Foreign Direct Investment

Measure	Argentina	Brazil	Chile	Colombia	Mexico	Venezuela
KF Stock (interest):						
MG est.[1]						
1987	46,000	31,000	2,000	7,000	84,000	58,000
	(2,682)	(1,807)	(107)	(408)	(4,897)	(3,381)
WB est.[2]						
1988	46,865	69,941	−8,498	−1,830	132,930	38,695
	(3,126)	(4,665)			(8,866)	(2,581)
1989	58,769	71,844	−10,852	−3,229	136,285	41,971
	(4,766)	(5,827)			(11,053)	(3,404)
HM est.[3]						
1988	8,085	−4,516	−20,186	−9,673	77,302	−8,801
	(539)				(5,156)	
1989	16,012	−2,123	−23,381	−10,894	82,638	−6,385
	(1,299)				(6,702)	

Residents' Deposits, U.S. Banks (interest):

1988	7,804	5,314	2,936	4,374	15,185	9,147
	(521)	(354)	(196)	(292)	(1,013)	(610)
1989	7,304	6,334	3,212	4,563	15,399	9,468
	(592)	(514)	(260)	(370)	(1,249)	(768)
1990	7,365	5,834	3,145	4,435	16,650	12,271
	(553)	(438)	(236)	(333)	(1,250)	(922)
1991	7,758	5,942	3,284	4,662	19,957	13,181
	(420)	(321)	(178)	(252)	(1,080)	(713)

Foreign Direct Investment avg:

1980–87	442	1,349	179	440	1,197	18
1988–90	1,337	1,258	191	397	1,944	65
1980–90	686	1,354	183	428	1,401	31

SOURCES: [1]Morgan Guaranty Trust, *World Financial Markets* 1988:7 (30 Dec.), using 6-mo. LIBOR or, if greater, increase of reported stock of external nonbank nonreserve assets (1977–87); [2]based on annual World Bank residual, corrected for misinvoicing (1971 to y); [3]based on yearly "hot money" estimate (+ misinv., same years). World Bank IECDI data base. FDI: IMF, *Balance of Payments Yearbook* (Washington, D.C.: IMF) (direct investment).

NOTES: All quantities in millions of U.S. dollars. Interest rates are U.S. T-bill rates for grossing-up of annual flow figures; for listed years above, as follows: 1987, 5.83%; 1988, 6.67%; 1989, 8.11%; 1990, 7.51%; 1991, 5.41%.

Table 4.5 Hypotheses and Mechanisms Linking Mobile Capital to Liberal Reform

Hypothesis	Predicted Pattern of Reform	Causal Mechanism		Anomalies
		Political Economy	Economic Trends	
Capital mobility	Extent of reform correlates with amount of net capital flight (or with degree of financial internationalization)	Power of holders of foreign assets (expatriate capital); power of MNCs, domestic holders of foreign assets; general effects of asset liquidity on preferences	Interest-rate sensitivity, market reactions; fiscal/ financial crises aggravated by capital flight; learning	Chile, Colombia
Ideology	Reform comes as ruling group accepts ideas for domestic reasons or learning	Attractiveness of ideas, success of liberal exemplars, leadership		All cases of "pirouettes" (Arg, Ven), Mexico
International pressure	Reform correlates with exposure to IFIs	Explicit conditionality and general shaping of how problems are viewed, tools available to solve them		Chile, Colombia, Brazil

Wriston's formulation obscures.[48] It describes the enhanced influence of both globally oriented transnational corporations and domestic holders of foreign assets. While it could also refer to countries with no (or negative) accumulated net capital outflows, the more common version of this idea involves countries that have experienced a lot of capital flight. Here, the argument goes, owners of expatriate capital can effectively make the adoption of liberal economic policies a condition for capital repatriation.[49]

The charge that Latin American development has been distorted by an internationalized bourgeoisie, a kind of financial fifth column, is an old complaint of nationalists and the Left. From this perspective, today's international capital mobility can be seen as a final consummation of the internationalization process, the creation of a new class that Petras and Morley call "the transnational capitalists," who benefit from austerity programs, good relations with the banks, and who "influence government decisionmaking" on these questions.[50] Indeed,

48. This argument is a version of what Bates calls "the partisan model." See Williamson, ed., *The Political Economy of Policy Reform*, pp. 31–33.

49. This idea is quite common. See Robert Kaufman's comment that Mexicans with assets abroad had little to lose by keeping pressure on the government to adhere to economic orthodoxy in "Economic Orthodoxy and Political Change in Mexico," in *Debt and Democracy in Latin America*, ed. Barbara Stallings and Robert Kaufman (Boulder, Colo.: Westview Press, 1989), p. 123; viewing Argentina, Roberto Bouzas puts it this way: "[T]he significant weight of these [foreign asset-holding] sectors was converted, in economies that had become very fragile, into a powerful incentive not to introduce additional elements of instability and conflict." He goes on to observe that countries with less flight had an easier time generating durable coalitions to reject recessionary adjustment policies, Brazil being his key example. See "América Latina y la Crisis de Endeudamiento Externo—A Modo de Introducción," in *Entre la Heterodoxia y el Ajuste: Negociaciones Financieras Externas de América Latina (1982–1987)*, ed. Roberto Bouzas (Buenos Aires: Grupo Editor Latinoamericano, 1988), p. 23. Considering the problem generally, Manuel Pastor, Jr., calls it an "elite veto." See "Capital Flight from Latin America," *World Development* 18, no. 1 (1990): 14. It extends to accounts such as that of Rogelio Hernández, who concludes from survey data that economic uncertainty was not a major factor in capital flight from Mexico in 1985, rather that "the placement of capital abroad is the best weapon of businessmen against the State." "La Política y los Empresarios Después de la Nacionalización Bancaria," *Foro Internacional* 27, no. 2 (1986): 258. The view of capital flight as intended to pressure is shared by many observers on the Mexican Left and in the PRI. See, for example, Gaston García Cantú, *El Desafío de la Derecha* (Mexico City: Joaquín Mortiz/Planeta, 1987), pp. 20, 154–55.

50. James Petras and Morris Morley, *U.S. Hegemony Under Siege: Class, Politics, and Development in Latin America* (London: Verso, 1990), pp. 198, 24. While proven wrong in their bold prediction that "the wholesale restructuring of economies . . . will not be implemented," Petras and Morley added that "the growth and consolidation of a transnational capitalist class in Latin America has created permanent and powerful spokespersons for liberalizing trading and investment regimes" (p. 208). A sympathetic

this argument comes not only from the Left. Asking why Latin American governments had shown a "general timidity" toward creditors while imposing large economic sacrifices on their citizens, *The Banker* suggested that

> a more important reason has been the deep interest of LDC's internationalized upper classes in keeping personal links with industrialized countries. And as a result of the past decade's capital flight, tens of thousands of middle-class savers have interests (material and psychological) on the creditor side of the ledger. They think of themselves as not just citizens of debtor nations but also depositors in international banks.[51]

Of course, these upper classes would include top positions in government, too—not only the widely publicized embezzling presidents and their cronies but also the average high official pursuing the "rational" course. As an ex-senior advisor to de la Madrid told a reporter, "Well, where do you think I have my money?"[52]

By this reasoning, the government bailouts of the 1980s would have fortified the liberal interest. They would have turned many erstwhile net debtors (who would have been potential allies of indebted governments against the banks) into net creditors of the international financial system, and thus into proponents of accommodation. In addition, it is likely that most domestic beneficiaries of government rescues also owned significant assets abroad.[53] In Argentina many holders of back-

---

reader would argue that the authors erred only in underestimating the strength of this class. A bitterly critical though entertaining treatment of this theme for Argentina is Norberto Galasso, *De Martínez de Hoz a Cavallo: Gatos y Sardinas en la Economía Argentina* (Buenos Aires: Editorial Fraterna, 1992).

51. Richard Feinberg and Mary Williamson, "Whose Finger on the Trigger?" *The Banker,* September 1987, p. 43; compare Carlos Díaz-Alejandro, "Latin American Debt: I Don't Think We Are in Kansas Anymore," *Brookings Papers on Economic Activity* 2 (1984): 382. A Brazilian official, complaining of domestic establishment opposition to the 1987 moratorium, comments on the elite's "tendency to underestimate the capacity for influence of the country," finding in Latin America generally an "incapacity of the dominant classes of the region to react to the breadth of the challenge represented by the debt crisis." See Paulo Nogueira Batista, Jr., *Da Crise Internacional A Moratória Brasileira* (Rio de Janeiro: Paz e Terra, 1988), p. 124.

52. James Henry, "Poor Man's Debt, Rich Man's Loot," *Washington Post,* 11 December 1988, p. C2.

53. Before becoming planning minister of Venezuela (where he fought to cut subsidies to private debtors), Miguel Rodríguez estimated a "90 percent overlap" in his country between holders of overseas capital and beneficiaries of debt bailout. Interview, January 1988.

to-backs (whose corresponding balances were, of course, not reported to the authorities) won an additional windfall at public expense.[54] Across Latin America one could find a peculiar combination of "wealthy businessmen and bankrupt businesses"; when in December 1987 a Mexican reporter made this observation to COPARMEX president Bernardo Ardavín, he responded that nothing would be gained by having businessmen miserable too.[55]

It must be admitted that the picture glosses over several important analytical issues. It is obviously simplistic to deduce a person's political preferences from the location (or currency denomination) of his savings. Aggregating this deduction to predict more extensive reform in countries with a lot of expatriate capital further supposes that such preferences get translated into policy without substantial mediation by parties or the state. It is true that to avoid positing an invisible state we could instead posit a complicitous one—with state officials, like the ex-presidential advisor quoted above, acting out of concern for *their* foreign assets. This does not make the generalization less crude. Since these issues lie beyond the scope of this chapter, let us consider the "transnational capitalist" scenario a shorthand for a broader change in the dominant class. With capital abroad and the state experiencing fiscal crisis, the ties of this class to government largesse weaken while its connections to international finance do the opposite.

Before considering the second possible mechanism we should note that to posit a political-economic influence on policy does not require that we appeal to net capital flight as the fundamental economic datum. The interests of the dominant class may become international-

---

54. Adolfo Canitrot, "Economic Policy Under Conditions of High Uncertainty: The Case of Argentina in the 1980s," *Quarterly Review of Economics and Business* 31, no. 3 (Autumn 1991): 244. This was a typical pattern. One account describes a meeting between an Argentine official and his agitated U.S. counterpart, the latter complaining about Argentine businessmen "who leech off the state and then take the money to Switzerland." When the Argentine objected, the North American surprised him with detailed information showing that many of the same people whose firms were far behind in their payments for government services were also buying expensive paintings in the exclusive auction houses of New York (Morales Solá, *Asalto a la Ilusión,* pp. 49–50). In 1990 unpaid debts to the central bank were found to have an estimated total of $67 billion, more than the foreign debt, with 80 percent owed by the private sector. Debtors included important banking and commercial interests. *Financial Times,* 12 September 1990, p. 7; *Review of the River Plate* no. 4504, 29 April 1992.

55. The quoted phrase is Sylvia Maxfield's. See her discussion in "National Business, Debt-Led Growth, and Political Transition in Latin America," in *Debt and Democracy in Latin America,* ed. Barbara Stallings and Robert Kaufman (Boulder, Colo.: Westview Press, 1989), pp. 76–78. On Ardavín, see *Proceso* 582 (28 December 1987): 9.

ized without a net outflow of capital, as long as capital has flowed in from other sources over the same period.

The second mechanism refers to the economic consequences of globalization that are important for policymakers as managers—the behavior of interest rates and stock markets, as well as the more diffuse ways mobile capital affects the priorities of the state. It begins from the obvious correspondence between Latin America's unprecedented financial crisis and its equally unprecedented shift toward neoliberalism. As Paul Volcker remarked, it "seems evident to most experienced observers . . . that the agony of the debt crisis provided the jolt necessary for Latin American leaders to rethink their old approaches and set off in fresh and much more promising directions."[56] Capital flight enters the explanation insofar as it contributed to the agony. Wherever observers like Volcker (and Wriston) do not dismiss capital flight as a mere symptom of policy errors, they implicate its economic rather than its political-economic effects: countries with more flight, having lost national savings at a critical time, would have had more severe economic problems, and these would have induced reforms in turn.

The picture is a bit more complicated than this implies. Most governments quickly turned their primary fiscal deficits into primary surpluses. Yet the debt overhang represented a large and destabilizing burden: it drained reserves, accentuated depreciations, and reduced domestic investment; it prompted desperate government actions that provoked additional waves of flight and created enduring private-sector distrust. Most seriously, the combination of borrowing and capital flight implied large public foreign obligations that had no counterpart in taxable or productive domestic resources. This was especially significant where governments ended up taking over private-sector foreign debts after the crisis broke out. Such moves added to the unprecedented transfer of wealth from public to private hands, as governments offered exchange subsidies for debtor firms (including foreign multinationals), or simply assumed the private debts.[57] Accord-

56. Paul A. Volcker and Toyoo Gyohten, *Changing Fortunes: The World's Money and the Threat to American Leadership* (New York: Times Books, 1992), p. 188. Or, as Nicolás Ardito Barletta said, "ultimately it was the debt and liquidity crisis of 1982–85 that permitted the new economic thinking to take hold" (in Williamson, ed. *The Political Economy of Policy Reform*, p. 459). See also Laurence Whitehead, "On 'Reform of the State' and 'Regulation of the Market,'" *World Development* 21, no. 8 (August 1993): 1381.

57. Here I do not include up-front insurance (Brazil's Resolution 432) or government

ing to one estimate, bailouts increased the region's fiscal burden of the foreign debt by 44 billion dollars, or about 25 percent of public foreign debt obligations.[58]

All in all, the larger the amount of flight as a proportion of total indebtedness, the tighter the hobble placed on efforts to "grow out of the debt" through domestic resources, and the more likely that the avoidance of liberal reform would lead to frustration. In the words of one observer of Argentina, "the perennial cap-in-hand trips by government officials to the IMF and foreign banks . . . [are] vital to keep the system liquid in the absence of adequate domestic savings"; another noted how the flight of Argentine savings into dollars made the government vulnerable to hyperinflation.[59] According to one economic model, by spurring inflation and shifting more of the adjustment burden onto the poor, capital flight helped drive the populace to accept

---

loans to overextended private firms before mid-1982, loans ultimately funded by foreign public borrowing. On the multinationals whose debts were assumed by the Argentine government, the hard-line nationalist *Revista Argentina de Política y Teoría* counts debts of U.S. companies worth $1.77 billion, of Dutch companies worth $1.35 billion, and of British companies worth $0.86 billion. See "Información Sobre la Deuda Externa," Year 3, no. 8 (December 1985–February 1986): 45–46. Instances of the assumption of debt include an episode in Argentina, when the central bank could not afford to pay on its generous offers of exchange insurance, and in Chile where the state took over the management of broken banks, their foreign liabilities, and their distressed local assets. On Argentina, see World Bank, *Argentina: Reforms for Price Stability and Growth* (Washington, D.C., 1990), 9 n. 6; p. 53. The bank noted that the scheme was enacted "at the urging of foreign creditors and domestic borrowers."

58. David Felix, "Half-Hidden Dimensions of Latin America's Debt Crisis," Working Paper no. 150, Dept. of Economics, Washington University (St. Louis, March 1990), pp. 6–10; and his "Debt Crisis and Adjustment in Latin America: Have the Hardships Been Necessary?" Working Paper no. 170, Department of Economics, Washington University (St. Louis, September 1992), p. 15 and table 1. A careful analysis by Robin Ann King presents lower estimates for Mexican subsidies under the Mexican exchange risk insurance scheme than does Felix. See "Mexican Private Sector Foreign Financing Trends of the 1980s and Public Sector Policy Response," Paper presented at the LASA Congress, Los Angeles, September 1992, p. 25. On the overall fiscal burden, see UN ECLAC, "Public Finance in Latin America in the 1980s," *Economic Survey of Latin America and the Caribbean 1990*, vol. 1, pp. 185–90.

59. Tim Coone, "Pride in Argentine Market Belies Reality," *Financial Times*, 23 June 1988, p. 33; Canitrot, "Economic Policy Under Conditions of High Uncertainty," p. 245. Coone goes on to note that the government was reluctant to declare a debt moratorium in this situation because it would end up with chaos "without creditors even having to bother to retaliate." The debt-without-resources effect was further aggravated by the fact that in the wake of the debt crisis many Latin American states were driven to rescue the private sector, at substantial cost to their own solvency.

policy changes it would have rejected earlier.[60] These ideas may allow us plausibly to connect capital mobility and liberal reform without referring to the political influence of those with foreign assets.

Our task now is to decide between political-economy and economic explanations for liberal reform. What evidence do we have regarding the relative weight of political influence or economic factors in bringing reforms about?

Annual figures for three macroeconomic variables in each country appear graphically in Figures 4.2A–F and 4.3: the level of investment as a percentage of GDP and GDP growth rates in the first series of graphs, and the consumer price index in the second. These show some indication of the degree of crisis in the economy (although here I omit the less reliable or comparable data on reserve and domestic debt levels).

We can see that the three most decisive reformers of 1988–93—Argentina, Mexico, and (to a lesser extent) Venezuela—were those that found themselves in financial straits that left them with few choices. The main short-term problems were spiraling and volatile domestic debt costs (especially Mexico by 1988), a reduction of exchange reserves to minimal or negative levels (Argentina and Venezuela by late 1988), and open panic in the exchange market (Argentina in mid-1989).[61] Longer-term difficulties included depressed growth and investment (Argentina 1984–89, Mexico 1985–86, Figure 4.2), debt service arrears (Argentina), a buildup of expensive foreign commercial credits (Venezuela), and hyperinflation (Argentina 1989, Mexico nearly so in 1987; Figure 4.3).[62] Governments in these three

60. Raúl Laban and Federico Sturzenegger, "Distributional Conflict, Financial Adaptation, and Delayed Stabilization," University of California at Los Angeles, July 1992, mimeograph, cited in Dani Rodrik, "The Positive Economics of Policy Reform," *American Economic Review* 83, no. 2 (May 1993): 358.

61. On Argentina in late 1989, see *Latin American Weekly Report,* various issues, and the comments of Sebastian Edwards in Williamson, ed., *Latin American Adjustment,* p. 178. Mexican domestic debt amortization as a share of GDP rose from 0.062 in 1987 to 0.104 in 1988 and 0.17 in 1989. See International Monetary Fund, *Government Finance Statistics Yearbook* (Washington, D.C.: IMF, 1994). On Mexico, see also the contribution of Javier Beristain and Ignacio Trigueros in Williamson, ed., *Latin American Adjustment,* pp. 158–64; on Venezuela, see the contribution of Ricardo Hausmann, pp. 226–28, and Miguel Rodríguez in Williamson, ed. *The Political Economy of Policy Reform,* pp. 378–79. In Mexico the internal debt reached the point that in 1988 the private sector received more in interest on the public debt than it paid in taxes. See Héctor Guillén Romo, *El Sexenio del Crecimiento Cero, 1982–1988: Contra los Defensores de las Finanzas Sanas,* Colección Problemas de México (Mexico City: Ediciones Era, 1990), p. 89, citing Michel Husson in *Problemes d'Amerique Latine* 92, no. 2 (1989): 86.

62. The domestic debt problems and hyperinflation characterize Brazil at this writing.

countries had limited their previous adjustments to the debt crisis by issuing domestic debt, calling on oil revenues, building up arrears or other credits, raising some taxes, and printing money. These measures postponed the basic fiscal adjustment by paying for relatively cheap foreign debt service with more expensive forms of credit.[63] When they finally enacted liberal reforms, these presented the only feasible way out: to reduce domestic interest rates by cutting fiscal deficits and retiring debt (privatization, fiscal discipline, tax reform), to attenuate inflation (fiscal discipline, exchange reform, trade liberalization, financial liberalization), to encourage domestic saving and investment (liberalized FDI rules, financial liberalization), and to finance the public investments that had been postponed for almost a decade (privatization, tax reform).

However, this should not obscure the fact that there was a powerful domestic constituency for reform among businessmen who openly linked the return of flight capital to liberal economic policies that were later adopted. In the mid-1980s Mexico's Partido Acción Nacional (PAN) took to calling Mexican private foreign assets a "capital reserve for future investments in Mexico," available to the country as soon as its owners had confidence in the government and received guarantees of security for their property.[64] (Like so much of the PAN platform, this view was later adopted by Salinas.) In November 1985, during a bout of capital flight, COPARMEX president Alfredo Sandoval ascribed it to disordered government finances, subsidies, and the slow pace of the promised privatizations. A week later, the vice president of the National Federation of Chambers of Commerce spoke of the need for "guarantees" for the private sector, and added his own list of additional causes of flight.[65] In 1989, after ascribing flight to statism, economist Luis Pazos recommended reprivatization of state assets; legal and constitutional changes protecting private property, internal commerce, and investment; an end to the state's agricultural land

Already by mid-1989 Brazil's internal debt service far exceeded its external costs. See *Latin American Weekly Report,* 1 June 1989, p. 12.

63. This point is made by William Cline and others in Williamson, ed., *The Political Economy of Policy Reform.*

64. See, for example, E. Juan del Campo, "¿Así Se Hacen los Milagros?" *La Nación,* Órgano del Partido Acción Nacional, Year 45, no. 1729 (15 April 1987): 12.

65. Sandoval, *Excélsior* (Mexico City), 1 November 1985, p. 16-A. Díaz de León, speech to National Association of Financial Executives, reported in *Excélsior,* 9 November 1985, p. 1-A, and *Unomásuno* (Mexico City), same day, p. 15. Díaz de León faulted the government for seizing lots in the capital after the earthquake, for allowing a land invasion on the Sinaloa property of Manuel Clouthier, and for inviting Daniel Ortega to visit Mexico.

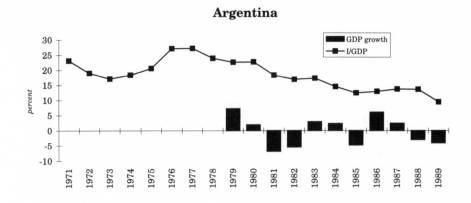

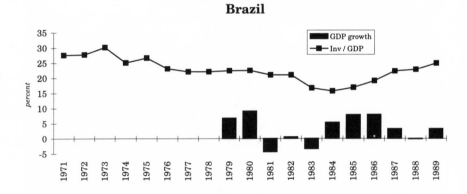

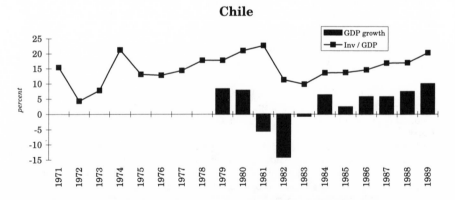

Figs. 4.2A–F.   GDP growth and investment as a percentage of GDP,
1971–1989. Investment is defined as gross fixed capital formation from IMF,
International Financial Statistics (Washington, D.C.: IMF), various issues.

Colombia

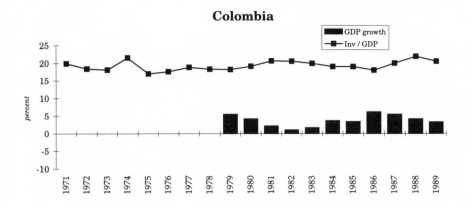

Mexico

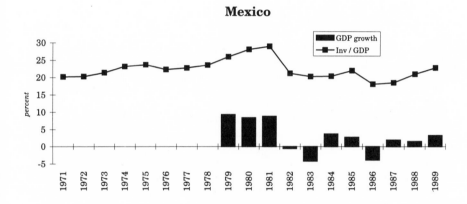

Venezuela

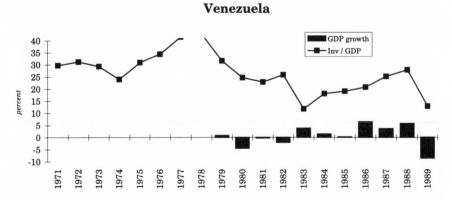

Figs. 4.2A–F.   (continued)

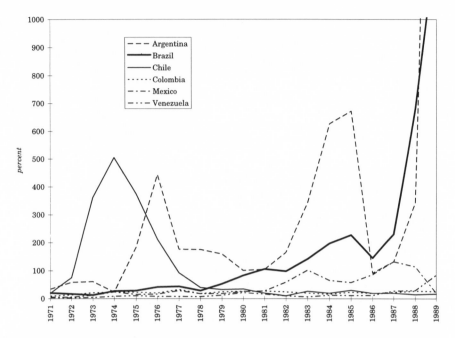

Fig. 4.3.   Annual change in Consumer Price Index, 1971–1989. IMF,
International Financial Statistics, various issues.

monopoly; and a free trade agreement with the United States. The
last would serve to "make permanent the changes above by subjecting
Mexico to market competition."[66] In Argentina the liberal economist
Roberto Alemann argued in 1984 that the Argentine debt would only
be paid if substantial capital could be induced to return. This, he
thought, required guarantees on property, possibilities for profit comparable to those available internationally, and the elimination of
restrictions on capital account.[67] Nearly all of the measures noted here
were later adopted.

   In many cases it is impossible to disentangle the play of interest
from the spur of crisis. The intersection of economic and political
expediency can be seen clearly in privatization. The connection between crisis and reform seems especially clear for such decisions:
privatization provided a way to reduce domestic financial pressure, to
win Brady-linked debt relief (reducing future capital payments), and
to support rapid stabilization. One analysis of Argentina concludes

66. *Christian Science Monitor,* 5 October 1989, p. 19.
67. *Mercado* (Buenos Aires), 18 October 1984, pp. 28–29.

"the speed of the Argentine privatizations and some of their characteristics can be understood only if one accepts that these privatizations were, in large part, a financing instrument for stabilization policies."[68] Even active promoters of privatization attribute its popularity to the crisis (though it would arguably serve their purposes better to point to ideological conversion). One advocate notes that governments in Mexico, Argentina, Brazil, and Venezuela had "little choice" and were driven to privatize by a lack of capital to invest in, or even maintain, deteriorating publicly owned assets.[69] Yet at the same time, political allies of the executive have often figured prominently among the local buyers of state firms. Sales of underpriced assets or poorly regulated natural monopolies have attracted attention as new forms of political patronage.[70]

In the end the crucial argument for the more decisive importance of crisis, rather than political influence, lies in the timing of the major reforms. If we suppose, rather simplistically, that transnational capitalists exerted influence over policy in proportion to the weight of foreign assets in nationally held wealth, this does not adequately explain why the main policy reforms did not take place in most countries until after 1988. In the sense used above, the relative political importance of transnational capitalists would have been mostly established by 1984, if we follow the capital flight estimates used in Chapter 1. So what had changed by 1988? It was the exhaustion of those expensive alternatives to foreign credit—primarily the inflation tax and domestic debt contracted at ever-shorter terms, at increasingly volatile prices, and more and more in instruments linked to foreign currencies. This brought on a second crisis, one that struck hardest (in terms of foreign exchange shortage and investment slump) in countries that had suffered the most capital flight over the previous

68. Alberto Petrecolla, Alberto Porto, and Pablo Gerchunoff, with the assistance of Guillermo Canovas, "Privatization in Argentina," Texas Papers on Latin America, no. 93-07 (Austin: Institute of Latin American Studies, University of Texas, 1993), p. 2.

69. Miles Wortman/Business International Corporation, *Privatization in Latin America: New Competitive Opportunities and Challenges* (New York: Business International, 1990), pp. 42, 86, 111, 128. He offers no evidence that international trends in ideology account for increased public support for privatization in Venezuela and Argentina; nor does he implicate IMF prodding. For a similar view, see Luis R. Luis, "Why Privatize in Latin America?" in *Privatization in Latin America,* supplement to *Latin Finance* (Coral Gables, Fla.: International Financial Publishing Corp., March 1991), pp. 5–6.

70. José Ignacio Rodríguez describes as a "big surprise" of the 1988 Mexican presidential campaign the unabashed public participation and financial support of important businessmen, and goes on to note that many of them benefited handsomely from privatizations. See *Este País* 10 (January 1992): 2, 4. See the discussion in Chapter 5.

decade. With private banks now less cooperative and the IFIs both more sympathetic and more assertively liberal, the threats and promises of local transnational capitalists found a willing audience.

Mobile Capital, Public Opinion, and Liberal Reform

We should not end this discussion without mentioning that reasonable arguments, based on political expectations, predicted capital flight during the 1980s to have a very different result than the one welcomed by Walter Wriston and others. In 1984 Carlos Díaz-Alejandro warned,

> public debt is public in that it is both the responsibility of the state and highly publicized. Private assets belong mostly to households and are surrounded by secrecy; the income they generate is frequently exempt from taxes. This situation reduces the political legitimacy of efforts to service the external debt; indeed, it has generated a crisis of legitimacy for the role of the private sector in Latin American development.[71]

Apart from the bank nationalization in Mexico, there was relatively little evidence of such a crisis for the private sector; quite the contrary. A full understanding of this would require a summary of the political fate of popular movements, labor organizations, and Left parties during the last decade, and is beyond the scope of this book. Let us nevertheless note a few of the more obvious reasons why the supposed loss of legitimacy of the private sector did not arrest the rise of liberal economics. In doing so we can see how economic crisis helped create political support for many of the liberal reforms (although here Venezuela is instructive).

Díaz-Alejandro was partly right: in the wake of the debt crisis there *was* significant public resentment against "speculation," especially when the latter could be linked to currency devaluations. As is well known, the major justification given by López Portillo for nationalizing the banks was their reputed role in encouraging flight, and the action was a popular one at the time. So was the effort to reveal the names of big *sacadólares,* and it remained a major topic until de la Madrid took

71. "Latin American Debt: I Don't Think We Are in Kansas Anymore," *Brookings Papers on Economic Activity* 2 (1984): 378–79.

over in December 1982.[72] Official declamations against speculators reappeared when capital flight revived in Mexico in late 1985 and again in late 1987. In Argentina, politicians' desires to play to popular revulsion against capital flight and devaluation also lay behind the inquiries into "illegal debt." In Venezuela, government bailouts and subsidies of private foreign debts faced related objections, since many in Acción Democrática (AD, President Lusinchi's party), and labor took them to reward holders of foreign assets with an additional publicly funded windfall. We can see this in the long saga of the multiple exchange-rate system and the fight to establish the concept of "net [private] debt" in the country's negotiations with foreign bankers.[73]

Still, governments ultimately accommodated mobile capital rather than confronting it. Although it is very hard to generalize here, the reasons included a combination of economic crisis and popular distrust of politicians. Those who had been willing to claim credit for what borrowed money could buy, or to don the mantle of international approval on the strength of their ability to borrow freely, could not escape the attribution of responsibility when the party ended. People saw politicians get rich during the crisis and they discovered the hypocrisy of some of the same presidents who most reviled the dollar buyers. While private bankers could serve as popular scapegoats for a time, as economic deterioration went on the futility of thundering against the holders of overseas capital became apparent. Indeed, the antistatist worldview also implied a different, sunnier story about

---

72. Making the list preoccupied a group of outgoing officials in the executive, and in October a Chamber of Deputies committee suggested the creation of a U.S.-Mexico interlegislative panel to work on it also. A much reduced version of the list was finally leaked to *Excélsior* in 1986 (see Chapter 5).

73. The amount in question was originally $3.5 to 4 billion of private financial debt. Central bank President Díaz Bruzual opposed granting the favorable rate, arguing that the debt originated in speculation (*Latin American Weekly Report*, 5 August 1983, p. 2). The controversy continued in 1986 when the government tried unilaterally to cut debt service subsidies to the private sector. A similar controversy arose later the same year as favorable exchange rates on private-sector debt came under fire in the cabinet and from labor leaders (*Financial Times*, 2 December 1986, p. 6). It flared for the last time under Carlos Andrés Pérez, as Miguel Rodríguez opposed central bank president Tinoco on the issue and won a drastic reduction of the subsidy (*Latin American Weekly Report*, 28 June 1990, p. 7; 19 July 1990, p. 7; 6 December 1990, p. 7). Given the circumstances of the Venezuelan debacle, it is understandable that considerations of apparent fairness, rather than merely a "refusal to acknowledge the state's role in the debt crisis," could have motivated the doubts about the subsidy. Quote from Robert E. Looney, "Venezuela's Economic Crisis: Origins and Successes in Stabilization," *Asian Political and Economic Studies* 11, no. 3 (Fall 1986): 336.

capital flight: it was a way that prudent private savers had placed the national patrimony beyond the reach of a grasping and corrupt political class.[74]

Without the economic crisis, then, it seems unlikely that liberal reforms would have had much popular support. We have already noted one model that sees capital flight as a key ingredient in wearing down popular opposition to reform.[75] In Venezuela the riots of February 1989 have been blamed on the fact that the crisis had not yet become generalized when Carlos Andrés Pérez introduced his *paquete*.[76] Although inflation was moderate and growth positive, the central bank had almost no available reserves and price controls had led to widespread shortages. Surprised by the parlous state of the government's finances, the new president had little choice but to betray the expectations of his supporters.[77] In several other countries inflation became a popular issue and the state got most of the blame for it. Hyperinflation, as Haggard says, expanded the "group of potential winners" from the introduction of a neoliberal package; moreover, it became regressive and arbitrary as it fell hardest on those who had no choice but to hold local currency.[78] In general, popular disenchantment with the economic role of the state was greater in proportion to the severity of

74. This was noted in the philosophy of the Mexican PAN, above, and is also the premise of Leonardo Auernheimer, "On the Outcome of Inconsistent Policies Under Exchange Rate and Monetary Rules: Or, Allowing the Market to Compensate for Government Mistakes," *Journal of Monetary Economics* 19 (1987).

75. Laban and Sturzenegger, "Distributional Conflict."

76. This is widely asserted; it is noted, for instance, by Felipe Larraín in Williamson, ed., *Latin American Adjustment,* p. 249, and by Williamson and Haggard, "The Political Conditions of Economic Reform," p. 585.

77. In other accounts the awkwardness of the introduction of the measures, and the lack of any effort to attain political consensus, added to their bad public reception (*Latin American Weekly Report,* 9 March 1989, pp. 6–7). Robert Graham, "An Old Hand Gets Off on the Wrong Foot," *Financial Times,* 4 March 1989, p. 2, notes that while CAP might have fortified the existing subsidies, this would have undercut the IMF and U.S. Treasury support, "which he deemed essential for any deal." See also Naim, *Paper Tigers and Minotaurs,* pp. 28, 31–36, 38; Fred Rosen, "The Temperature Rises in the Crucible of Reform," *NACLA Report on the Americas* 27, no. 5 (March/April 1994): 27. Given the above considerations, it is hard to see what alternative CAP would have had.

78. Stephan Haggard in Williamson, ed., *The Political Economy of Policy Reform,* p. 469. See also Guillermo O'Donnell, "On the State, Democratization, and Some Conceptual Problems: A Latin American View with Glances at Some Postcommunist Countries," *World Development* 21, no. 8 (August 1993): 1366. The latter part of the statement is made most often with reference to Brazil, but see for a general statement Hojman, "The Political Economy of Recent Conversion," pp. 213–14. Referring to Argentina, Mario Brodersohn makes a similar observation in "Developing Countries' Delicate Balances," in *Tax Policy in the Twenty-First Century,* ed. Herbert Stein (New

the crisis—inflation, unemployment, and stagnation—in the real economy.

In particular, the popularity of privatization had much to do with the state's fiscal crisis. The crisis brought pressures to raise the costs of public services and to cut the investment in their maintenance.[79] After 1982 Latin American middle and lower middle classes, whose main daily contact with government came as they used urban public services and enjoyed regulated basic prices (bread, flour, cooking oil, fuel), paid more and more for less and less. Thus a politically important stratum increasingly faced unreliable power, inoperable telephones, bad water, surly bureaucrats, and larger bills for everything. By the end of the decade public opinion polls showed increased support for privatization (although Brazil lagged in this regard).[80] And in Mexico efforts to coax capital home through free-market reform be-

York: John Wiley, 1988), pp. 122–23. For figures on Mexico for the period before the debt crisis, see Jesús A. Cervantes González, "Inflación y Distribución del Ingreso y de la Riqueza en México," *El Trimestre Económico* 200 (1983): 2026; Francisco Gil Díaz, "Some Lessons from Mexico's Tax Reform," in *The Theory of Taxation in Developing Countries,* ed. David Newbery and Nicholas Stern (New York: Oxford University Press/World Bank, 1987). During the 1980s the inflation tax suffered a decline in its base for reasons related to the main theme here, as capital fled abroad and governments accommodated this mobility with domestic dollar-linked bonds and high interest rates.

79. Wortman, *Privatization in Latin America,* pp. 87, 128. The opinion is shared by a wide variety of observers of the privatization process. On Argentina, see Naúm Minsburg, "Política Privatizadora en Argentina," *Comercio Exterior* 43, no. 11 (November 1993): 1066–67; on Venezuela, see Luis Alvaray (vice president of MAS) in *Viernes,* November 1991, reprinted in *Foreign Broadcast Information Service Latin America,* 27 December 1991, pp. 41–42. Alvaray also notes the de facto "unofficial privatizations" stemming from the "dangerous crumbling of public functions" in health care, higher education, police, and water (p. 45).

80. In 1991 in Mexico a nationwide survey showed 39 percent to believe that the move would help people like themselves, 29 percent to think it would hurt, and 17 percent to expect no effect. *Este País* 9 (December 1991): 5. N = 1546, 61 locations, September 1991. Surveys in greater Buenos Aires showed a rise in enthusiasm for privatization: in July 1986 (N = 401) 16 percent said no state enterprises should be privatized, 53 percent said only some should, and 27 percent said as many as possible should; in March 1989 (N = 405) 18 percent said none should be privatized, 36 percent said some should, and 38 percent said that all should (Hugo I. Kolsky, *Sistemático,* nos. 2, 11; 1986, 1989). It should be noted that in Mexico, according to the survey above, support for privatization in the capital was higher than anywhere else, so the greater Buenos Aires figures may overstate the national trend. Gary Mead reported that in 1990 "all public opinion polls" showed over 70 percent in favor of sale of nationalized companies (he does not distinguish "some" or "all"). See "Peronism Takes a Back Seat in Privatization Drive," *Financial Times,* 30 March 1990, p. 4. For Brazil one survey in São Paulo and Rio in October 1989 showed about 2:1 support for keeping the telephone and railroads public (DataFolha, N = 1801).

came more popular, too. In early 1990 a survey of four Mexican cities found the planned reprivatization of the banks approved by 63 percent of respondents, with 54 percent expressing a belief that the move would bring capital back to the country.[81]

Before moving on, however, we should remember that Díaz-Alejandro was not merely predicting political events on the basis of his own moral outrage. He anticipated both the justification and the medium-term success of liberal reforms. Discussing the power of mobile private assets to circumscribe state action, he warned that "all of this seems like a new stance for overcoming the uncertainties of underdevelopment and erratic government but one which seems vulnerable to nationalist fury and to the anger of the majority without wealth abroad."[82] He then recalled that Argentina's perceived capitulation to British pressure in the Roca-Runciman accords, although followed by nearly a decade of conservative economic management, later became the focus of revived "memories of wounded national pride" after the June 1943 coup.[83]

Conclusion

I began by noting that the idea of mobile-capital-as-discipline was one of several general explanations for the remarkable advance of liberal economics in Latin America. After describing a moderate correspondence between the degree of past capital flight and the extent of liberal reform, and presenting some evidence to show that worries about expatriate capital probably outweighed concern for foreign investment in general, I suggested two plausible causal mechanisms behind this relationship. The first sees reform in terms of policy responses to economic challenges, and the second traces reform to changes in the constellation of societal interests and in their relation to the state. In

81. Survey by Opinión Profesional, reported in *Excélsior* (Mexico City), 9 May 1990, pp. 1A, 32A, 38A, reproduced in *Foreign Broadcast Information Service Latin America*, 20 June 1990, pp. 17–18. N = 2500, sample matched to census classifications. One might interpret the number on the return of flight capital as referring only to the measure's likely effectiveness, independent of the respondent's approval or disapproval. The strong positives for both questions suggest not. It seems implausible to interpret the modal response as combining favor toward the bank privatization with pessimism about its ability to elicit similar confidence among holders of foreign assets.

82. "Latin American Debt," p. 380.

83. Ibid., p. 389. This argument resembles the one that is implied when Carlos Salinas is compared to Porfirio Díaz.

the name of completeness I have somewhat awkwardly entertained more analytical distinctions than I could justify empirically. Nevertheless, let us examine the main conclusions.

Neoliberal reform has obviously been more widespread in Latin America than has massive capital flight. This could argue for the independent role for ideas in the process of policy reform. Governments in Colombia and Chile liberalized and privatized with moderate debt burdens and having experienced little or no net flight. While there were some problems in Colombia on the eve of its reforms and while the role of the World Bank in promoting freer Colombian trade has been discussed, it would be hard to argue that Gaviria in 1990–92, or Pinochet in 1984–89 and Aylwin thereafter, had little choice. Despite the obvious differences in market size and autonomous capital formation, the divergence of Brazilian policy (at least for a time) appears to confirm that such choices exist.

Yet by 1988 a convergence of circumstances, among them capital flight, had narrowed the range of choice drastically for several countries. I have argued that the most important reason for the correspondence between capital flight and subsequent liberal reform was the contribution of flight to deepening and extending the debt crisis. There have always been strong advocates of liberal policies in Latin America, and while capital flight made them more vocal and numerous, it was economic crisis that made governments listen. The timing of the reforms shows this. By around 1988 the combination of economic stagnation, reluctant banks, declining reserves, and the exploding cost of other modes of financing began to prove decisive. This combination presented itself most forcefully in countries that had experienced a lot of capital flight. Moreover, expatriate capital represented an enormous prize to be awarded to governments that chose the right policies, while the holders of this capital, along with the international financial institutions, assiduously reminded policymakers what these policies were.

To this I would like to add a final observation. In disentangling the role of ideology, I earlier noted the close and reciprocal relationship of ideology and beliefs about what is possible. Insofar as policymakers became convinced that the reign of mobile capital had begun, they may have elected liberal policies in the same way that a person in a canoe avoids paddling against what appears to be a strong current. Yet the current in this case was not a fact of nature but an artifact of human institutions. Two World Bank economists recently advised that developing countries forgo taxation of financial income, wealth, or transactions so as not to "create strong incentives to move funds abroad." They also recommended removing or reducing any "restrictions that inhibit the flexibility of wages and the prices of goods and assets."[84] As this suggests, whether the Wriston argument about the reign of mobile capital is right or not, people in high places think it is, and for prudent developing-country governments this has to matter a great deal.

84. Donald J. Mathieson and Liliana Rojas-Suárez, *Liberalization of the Capital Account: Experiences and Issues,* Occasional Paper 103 (Washington, D.C.: International Monetary Fund, March 1993), p. 2. Of course the worries here involve only the flexibility of wages downward and of asset and goods prices upward.

5

Mobile Capital and Political Institutions

Latin America has witnessed a reawakening of enthusiasm for constitutional and juridical reform. Analysts and politicians talk often about the rule of law.[1] Some emphasize its status as a defining attribute of a democratic polity, while others look to legal reform to secure property rights and encourage investment. Among the latter, some have also suggested that today international market constraints, especially those emerging from the international mobility of capital, are helping

1. It would be fair, in this context, to draw the broad conception of the rule of law from Friedrich Hayek: not "mere legality of government action" but rather that "all laws conform to certain principles," of which a crucial one is "government must never coerce an individual except in the enforcement of a known rule." Friedrich A. Hayek, *The Constitution of Liberty* (Chicago: University of Chicago Press, 1960), p. 205. Since the other principles upon which laws are based are those accepted at large in the culture, it follows that rules do not often change (pp. 61–65, 205–7).

to advance legal and political institutionalization. This seems plausible: politicians need to win the trust of newly footloose international investors, and they may well find that by renouncing discretionary powers and creating new technocratic or juridically impersonal institutions they can calm currency markets, reduce borrowing costs, and attract productive investment.[2] If this is right, and if we accept that the reign of mobile capital has truly begun, then the reign of law cannot be far behind.

This chapter begins approximately where the last one left off, with the proposition that in their conduct of economic policy, governments today must operate under the discipline of internationally mobile money. Here, however, I ask about the effect of this discipline not on policies but on law and on political institutions. I draw from, among other sources, writings in the new institutional economics (although I define "institution" more strictly, confining it to what they call the "formal" type). I will not dwell on the echoes of Whig history in some of the current thinking in this area, although I would say that some present-day liberal institutionalists may be faulted for asserting that in Latin America liberal ideas have never really been applied.[3] In the

2. Dianne Solis, "Zedillo, Sworn in as Mexican President, Vows Reform of Troubled Justice System," *Wall Street Journal*, 2 December 1994; more to the point, the rule of law and checks on presidentialism were prominent themes in a profile of Zedillo sent to foreign investors in April 1994. Partido Revolucionario Institucional, Secretaría de Asuntos Internacionales, Consejo Ejecutivo Nacional, "Ernesto Zedillo: Architect of a Modern Mexico" (Mexico City: PRI, 1994), pp. 20–22. But see *Proceso* 914 (9 May 1994): 11.

3. While recent historiography of the nineteenth-century liberal period has reduced the estimate of its distinctiveness, it does not go as far as the accounts of unremitting "mercantilism" in *The Other Path* (cf. Vargas Llosa in the foreword to the paperback edition, pp. xiv–xv, and de Soto, pp. 235–37) and the picture of Latin America in Douglass North, *Institutions* (in which the region saw a "gradual reversion, country by country, to bureaucratic centralized control" in the nineteenth and twentieth centuries, p. 103). See Hernando de Soto in collaboration with the Instituto Libertad y Democracia, *The Other Path: The Invisible Revolution in the Third World*, trans. June Abbott (New York: Harper and Row, 1989), and Douglass C. North, *Institutions, Institutional Change, and Economic Performance* (New York: Cambridge University Press, 1990). One recent balance describes a "symbiotic relationship between liberalism and its ancient adversaries." See Joseph L. Love and Nils Jacobsen, *Guiding the Invisible Hand: Economic Liberalism and the State in Latin American History* (New York: Praeger, 1989), p. ix. Or consider the following from another summary: "[T]he growth that did occur took place within the institutional framework that Latin American liberals had erected in place of the vestiges of Hispanic colonial corporatism that had been cleared away in 1820–80. . . . the enactment and more or less consistent application of civil legal codes in most Latin American countries in the third quarter of the nineteenth century made the assessment of risk easier and the enforcement of contractual obligations more certain."

spirit of at least some of this writing, in this chapter I stay mainly at the level of models and examples. The latter draw mainly from Argentina and Mexico.

I argue that in Latin America there are good reasons to expect that mobile capital's positive role in promoting institution-building will remain confined to financial markets and to areas relating directly to the security and profitability of foreign investment. The main problem, it seems to me, is that where wealth is very highly concentrated, the very actors who constitute the markets are those who usually also enjoy lots of informal access to politicians and judges. If this is so, there would be little reason for such markets to demand that the state exercise power transparently and impersonally. Let me expand on this briefly before proceeding.

In the discussion of Mexico in Chapter 3 I noted Carlos Arriola's suggestion that the dominance of the PRI machine over representative institutions in Mexico led Mexican businessmen to influence policy through other channels, such as withholding investment or sending capital abroad.[4] As I have already argued, I do not believe this a full description of most Mexican capital flight, since it misses the risk and profit motivations for what are usually individual portfolio decisions. Nevertheless it does capture the political sense of the argument that mobile capital curbs "irresponsible" policies. Expressed in terms of nineteenth-century Western politics, this is mobile capital as a kind of virtual senate, an arm of large property against the dangerous tendencies of the executive or popular chamber, and therefore good for economic development.

Important limits to the creative power of mobile capital relate to this idea. One is that when property is held very narrowly and the state is open to informal influence, it is much more likely that the same people with dominant power in asset markets also wield informal political power (especially in times of financial crisis). If so, they may often prefer this combination to more institutionalized avenues, and to the extent that they do, they will have little reason to use their market power to promote these avenues. When a judge's decisions go to the highest bidder, it may not pay the rich, who would generally win, to change the system. Insofar as existing formal bodies channel popular voices, it makes sense for big investors to seek assurance

David Bushnell and Neill Macaulay, *The Emergence of Latin America in the Nineteenth Century* (New York: Oxford University Press, 1988), pp. 287–88.

4. *Los Empresarios y el Estado, 1970–1982*, 2d ed. (Mexico City: M.A. Porrúa, 1988), p. 47.

outside of them.[5] For these and other reasons I will argue that pressure from asset markets alone will likely make a rather limited contribution to transparency and the rule of law in Latin America. The same logic also leads me to suggest that leaders with weak ties to big business, and foreign (rather than domestic) investment, may be better for institutional development.

The chapter begins by describing recent trends that support a hopeful interpretation of mobile capital as engine of institutional development in Latin America and elsewhere. It then describes a simple model of institutionalization in the presence of mobile capital and goes on to discuss its implications. The second half of the chapter takes up the relation between mobile capital and formal representative institutions. Referring mainly to Mexico, it discusses the limits of the hopeful view with relation to legislatures and judges. It then discusses how the model's implications differ with respect to foreign and domestic capital.

Market Constraints and Institutional Development

Today it is common to encounter the argument that *more* international market constraint solves development problems better than less. Mining the same vein as Wriston, McKenzie and Lee predict that in the world of "quicksilver capital" firms will seek greater liquidity—by downsizing, outsourcing, seeking fixed investments with shorter-term payouts, and establishing subsidiaries in many governmental units, "so that production can be moved in response to changes in government policies" more quickly. As many firms gain the ability to respond to government policies in this way, the policies become more predictable. Under the lash of mobile capital, the authors conclude, governments obey.[6]

Others extend the hopeful scenario to embrace the development of institutions. One position holds that free trade reduces corruption and state arbitrariness because the unpredictable costs of these become less tolerable to local firms newly exposed to trade competition, driving

5. A related argument about democracy and the market appears in José Antonio Ocampo, "Reforma del Estado y Desarrollo Económico y Social en Colombia," *Análisis Político* [Bogotá] 17 (September–December 1992): 31–34.

6. Richard B. McKenzie and Dwight R. Lee, *Quicksilver Capital: How the Rapid Movement of Wealth Has Changed the World* (New York: The Free Press, 1991), p. 243.

businessmen to fight corruption actively.[7] Another account, decrying the institutional uncertainty that leads to capital flight and finding that "democracy does little to limit the discretionary power of the state," places its greatest hope in external forces—competition from Asia and international conditionality that, it is hoped, "will pave the way for institutional reform."[8] Still another suggests that since mobile international capital blurs the line between capital-exporting countries (which support protection of international property rights) and capital-importing ones (which may seek to limit such rights), it will lead to a convergence of interests around rules protecting property.[9] And yet another holds that free markets propagate crises that depreciate institutionally specific, rent-producing assets, weakening the incentive of favored groups to defend the old order and permitting new, better institutions to emerge.[10]

The arguments cited above also agree about what international market constraint is supposed to accomplish. It should cut patronage and discourage rent seeking and graft, but its main benefit derives from its reduction of state discretion and the fortification of guarantees on private property rights. While the main thrust of much recent writing in institutional economics derives from an appreciation of the

7. This is argued by Stephen P. Morris, "Corruption and the Mexican Political System," *Corruption and Reform* 2 (1987): 12. Though not explicit on this point, the argument assumes that the tradeables sector takes the lead.

8. Silvio Borner, Aymo Brunetti, and Beatrice Weder, *Institutional Obstacles to Latin American Growth* (San Francisco: ICS Press, 1993), pp. 23, 29, 39. Although the authors do not explicitly tie capital flight to external constraints, they assume that it is the dire need for investment that prompts states to fulfill institutional requirements beyond stabilization in order to win renewed growth.

9. Deepak Lal, "The Migration of Money from a Libertarian Viewpoint," in *Free Movement: Ethical Issues in the Transnational Migration of People and of Money*, ed. Brian Barry and Robert E. Goodin (University Park: The Pennsylvania State University Press, 1992), p. 106.

10. Ralph Bradburd, "Why Things Have to Get a Lot Worse Before They Can Get Better: Institutions, Investments, Crisis, and Reform," Williams College, 8 February 1994, photocopy. I hesitate to place *The Other Path* in this category. While de Soto does refer to capital flight as showing rejection of arbitrary and redistributive "mercantilism" (p. 199), he does not dwell on this point and the book itself testifies to the belief that international market discipline is not enough without the ability to draw the proper lessons from it. In addition, his dominant rhetorical preoccupation with informals lends the book a more democratic flavor than it would have had if he had written only in defense of property rights as he does in the later chapters. (The gap between democrat and the defender of property is bridged in subtle ways, such as in the usual reference to land invasions on public waste land [p. 178], for example—a proximity to myths of primitive appropriation that can only be achieved in the dune-covered outskirts of Lima.)

ways in which the rule of law promotes markets (a prominent theme being the effective enforcement of contracts[11]), the ideas that concern us here posit the opposite relation—ways in which markets, though perhaps indirectly, promote the rule of law. Here is a vision of institution building in which states extend some powers (for example, law enforcement, intellectual property rights) while renouncing others (discretionary power over economic matters). Internationally mobile capital is to play a leading role in bringing this about, by encouraging governments to erect legal systems that international investors trust and by providing a way for markets, in the form of capital flight, to police government promises.

There is some evidence that such institutionalization has taken place. *Business Latin America* observed in 1993 that regulatory frameworks and capital markets in the region are "coming into line with the developed countries."[12] John Goodman and Louis Pauly note that the obsolescence of capital controls in rich countries has been driven by the ability of private firms to evade them or invest elsewhere, so that governments saw the usefulness of controls decline as their costs rose. They add that in Italy the government passed legislation aimed at limiting its own power to reimpose controls in the event of a currency crisis.[13] Sylvia Maxfield has argued persuasively that the rush to create independent central banks all over the world in the 1989–93 period can be linked to the power of international capital. Governments seek to reduce their costs of financing as their bonds compete against everyone else's, and central bank independence constitutes a relatively cheap way to assure investors and reduce interest costs, or (for some countries) to make borrowing feasible at all: "[T]o signal their commitment to create and maintain a creditor and investor-friendly environment, they are ceding authority to their nation's central banks."[14] (Of course, the incumbent of the newly independent

11. To Douglass North, "the inability of societies to develop effective, low-cost enforcement of contracts is the most important source of both historical stagnation and contemporary underdevelopment in the Third World" (*Institutions*, p. 54).

12. 12 April 1993, p. 1.

13. John B. Goodman and Louis W. Pauly, "The Obsolescence of Capital Controls? Economic Management in an Age of Markets," *World Politics* 46, no. 1 (October 1993): 51, 78.

14. "International Sources of Central Bank Convergence in the 1990s," paper presented at the LASA XVIII International Congress, 10–12 March 1994, Atlanta, p. 9. It is hard to impute mobile capital as a cause when international imitation is obviously taking place. But by the same token international competition for capital also implies that advantageous innovations will be rapidly copied for defensive reasons. It is also true, as Laurence Whitehead observes, that the establishment of independent central

post must have a reputation for orthodoxy or the juridical independence will be wasted.[15]) Here is a clear restriction of the sphere of
legislative power in favor of a "representative" of the moneyed interest
at an independent central bank.

In a few Latin American cases the renunciation of discretionary
power has been quite remarkable. In the early 1990s governments in
Mexico and Argentina deliberately limited their own sovereignty over
economic policy in order to win the confidence of potential investors.
Following the Bolivian example, in April 1991 the Argentine central
bank decreed that it could not issue any pesos not backed up by dollars
it held as reserves. That is, surmising that Argentine and foreign
asset holders did not trust the authorities to print money prudently,
the Menem government publicly abandoned this power.[16] In Mexico
President Salinas made it a prominent public justification for the
North American Free Trade Agreement (NAFTA) that the treaty
limited his ability, and that of future Mexican presidents, to reverse
free-market economic reforms.[17] Other countries have followed this
logic in pursuing regional trade agreements and in seeking admission
to a Western Hemisphere trading bloc.[18] In each case the action was

---

banks does not necessarily have antipopular implications. If monetized deficits fund
subsidies for the rich while the poor suffer inflation, his objection is clearly valid. The
purpose of independence clearly does involve circumscribing the sphere of "political"
decision making, however. Ironically, as more politicians discover the electoral benefits
of conquering inflation, central bank independence may become less necessary in Latin
America—more an investor insurance policy than an institutional barrier against
popular passions. See Whitehead, "On 'Reform of the State' and 'Regulation of the
Market,' " *World Development* 21, no. 8 (August 1993): 1387.

15. This could be seen in the controversy after the resignation of Ruth de Krivoy as
president of the Banco Central de Venezuela in April 1994.

16. For a discussion of the Cavallo Plan as a way of fencing in a distrusted political
class in order to win investor confidence, see Eduardo R. Conesa, *La Crisis del 93: Una
Agenda de los Riesgos que Enfrentará la Economía Argentina* (Buenos Aires: Planeta,
1992), pp. 105–12. In February 1995 some argued for a similar currency board in
Mexico: "[U]nless a monetary straightjacket is imposed, investors will not return there
in the same numbers." Nathaniel Nash, "A Strong Leash for Currencies on a Rampage,"
New York Times, 5 February 1995, p. F3; see also Alberto F. Ades, "Currency Boards
and Implications for Argentina," Goldman Sachs Economic Research, Latin America
(New York: February 1995).

17. Such actions also intended to influence exchange-rate expectations: in Argentina,
by seeming to promise that deflation would precede devaluation if reserves were to fall
significantly in the future; in Mexico, by raising the (likely) possibility that the
equilibrium exchange rate for a Mexico fully integrated into North American trade
would be an appreciated one. But their more important function lay in what they did
for the broader policy commitment.

18. On the former, Miguel Urrutia argues that Colombian officials saw free trade

intended to make credible the government's commitment to policies that favored internationally mobile capital.

Consider the logic of the Argentine Convertibility Plan, a typical currency-board scheme. In the face of international investors who suspected, much as I suggested in the last chapter, that his marriage to neoliberalism was mainly one of convenience, Carlos Saúl Menem legally limited the central bank's power to print money and to act as lender of last resort.[19] In doing so, Menem acknowledged that while investors may have trusted the overall mobility of capital to keep him generally in line, before any of them dared to invest (especially in illiquid assets) he would look for a credible promise to keep the Congress, or even the central bank itself, out of monetary policy. There is surely more to the Argentine investment problem than this, but this renunciation is one of its most interesting aspects.

However, the idea that mobile international money promotes institutional development contains a paradox. Surely it makes sense to say that stable rules and institutional safeguards for property will attract capital. This is what governments often hear from managers of multinational firms and the IMF, not to mention Kissinger and Associates or *The Economist*.[20] But the same capital mobility that makes government promises credible, since it punishes broken ones, also might make investors less likely to solicit such promises, since the possibility of flight is a form of insurance. If capital mobility suffices to "take away free lunches," who needs institutions that do so?[21]

---

with Venezuela as strengthening the presumption that this policy would "make it necessary to maintain a more general trade opening." See John Williamson, ed., *The Political Economy of Policy Reform* (Washington, D.C.: Institute for International Economics, 1994), p. 286. See the discussion in Peter Hakim, "Western Hemisphere Free Trade: Why Should Latin America Be Interested?" *Annals of the American Academy of Political and Social Sciences* 526 (March 1993): 129–30. Hakim dismisses doubts about lost sovereignty as ideological, noting that North American countries lose autonomy in the NAFTA also, a mutual renunciation common to all treaties. He expects that a treaty-bound stability of liberal rules should then encourage investment flows (pp. 130–31).

19. For a good discussion of the system under stress, see Matt Moffett and Jonathan Friedland, "Taking a Huge Risk, Argentina Intentionally Deflates Its Economy," *Wall Street Journal,* 21 March 1995, p. A1.

20. For a sense of MNC managers' frustration with changeable rules and weak protections for intellectual property, see the comments of Robert Walter of Monsanto and William Wells of McDonald's in *Quarterly Review of Economics and Business* 31, no. 3 (Autumn 1991): 59, 62, 136–37; see also Nancy Stoetzer, "Patently Obvious: Venezuela's Outdated Intellectual Property Laws Are Scaring Away Potential Investors While Giving the Pirates a Free Hand," *Business Venezuela,* May/June 1991, p. 27.

21. I assume here that we refer to institutions apart from those that allow or facilitate

The short answer is: anyone who contemplates long-term or fixed investment, and therefore any government trying to encourage such investment. In this domain the crucial distinction becomes one between the liquidity of a particular asset and the average liquidity of the market. The power to keep the government honest is held by the latter. To the extent that his investment is illiquid, the investor who trusts in the lash of mobile capital to protect it is trusting in the aggregated power of the holders of more liquid assets, who can punish the government by selling them off. Because he relies on others, the investor in illiquid assets may not feel as secure as someone who could liquidate his own asset immediately at low cost, so he may welcome some other form of security. Moreover, over the life of his investment the government might build up a cushion of reserves that insulates it from the immediate effects of any but the most cataclysmic flight of capital—from the investor's point of view, allowing it to fall into populist temptation. The holder of long-term illiquid assets thus looks for some other guarantees, and, needing long-term illiquid investment, the government has a strong interest in offering them. They take the form of institutionalized promises, commitments represented in treaties and constitutions by which the government voluntarily raises the cost of breaking a promise, thereby granting the promise some value independent of the expected effectiveness of other policing mechanisms.

This argument is represented more formally as a simplified matrix in Figure 5.1. As capital mobility rises, the punishment that can be taken against the government (here, "p") also increases, and hence the payoff to bad government behavior (arbitrarily valued here at "5-p," lower left) falls below what the government would gain by renouncing a threat or new tax (4, upper left). Since in the right column both cells are the same, the high ("p" greater than one) punishment capability leads one to expect the government to choose the upper row, the dominant strategy. An institution that codifies this choice would be credible. Then, if the expected profits from illiquid investments offer a suitable premium ("r" is highly positive), they are made.

Before moving on we should note that whether or not to call this a "bargain" is an important problem. It is the government's decision to respond to a situation of suboptimal investment with legal or institutional changes. The private sector's power mainly lies in pro-

---

the mobility of capital. As noted below, the key point here is that capital controls are declining in efficacy and rising in cost, so the likelihood that they will be imposed out of prudence falls.

Asset Holder

		Invest Within	Invest Abroad
Government	No Threat or Tax	4, (5+r)	0, 5
	Threat or Tax	(5–p), (5+r–t)	0, 5

Fig. 5.1.   Simplified payoff matrix for governments and global asset holders.

ducing the situation. It need consider itself under no obligation to invest, even if the government reforms thoroughly and credibly.

The most important general result of this analysis is that the sustainability of a liberal reform program depends on some combination of policing and commitment. It has been widely observed that, to the extent that reforms come about only as a response to crisis, the abating of crisis puts their survival in danger.[22] If liberal reforms are to succeed beyond mere price stabilization and short-term fiscal balance, they have to encourage capitalists to invest in long-term bonds and fixed, productive assets.[23] Leaders need to convince investors that structural problems have been solved and liberal rules are solidly in place, yet they must also persuade labor and others that, despite the passing of crisis, the time is not yet ripe for redistributive measures.[24] Hence, in order to reassure potential investors that they

22. See Richard Webb's comments on Peru in Williamson, ed. *The Political Economy of Policy Reform,* pp. 373–74.

23. According to the president of the Argentine Business Council, in mid-1993 Domingo Cavallo created an investment foundation whose necessity derived from the fact that "until now most investments have been made in privatizations." *Buenos Aires Herald,* 26 June 1993, reprinted in *Foreign Broadcast Information Service Latin America,* 29 June 1993, p. 26. Between year-end 1990 and 1993 privatizations yielded about $9 billion in cash to the government (the current account deficit in the same period totaled about $20 billion). On cash and debt: *Somos* (Buenos Aires), 20 December 1993, pp. 68–70. On the current account: International Monetary Fund, *International Financial Statistics,* May 1995. On instability as a barrier to investment: *Business Latin America* (New York), 22 March 1993, pp. 6–7.

24. Carlos Acuña and William C. Smith, "The Political Economy of Structural Adjustment: The Logic of Support and Opposition to Neoliberal Reform," in *Latin American Political Economy in the Age of Neoliberal Reform: Theoretical and Comparative Perspectives for the 1990s,* ed. William C. Smith, Carlos Acuña, and Eduardo A. Gamarra (New Brunswick, N.J.: Transaction Publishers/University of Miami North-South Center, 1994), pp. 37–38. As my colleague Ralph Bradburd has noted, the felt need for redistribution after the first stage of liberal reform depends on the proposition that the alternative to reform would have meant less sacrifice for wage earners—a

will not yield to such pressures, the argument goes, leaders bind their hands by codifying many of the new rules in laws and constitutions.

Implications

I would like to note three implications of this argument for institutionalization: the abating of crisis will reduce the incentive to build institutions; the existence or creation of some institutions at least temporarily reduces the incentive to create more; and the greatest amount of institutional development may take place when leaders with the *weakest* credibility are at the helm.

The first two are obvious. A leader who achieves stabilization and enjoys a positive capital account may find that these suffice for electoral success, at least within his time horizon, especially if the inflation he "conquered" was very bad. In this situation further renunciation of autonomy, in the pursuit of longer-term benefits, may be made less likely by near-term success. In addition, innovations such as independent central banks and monetary rules may promote inward capital flows enough to end the immediate incentive for change. (Of course, it is possible for international market competition to ratchet up the institutional requirements to attract a given size of capital flow.)

The third implication is less obvious. Some economists have posited that reformers with poor credibility, if they wish to prove their seriousness and have their policies succeed, will have to push harder and longer, and perhaps pay an obvious political price.[25] And, in fact, much of the vigor of the money-courtship in the Argentine and Mexican reforms could be attributed to the past records of the parties, politicians, and ministers in question. The PRI, given its presidentialism and past record, had to go to great lengths to prove its capitalist *bona fides*. So did Carlos Menem, a Peronist with a well-known record of

---

proposition impossible to prove and perhaps highly doubtful if reform begins in a hyperinflation. Here politics is about persuading people of the relevant counterfactual.

25. See the remarks of de Pablo in John Williamson, ed., *Latin American Adjustment: How Much Has Happened?* (Washington, D.C.: Institute for International Economics, 1990), pp. 113–14; Dani Rodrik, "Promises, Promises: Credible Policy Reform via Signalling," *Economic Journal* 99, no. 397 (September 1989): 756–72. The issue was common in the 1989–91 period as governments initiated reform drives; cf. Iwo Dawney's discussion of the symbolism of Sarney's closing of ministries in *Financial Times* (London), 17 January 1989, p. 5.

extravagant public-sector patronage as governor of La Rioja.[26] When he replaced former Bunge y Born vice president Néstor Rapanelli as economy minister with longtime *menemista* Antonio Erman González, a politician instead of an important businessman, his policy turned in an even more liberal direction. His next appointment in that office, Domingo Cavallo, had to tie his own hands with the Convertibility Plan—understandably, in view of the 1982 events colloquially known as the *cavallazo* (described in Chapter 3). Of the Menem privatization program it was observed that "the unprecedented speed of the process of liquidating assets can also be explained by the government's need to 'buy' a reputation."[27]

Within limits, institutional change may follow this same logic. Would "the markets" have been more insistent in demanding an end to Mexican presidentialism if they had expected the sash to be donned in 1994 by a Zedillo or by a Cárdenas? Would Brazilian asset holders have discovered new reasons to restrict presidential decree power if they had expected Lula to be their next president? Under conditions of international financial constraint, leaders whose political affiliations or personal reputations *cannot* soothe the markets have the most to gain by making institutionalized commitments.[28] This would also

26. Especially after his government decreed the forced refunding of its BONEX instruments (domestic debt denominated in foreign currency) in December 1989 and January 1990, effectively confiscating savings. The central bank was out of reserves to pay off the maturing bonds in foreign exchange. These incidents, and their effect on credibility, are described by John Welch and Robert Walter in comments in *Quarterly Review of Economics and Business* 31, no. 3 (Autumn 1991): 61–62. After the freeze ordered by Collor de Melo in Brazil, the *Wall Street Journal* carried an Associated Press story referring to it, the Mexican 1982 freeze, and the one on Argentine 7-day CDs in January 1990. The article concluded, "that is why Latin Americans have more than an estimated [*sic*] $200 billion" abroad (16 April 1990, p. 18C). While true in part about Mexico, this generalization obviously exaggerates the link between legal insecurity and capital flight, though it typifies the emphasis many business representatives often place on government arbitrariness as the root of the problem.

27. The authors continue, "he did not win [business] confidence immediately, mainly because of the complete turnabout that the new policies represented in comparison with Menem's discourses in the months before assuming the presidency." See Alberto Petrecolla, Alberto Porto, and Pablo Gerchunoff, with the assistance of Guillermo Canovas, "Privatization in Argentina," Texas Papers on Latin America, no. 93-07 (Austin: Institute of Latin American Studies, University of Texas, 1993), p. 9. Roberto Bouzas points out the actions that left the Menem government little other choice if it wanted to finance its deficit—two hyperinflations and the forced consolidation of BONEX (foreign-exchange indexed 7-day instruments). See "¿Más Allá de la Estabilización y la Reforma? Un Ensayo Sobre la Economía Argentina a Comienzos de los 90," *Desarrollo Económico* 33, no. 129 (April–June 1993): 17.

28. In the postwar period it was often the case that legal restrictions of presidential

apply to leaders whose reputations have suffered, say, in the wake of a sudden devaluation of the currency. (By this logic, sitting leaders will also face a choice between creating institutions and working on their reputations, a possibility I will discuss below.)

Mobile Capital and Representation

Let us now address the case of a clearly political institution. Does increased capital mobility tend to fortify formal bodies of representation? One's first impression ought to be negative: after all, it is mainly from such bodies that many central banks have recently become independent. Beyond this, Hirschman's analysis of exit and voice predicts that those who seek voice have high costs of exit. If capital's international exit costs have fallen, there would be less reason for its owners to solicit representation.[29] In a world in which capital moves more easily and quickly, and firms undertake strategies to take advantage of this, it would seem that investor pressure for channels of voice would decline. So the above suggestion might be dismissed as another awkward attempt to conjure democracy out of free markets.

Yet this may not be the whole story. Increased capital mobility may prompt states to grant formal representation in exchange for something they want. According to Bates and Lien,

> revenue-seeking governments may well find it to their advantage to strike bargains with citizens whose assets they seek to tax. To induce a greater willingness to pay taxes, they may defer to the citizens' policy preferences. Such bargains may become more beneficial from the citizens' point of view the more mobile the assets the citizens hold.[30]

---

power were proposed or enacted after a leftist came to power. However, the changes were not meant to be permanent, only to restrict a Goulart or an Allende.

29. Albert O. Hirschman, *Exit, Voice, and Loyalty: Responses to Decline in Firms, Organizations, and States* (Cambridge, Mass.: Harvard University Press, 1970), chaps. 3 and 7. Jeffry Frieden also links the possession of specific fixed assets to the tendency to exert more pressure on government policy, since the owners of such assets cannot liquidate to avoid losses from unfavorable policy changes. See his *Debt, Development, and Democracy: Modern Political Economy and Latin America, 1965–1985* (Princeton: Princeton University Press, 1991), pp. 19–22, 33.

30. Robert H. Bates and Da-Hsiang Donald Lien, "A Note on Taxation, Development, and Representative Government," *Politics and Society* 14, no. 1 (1985): 53.

In medieval Europe the bargain involved representation in exchange for taxation, or at least taxation of movables: "[I]n both England and France it was the taxation of 'moveable' property that promoted the conferral of political representation by revenue-seeking monarchs."[31] In this spirit the ideal institutional guarantee for property would be a new upper house that mirrored the distribution of wealth.[32]

And, in fact, there is some evidence that in Latin America, holders of internationally mobile capital, and governments that want to please them, draw a connection between formal representation and the security of property. In 1991, when Carlos Andrés Pérez rescinded an old decree suspending economic guarantees and thereby returned power over these matters to the Venezuelan Congress, he publicly hoped that the move would "propitiate the confidence of national and foreign investors."[33] In the mid-1980s Mexican business leaders commonly linked the recovery of investment and the return of capital to the ability of business representation to restrain the executive: as the president of COPARMEX put it, a "maturation, participation, and modernization" in politics.[34]

Indeed, Mexico appears to support the argument quite well. To many, events of the 1970s and 1980s showed a clear connection between unaccountable presidentialism and assaults on property. Informal arrangements, it turned out, could be broken or allowed to lapse, as business groups found out when they complained that they had not been consulted about Luis Echeverría's tax reform bill in 1971. The president responded by reminding them that he was under no constitutional obligation to do so—he had only to bring it to the PRI-dominated legislature. (A leading member of COPARMEX, the Monterrey-dominated business organization, later remarked bitterly, "obviously the established pattern of exchange between the government and the private sector which had functioned for over three decades had been cast aside."[35]) In 1982 the bank nationalization and

31. Ibid., p. 55.
32. To take the fancy a bit further, electors might qualify by paying a wealth tax, with its threshold frozen in real terms or programed to decline slowly over time, so that as economic growth proceeded, more would become eligible. The body would have less of a rural bias than some existing senates, would enhance confidence about the stability of rules and about long-term profitability, and would justify a wealth tax while providing an incentive for the rich to pay it.
33. Quoted in *Latin American Weekly Report,* 25 July 1991, p. 5.
34. Alfredo Sandoval, quoted in *Excélsior* (Mexico City), 13 February 1985, from Rogelio Hernández R., "La Política y los Empresarios Después de la Nacionalización Bancaria," *Foro Internacional* 27, no. 2 (1986): 262.
35. David R. Dávila Villers, "Les Conflits entre L'état et le Patronat au Mexique:

the freezing of Mexdollar accounts greatly amplified the call for new guarantees.[36] For many these events constituted the final demonstration of the incorrigible arbitrariness of the PRI party-state, and they put their capital abroad out of fear and distrust. Observers of the period concluded that "the problem of effective representation is at the center of Mexican business' current political renaissance," which "represents a break with the old government-business pact in which businesses exercised their political will subtly, behind closed doors."[37]

Looking at Mexico, then, one would conclude that executive discretion, one-party machines, and rubber-stamp congresses had a lot to do with the insecurity of property, and that mobile capital could help. If the need to attract foreign and expatriate capital could open such a system, international capital mobility might advance the democratic cause even if capital were seeking only the highest expected returns.[38]

Limits and Implications

Unlike the case of asset-market institutions noted above, here we find little support for a hopeful model that connects international asset mobility to stronger formal representation. It has been widely observed that representative institutions have generally become weaker, relative to presidents, during Latin America's recent period of radical economic reform.[39] The most obvious sign of the new presidentialism

1970–1976," Ph.D. thesis, Université de Paris, 1984, p. 22; Luis Bravo Mena, "COPAR-MEX and Mexican Politics," in *Government and Private Sector in Contemporary Mexico,* ed. Sylvia Maxfield and Ricardo Anzaldúa, Center for U.S.-Mexico Studies, University of California at San Diego, Monograph Series 20 (La Jolla: UCSD, 1987), p. 97.

36. Middle-class savers were especially bitter about the latter, since they had believed official assurances, felt sympathy with the stated goals of López Portillo, and held their dollar assets in Mexico rather than abroad. They heard the president growl about the big *sacadólares,* but they were the ones who got bit. Conversations with a Mexico City shopkeeper, a friend's uncle, July 1988. See also the comments of Manuel Clouthier (who later made it into a campaign issue) in *Expansión,* 1 September 1982, p. 54.

37. Matilde Luna, Ricardo Tirado, and Francisco Valdés, "Businessmen and Politics in Mexico, 1982–1986," in *Government and Private Sector in Contemporary Mexico,* ed. Sylvia Maxfield and Ricardo Anzaldúa, Center for U.S.-Mexico Studies, University of California at San Diego, Monograph Series 20 (La Jolla: UCSD, 1987), pp. 39–40.

38. I ignore for the moment the point that in most of the countries in question bona fide representative institutions already exist. By the argument above, mobile capital would not have been necessary as a protection of private property if these institutions had been adequately fulfilling that role.

39. Regarding the decision-making style common among reforming governments,

has been the remarkable surge in decrees or decreelike instruments (such as the *medida provisória* in Brazil). Peru and Argentina are obvious examples.[40] In Mexico presidential power grew under Salinas, although the Congress has been a party to reform and the process has been accompanied by an official discourse about modernization and liberty.[41] In general, old parties have been weakened, new ones have not fully replaced them, presidents dominate the media, and a kind of "delegative democracy" has taken hold.[42]

At the same time, evidence of the privilege accorded informal access abounds. Patronage and graft have often been conspicuous in the course of liberal reform, especially in connection with privatizations. With reference to Mexico, for instance, we have already noted the links between Salinas and prominent businessmen who later profited from sales of state assets at low prices. Monopolies have been built, while some natural monopolies have gone private under unsteady regulatory regimes. In Argentina the corruption under Menem has

---

Adam Przeworski has commented, "the effect of this style is to undermine representative institutions. When candidates hide their economic programs during election campaigns or when governments adopt policies diametrically opposed to their electoral promises, they systematically educate the population that elections have no real role in shaping policies. When governments announce vital policies by decree or ram them through legislatures without debate, they teach parties, unions, and other representative organizations that they have no role to play in policy making." *Democracy and the Market: Political and Economic Reforms in Eastern Europe and Latin America* (New York: Cambridge University Press, 1991), p. 186.

40. On Argentina, see, for example, Jeremy Adelman, "Post-Populist Argentina," *New Left Review* 203 (January–February 1994), especially pp. 82–86; *Clarín*, Edición Internacional, 12–19 June 1993, Suplemento Económico, p. 6. In Venezuela, Miguel Rodríguez recalls, only the "cabinet agenda" was carried through. Everything that required the agreement of Congress, where the president's own party led the opposition to reform, failed. See Williamson, ed., *The Political Economy of Policy Reform*, p. 380. In Colombia, Urrutia notes, much of the reform package, including trade liberalization, required no consultation with Congress; where it was required, on foreign exchange and tax reform, the Gaviria government showed considerable skill and succeeded. Williamson, ed., *The Political Economy of Policy Reform*, pp. 286–311.

41. See, for example, Lorenzo Meyer, "El Presidencialismo, del Populismo al Neoliberalismo," *Revista Mexicana de Sociología* 55, no. 2 (April–June 1993), esp. pp. 71–79; Víctor M. Bernal Sahagún, "Estado y Capital Transnacional," in *El Nuevo Estado Mexicano*, ed. Jorge Alonso, Alberto Aziz Nassif, and Jaime Tamayo, vol. 1, *Estado y Economía* (Mexico City: Nueva Imagen/Universidad de Guadalajara/CIESAS), p. 187 (on the installation of new foreign investment rules).

42. This is Guillermo O'Donnell's term; see his "On the State, Democratization, and Some Conceptual Problems: A Latin American View with Glances at Some Postcommunist Countries," *World Development* 21, no. 8 (August 1993): 1360–65.

been remarkable. In general, while fiscal crises reduced one kind of resource for patronage, they also justified emergency discretionary powers that impeded judicial or legislative checks and allowed politicians to tap other sources of gains—notably the kickbacks and graft from asset sales.[43]

So what is wrong with the model? Obviously, Latin America presents a historical panorama quite different from the prototypical picture of state formation derived from Western Europe. In twentieth-century Latin America one cannot equate parliaments with the representation of property. Advocates of free-market reform are more likely to complain of too much popular representation rather than too little.[44] After late 1987 in Mexico, when a leftist movement temporarily displaced the rightist PAN as the ostensibly most powerful challenge to PRI hegemony, business organizations rapidly changed (or muffled) their tune about democracy. The goal from capital's point of view is not just greater predictability but a more predictable profitability; it may favor deinstitutionalization of unions, left parties, and the leftist press.[45]

However, there is more to the failure of the hopeful scenario than a bad historical analogy. Any investor faces the obvious problem that liberal reforms made by decree can be unmade the same way. A

43. Luigi Manzetti, "Economic Reform and Corruption in LDCs," North-South Center, University of Miami, 1993, photocopy, pp. 5–10.

44. See, for example, the Asia survey of *The Economist*, 30 October 1993, survey pp. 20–22. The overall point was well formulated for me by an anonymous reviewer of a National Science Foundation grant proposal. Bates and Lien themselves observe that international capital can have "disproportionate influence." See "A Note on Taxation, Development, and Representative Government," p. 63. Another difference between the model and Latin America is obvious: the prosecution of wars played a historically much smaller role in Latin American state formation than it did in Western Europe, and war is obviously not driving institutional development today. Yet if we adhere to the model, the historical disparity may have a relevant implication for relations between states and economically dominant classes. In the medieval Europe of Bates and Lien the asset holder usually had a clear stake—the enjoyment of his property and his security—in the sovereign's victory. Cooperation had a higher payoff than mutual defection. However, in the absence of war, or especially if the potential threat to the assets comes from the same state that seeks to tax, there would be a greater incentive for the citizen to "defect," forgoing formal representation while avoiding tax.

45. Sergio Zermeño has argued that neoliberal reform in Mexico has seen a disorganizing of civil society and a retreat into often anomic private life by "deliberate action" on the part of the state to dismantle "inconvenient collective identities." See "La Derrota de la Sociedad: Modernización y Modernidad en el México de Norteamérica," *Revista Mexicana de Sociología* 2 (1993): 274.

revival of long-term investment requires solid guarantees, and institutionalized access would seem to be one of them.[46] Along with the
elementary difference in the constitution of formal representation,
there are three other reasons why asset market pressures may not
promote formal representation in contemporary Latin America: presi-
dencies are open to, and actively solicit, informal access by big business; capital is concentrated enough so that these informal ties can
usually suffice to reassure "the market"; and, I will speculate, the
formalization of the relationship between state and asset holders
might lead the latter to be placed under inconvenient obligations.
Under these conditions market pressure from *foreign* investors may be
more likely than that of domestic ones to advance transparency and
the rule of law. Let me elaborate.

The executive's cultivation of close informal contacts among the
upper reaches of the private sector is nothing new in Latin America.
But it was an especially prominent feature of the 1980s, because of the
conditions for reestablishment of elected regimes and because of the
economic crisis. As Whitehead has observed, the pacts that enabled a
transition from authoritarianism had to provide big business representatives with "easy access to, and confidence in the economic policy
makers."[47] In Mexico under Salinas the largest business interests
enjoyed frequent and regular informal (and corporative) access to the
president; enhanced formal democracy suited them less well.[48] And

46. Borner et al., *Institutional Obstacles to Latin American Growth*, pp. 38–39,
consider that the weak growth of investment and output in Bolivia since 1986 has
resulted from institutional insecurity. *Clarín*, Edición Internacional, 12–19 June 1993,
Suplemento Económico, reports a survey showing that 77 percent of executives felt
the country lacking in juridical security, with the proliferation of decrees a major
complaint (pp. 2–3).

47. Whitehead, "On 'Reform of the State,'" p. 1385. In this light, and to the extent
that mobile capital forces all states to reform economically, it should not surprise us to
find elected governments just as capable as dictatorships at undertaking adjustment
programs and attracting capital investment. On the former question, see Stephan
Haggard and Robert R. Kaufman, "Economic Adjustment in New Democracies," in
Fragile Coalitions: The Politics of Economic Adjustment, ed. Joan Nelson (New Brunswick, N.J.: Transaction/ODC, 1989), pp. 57–77; on the latter question, see Manuel
Pastor, Jr., and Eric Hilt, "Private Investment and Democracy in Latin America,"
World Development 21, no. 4 (April 1993): 489–507. By presenting the "democracy
without choices" argument I do not want to assume away the significant economic
autonomy that governments do have. I would suggest, however, that a demonstration
that elected governments are just as good as dictatorships at following IMF recipes does
not strike a blow for the autonomy argument—especially if the underlying presumption
is that all governments will have to pursue liberal reform sooner or later.

48. Ricardo Tirado and Matilde Luna, "El Estado y los Empresarios: De la Actuación
al Repliegue Político Relativo," in *El Nuevo Estado Mexicano*, ed. Jorge Alonso, Alberto

the most egregious example of this practice could be seen in Argentina in 1989. The appointment of two successive vice presidents of Bunge y Born as economy minister was not only the expression of an alliance between Menem and Jorge Born; it was also a gesture of good faith to the leading sector of Argentine business.[49]

Those with informal access or cabinet-level "representation" have a less compelling interest in stable rules or powerful legislatures. In her revealing studies of Chihuahua, Yemile Mizrahi describes the problem in greater detail, showing the division between small and large business on questions of representation and transparency. Small businessmen came away from 1982 intent on curbing the discretionary power of the presidency and making the government accountable; they mobilized in large numbers into active political life in order to "bind the government to the rule of law."[50] They did so for pragmatic reasons: as owners of small firms, they had "few economic or personalistic ties to the government" and hence sought greater formal representation outside the channels of the PRI. Meanwhile, however, big entrepreneurs enjoyed "privileged access" and could also "press the government by threatening to withhold investment and ship their capital out

---

Aziz Nassif, and Jaime Tamayo, vol. 3, *Estado, Actores, y Movimientos Sociales* (Mexico City: Nueva Imagen/Universidad de Guadalajara/CIESAS), pp. 22–23, 27–28. On the regular meetings of the Mexican Businessmen's Council with the president and cabinet members, see Roderic A. Camp, *Entrepreneurs and Politics in Twentieth-Century Mexico* (New York: Oxford University Press, 1989), pp. 167–70. Though referring only to business organizations, Camp's remark is appropriate here: "[S]atisfactory institutionalization will never take place until businessmen see themselves fairly represented in their organizations and rely on them rather than individual channels to present their demands" (p. 159).

49. While Born was surely different from the typical Argentine representative of big business, Morales Solá does mention an exchange between Menem and Born after the death of Miguel Roig, the first economy minister and a retired vice president of the firm. Menem is supposed to have said, "I need an explicit commitment with you. . . . the alliance should be evident with the designation of the new minister. Look what business has done with prices in a week—and with Roig at the Ministry. What would happen if the new minister is someone who binds nobody [*no compromete a nadie*]?" See Joaquín Morales Solá, *Asalto a la Ilusión: Historia Secreta del Poder en la Argentina desde 1983* (Buenos Aires: Planeta, 1990), p. 279; on Born, see pp. 272–73. Morales (p. 276) also casts doubt on the idea that Born advanced the government several billion dollars against future export receipts (cf. *Latin American Weekly Report,* 10 August 1989, pp. 2–3).

50. "Rebels Without a Cause? The Politics of Entrepreneurs in Chihuahua," *Journal of Latin American Studies* 26, no. 1 (February 1994): 150. On the business mobilization into politics, see Sylvia Maxfield, "Introduction," pp. 3–8, and Luna et al., "Businessmen and Politics in Mexico, 1982–1986," pp. 18–19, both in Maxfield and Anzaldúa eds., *Government and Private Sector in Contemporary Mexico.*

of the country."[51] They depended on state contracts and favors, too, so that openly opposing the PRI might have been unprofitable. Mizrahi reports that "when asked about the problem of accountability, lack of effective checks and balances, many of these entrepreneurs said that Mexicans are not really ready for democracy." Moreover, they valued informal contacts because these presented opportunities to win exemptions from the law; enforcement of the law appeared to these men as a second-best solution, one that bespoke a shameful lack of political access.[52]

As this suggests, in Latin America the same firms and people with power in the asset markets are also likely to enjoy informal political power. The membership of the Mexican Businessmen's Council can move the markets, and it can also sit down at a rather intimate dinner with the president and his chief economic ministers. Furthermore, the testimony above also suggests that the same rational calculus that leads a big investor to prefer personal access over the formal, public variety, may also lead him to expect little gain from the extension of impersonal norms in judicial and administrative decisions.[53]

A final obstacle to institutionalization may arise from an important asymmetry in the relationship between state and investor described in the first half of the chapter. The main payoff to capital comes from the premium on fixed assets (a positive "r" in Figure 5.1). But forces beyond the state's control, such as a rise in world interest rates or a fall in an export commodity price, could quickly turn the premium into a discount. Rapid outflows could bring a sharp rise in the government's interest cost, or a bad foreign exchange crisis, or a costly asset deflation—not only in the face of "irresponsible" policies but also in response to exogenous factors.

51. Mizrahi, "Rebels Without a Cause?" pp. 150–52.

52. Ibid., pp. 153–54. See also David Asman, "Mexico's Modernization: Phase II," *Wall Street Journal,* 5 October 1994, for a discussion of widespread rent or *"hueso"* seeking that depends on government favoritism. As the dependence on government contracts weakens, the value of informal ties to the government falls. But while this reduces the power of the government over the businessmen, the latter's market power has not been diminished. Besides, they may value their informal access as a way of assuring general policies relating to macroeconomic stability.

53. Moisés Naim asserts that in Venezuela the "small number of controlling parties in the private sector" provided an argument *against* sectoral policies and for a more arms-length, impersonal treatment of business: any sectorally targeted subsidies would be seen as favoring one conglomerate over another, which would "invite repercussions from those left out, adding to political instability." See *Paper Tigers and Minotaurs: Economic Policy Reform in Venezuela* (Washington, D.C.: Carnegie Endowment, 1992), p. 88.

Now, the hope for institutional solutions presupposes that the representatives of capital wish to have their influence made transparent. But there are good reasons why they might find this inconvenient. First, to the degree that market power is concentrated, its institutional equivalent (witness the complaints of small business within the Consejo Coordinador Empresarial in Mexico) may prove a political disadvantage in a democratic context. Second and more subtly, when business representatives call publicly for detailed changes in policies or institutions, people may understandably take them to be offering a bargain: do this and we will invest. Apart from questions about the credibility of the reforms, however, private wealth holders can be held to no such obligation. Waiting may be the rational option instead.[54] They would be keen to avoid the public perception that they have incurred a potentially inconvenient obligation to invest. This perception would be more likely if their policy suggestions were made in a formal setting. Here is another possible reason why they may prefer informal and market influence (especially if the latter could be presented as a message from the "public") to formal representation.

All of these reasons for avoiding institutionalization depend on relatively short-term considerations. From a longer-term point of view, informality remains a less than ideal solution. The combination of personalism and insecurity produces a suboptimal, nearsighted investment profile. At the extreme, crony capitalists take rapid and extravagant profits, since they cannot be sure how long their man and his laws will persist. Even the more established liberal interests fear unforeseen political changes, placing a great deal of importance on who occupies the presidency. However, given that big investors consider formal options less reliable, that the executive willingly consults them personally, and that the markets can be calmed by attending to a few large investors, the road to institutionalizing the political representation of capital appears long and rocky.

But in some countries there is a ready institutional alternative to the legislature: corporatism. In Mexico the CCE has become the preeminent representative of capital, and it notoriously overrepresents big, international conglomerates. It has not only served as the business representative in the agreements that began with the Pacto de Solidaridad Económica, but it was also deputized to coordinate the negotiations of the NAFTA for Mexico.[55] Jeffry Frieden has speculated

54. Cf. Raúl Laban, "Capital Repatriation and the Waiting Game," *Economics Letters* 37 (1991): 249–53.
55. Ricardo Tirado and Matilde Luna, "Los Empresarios en el Escenario del Cambio: Trayectoria y Tendencias de sus Estrategias de Acción Colectiva," *Revista Mexicana de*

that as global financial integration reduces the costs of exit, we may see "more political action by owners of capital as a class and less participation of capitalists in sectoral lobbying."[56] Corporatism may be the vehicle for this action.

Or it may not. Political action on nonsectoral, class issues (such as the level of interest rates or the extent of privatization) could easily take place informally—in those instances when, as Mizrahi reports, big investors use personal access to remind the government that their costs of exit have in fact fallen, threatening capital flight. Moreover, historically a key condition for corporatism has been a strong labor representative—either sitting at the table itself, or providing, through its organized power, the main incentive for an authoritarian arrangement that excludes it. As labor's strength wanes in Mexico and Argentina, the incentive to bargain in this way may decline.

All in all, under these conditions presidents may face a choice between making institutional commitments and working on their reputations. Assume, as we have done above, that legislatures are considered refractory and that at least some capital directly enjoys the insurance of flight (and the rest gains some protection from this). While sweeping liberal reforms may demand executive initiative, this process raises the possibility that presidents will reverse past decrees with future ones. The question of executive discretion reappears. Presidents face the following decision: either renounce power constitutionally or make the promise of stability credible in other ways. If a president prefers personal power, the latter route implies enhancing his reputation as a trustworthy free-marketeer. (For example, what did it mean that Menem publicly expressed admiration for Augusto

Sociología 55, no. 2 (April–June 1993): 247–50, 254. Camp, *Entrepreneurs and Politics in Twentieth-Century Mexico*, pp. 166–68. Others have seen the emergence of a "neocorporatism" also in the relative weakness of market criteria in privatization decisions. See Edmundo Jacobo Molina and Enrique Quintana L., "La Reestructuración del Poder Económico y sus Condicionantes," in *La Modernización de México*, ed. Arturo Anguiano (Mexico City: Universidad Autónoma Metropolitana, Unidad Xochimilco, 1990), pp. 243–44.

56. "Invested Interests: The Politics of Natural Economic Policies in a World of Global Finance," *International Organization* 45, no. 4 (Autumn 1991): 443; but see also his *Debt, Development, and Democracy,* esp. pp. 19–22, where he argues that holders of more specific assets have more intense preferences on government policy and thus (other things being equal) exert more influence over it. This seems to imply that a generalized shift toward greater liquidity in an economy would reduce sectoral constraints on the state and allow it more freedom of action; yet Frieden links liberalizing reforms most strongly to the aftermath of highly salient class conflict, as in Chile after 1973, a hypothesis less relevant for the 1989–94 period.

Pinochet while campaigning for constitutional changes that would allow his reelection?[57]) Insofar as the market trusts the sitting president, its pressure for constitutional restrictions on the presidency would abate, and presidents may try to take advantage of this.

Before leaving this subject, I would like to suggest a final implication of the discussion above. As trade integration proceeds, informal political access may prove to be more crucial as a competitive advantage of domestic capital. Political insider status could make some local firms formidable rivals for foreign ones or, perhaps just as likely, prized alliance partners in a transnational marketplace. If the former, foreign transnationals might become the best-endowed torchbearers of transparency (although in a relatively narrow sphere) as they sought to level the playing fields on which they expected to win. *Their* market pressure, and the diplomatic pressure of their home governments, might in fact conform to the hopes of the optimists. They would have the most to gain from (and offer as a reward for) institutional development, since they have lots of investment capital and expertise but little political access.[58] (Winning back the trust of foreign money managers burned by the Mexican devaluation of December 1994 was a decisive consideration in the decision to publish foreign-exchange reserve figures monthly.[59]) To take the argument a step further, it is

57. FBIS Latin America, 23 February 1993, p. 21, reporting a speech in La Rioja. Jeremy Adelman describes Menem as "wrapping himself in a political discourse which presents democratic checks and balances as obstacles to capitalist reform and political stability" ("Post-Populist Argentina," p. 91). Menem's renunciation of some decree and judicial appointment power was forced upon him not by the markets but by the agreement with the Radicals to secure his eligibility for a second term. He later had to deal with speculation that he might trade away economic reforms for the chance for reelection. The latter is noted in Thomas Kamm, "Menem Seeks Title of 'Mr. Indispensable,' " *Wall Street Journal,* 29 June 1993, A15. On hopes for checks and balances on Menem and the regret about their absence in Peru from the foreign investor's view, see *The Economist,* 16 April 1994, p. 17; on Menem, see interview with Stephen Fidler in *Somos* (Buenos Aires), 13 December 1993, pp. 24–25. Let me note that I am not saying that markets determine this outcome uniquely. It is their preference for personal authoritarianism that largely determines that such leaders would rather have the relatively unencumbered power that comes from trust in their person than the kind of trust that would derive from their promulgation (or recognition) of laws circumscribing the power of their office.

58. The U.S. government has used the protection of intellectual property rights as a condition for access to the U.S. market under the Enterprise for the Americas initiative. One problem here may be that companies *avoid* using the legal system of the host and instead call on the U.S. government, removing their incentive to push for reform of the system rather than of a narrow set of regulations. See *Business Latin America,* 25 January 1993, pp. 6–7.

59. On the decision, see *El Universal* (Mexico City), 10 January 1995, pp. 1, 6.

even conceivable that foreign calls for transparency could end up rhetorically and practically opposed to economic nationalism.[60]

Conclusion

I began this chapter by describing the benign view of mobile capital as that of a virtual senate, a guardian of big property against unpredictable presidents and populist legislatures. This formulation captures some of the reasons why mobile capital may be less effective in promoting the rule of law in areas beyond the financial markets. When economically liberal observers call for institutional reform in Latin America, they usually imply that the market signals the direction of necessary change. Inflation and rising interest rates show a need to restructure the state and make the government credible; capital flight means that the government should make property more secure and investment more profitable. Behind these observations there often stands this premise: by efficiently aggregating private decisions, the market represents the "public interest" better than does the political realm, which is encumbered by personalism, rent seeking, and the temptations of populism. Leaving aside the political problems with this assumption, we cannot take it to imply that the market will necessarily promote the creation of new political institutions. The same people and firms that can move asset markets may rationally prefer the informal political access they often enjoy. Or at least, to state it more generally, insofar as institutional reform responds to market power, we should also expect this reform to remain confined to areas in which those with market power have no ready substitute for institutions.

Let me end on two notes of qualified optimism. For one, international market constraints do seem to have reduced public tolerance for corruption in high places.[61] A populace that endures austerity and

60. Camp notes that some businessmen believed that nationalism "not only works against foreign companies' influencing government but also allows Mexicans a level of intimacy with the state unobtainable by foreign entrepreneurs." He cites a member of the Mexican Businessmen's Council who thought that if foreign entrepreneurs tried to influence government policy directly, "the consequences would be disastrous and produce the opposite of the result they desired." *Entrepreneurs and Politics in Twentieth-Century Mexico*, p. 235.

61. Manzetti, "Economic Reform and Corruption in LDCs," emphasizes the gap between rhetoric and performance of the politicians selling the market model (pp. 6, 17–19).

IMF homilies about "getting one's house in order" may understandably reach for a new broom to clean it. For another, institutions last longer when their power is circumscribed in predictable ways. If the need to please internationally mobile capital leads populists to change course immediately upon taking office, the promise of democracy, in the sense of the will of the electorate somehow expressed in public policies, may seem to have been flagrantly broken.[62] But confidence in the disciplining power of mobile capital may also dissuade moneyed elites and international actors from coup making. While voters may feel repeatedly betrayed when elected officials embrace the "realism" of acceding to market imperatives, realism has certain advantages when it comes to survival.

All things considered, the most likely result of the newly enhanced power of mobile capital, I believe, combines good financial housekeeping with the opaque influence of big business. We can expect to see strong guarantees for liquid, financial assets, as in the central bank independence and monetary rules already noted. International investors may also contribute to the advance of impersonal legality, although it is also possible that they will retreat from this quest as their informal access improves or as they ally themselves with the local economic elite in order to take advantage of the latter's political connections. Most likely, the energy for institution building will have to come largely from other quarters: from popular movements and farsighted leaders who value law and transparency even when they are not pushed to do so by international market forces.

---

62. We have what Bowles and Gintis have called "accountability without sovereignty," what others have labeled "democracy without choices" or an "emptying" of the concept. See Samuel Bowles and Herbert Gintis, *Democracy and Capitalism: Property, Community, and Contradictions of Modern Social Thought* (New York: Basic Books, 1987), p. 199. The "democracy without choices" phrase is that of Pablo González Casanova, "México: Hacia una Democracia Sin Opciones?" in *El Nuevo Estado Mexicano,* ed. Jorge Alonso, Alberto Aziz Nassif, and Jaime Tamayo, vol. 1, *Estado y Economía* (Mexico City: Nueva Imagen/Universidad de Guadalajara/CIESAS), p. 267. A critique of the *vaciamiento* thesis is Acuña and Smith, "The Political Economy of Structural Adjustment," pp. 19–20.

6

Mobile Capital,
Structural Dependence,
and Politics

In this book I have traced the political and structural causes and
consequences of international capital movements, looking mainly at
six major Latin American countries. Among causes of the 1982 crisis,
I have described changes in the international system and in governments' management of foreign exchange. As international capital
flows grew and became freer, they exposed the global financial system
to procyclical instability. Especially vulnerable in this regard were
Latin American countries whose exports remained concentrated in
one or a few commodities and whose openness to capital movements
was, for reasons of policy, culture, and wealth distribution, relatively
greater than their openness to trade. Governments that had responded
to export stagnation and volatile capital flows with exchange policy
reforms in the 1960s later suffered less capital flight while amassing
debt in the critical period (1980–82). After the crisis broke, capital

flight persisted or worsened for reasons connected to politics, the terms of the debt, and agents' expectations of fiscal burdens that would imply future taxes or inflation. Flight thus aggravated the debt crisis and narrowed the options for many countries, helping to drive them toward liberal economic policy reforms by the end of the 1980s. Along with these reforms, competition for mobile international capital also contributed to governments' decisions to deepen financial markets and to erect institutional safeguards against the political uncertainty that might unsettle potential investors. Beyond this, however, while increased capital mobility has represented a decisive constraint on policy, its role in advancing the rule of law, or in strengthening political institutions, will probably remain limited in Latin America.

In the following pages I summarize the major conclusions of the foregoing chapters, in light of the Mexican exchange crisis of 1994–95 and with relation to the literature on the political economy of development. The first section reviews the main comparative arguments of Chapters 2 through 4, highlighting their common focus upon matters of economic structure, and discusses what they have to say about the relationship between international forces and policy choices. The next section considers the capital flows to and from Latin America in the early 1990s and their connection with the reemergence of old patterns of foreign exchange policy. The rest of the chapter locates the arguments of this book in a broader context of political economy and suggests how some of them might fit into a model of international financial constraints on developing countries. The chapter ends by discussing mobile capital, the nation-state, and democracy in the future of Latin America.

Structures and Comparisons: Review

The connection between economic structure and policy outcomes has been drawn here in three dimensions, for two comparisons, and (for one of the latter) over two time periods. These are represented in Figure 6.1. Of the three dimensions, the first ("Exchange Crises") comprises the relative abundance of resources available to balance external accounts, the depth and recurrence of exchange crises, and the fortunes of the main export sectors in the world market. Another ("Sectoral Balance") relates to the relative size and organization of sectoral interests in civil society, mainly the balance between rural producers of tradeables, and urban consumers and industrial interests.

Finally, a third dimension involves what I have called financial cosmopolitanism, the degree to which national savings (whether held by firms or households) have taken on an international orientation, in which savings are held by agents who know about and are comfortable with foreign asset options. The two comparisons are between Latin America and East Asia (A), and among six Latin American countries (B). The time periods (B1 and B2) divide at the outbreak of the debt crisis in 1982.

For Latin America and East Asia before 1982, the second dimension corresponds to the Sachs argument recounted in Chapters 2 and 3. According to this argument, East Asian countries were more likely to pursue export-led strategies because of a populous rural tradeables sector, constituting a base for policies that overruled the preferences of urban ISI interests. The first dimension here represents a potential criticism that could be leveled at the Sachs thesis: the switch from ISI to an entry-level, low-wage export-oriented industrialization would have been easier in countries with less prosperous commodity export sectors because of the effect of abundant exports in appreciating the equilibrium exchange rate (making production costs higher in international terms). On the third dimension it was argued that for historical reasons Latin America has had a much higher degree of financial cosmopolitanism than East Asia. This resulted from the relatively early presence of multinational corporations, on the one hand, and, on the other hand, the greater concentration of national wealth in an elite that was as internationally oriented as it was narrow.

In addition, all three dimensions influenced the outcome of the international borrowing spree of the late 1970s and early 1980s. On the first, commodity booms and trade surpluses excited bankers. On the second, surviving ISI coalitions and their priorities helped push governments into projects intended to enhance self-sufficiency with borrowed money. As for the third, longstanding bank relationships with private- and public-sector borrowers facilitated the process of channeling petrodollars to Latin America. And the international orientation of Latin American private wealth contributed to the fact that capital flight was, relative to the larger East Asian countries, an easier and more familiar option.

Chapter 3 referred to two of the dimensions when comparing six Latin American countries before the 1982 debt crisis. (The third was assumed to operate equally across the countries.[1]) Structural

1. The difference in income distributions between Argentina and other countries

characteristics of the export sector, mainly the seriousness of world market stagnation of the main traditional export (which led to repeated exchange crises), constituted an important element in shaping policy change. Crises and commodity gluts put export diversification on the agenda and their recurrence helped keep it there, leading governments to consider policies, such as a crawling-peg exchange-rate system, that bore a greater political cost than the typical subsidies and exhortation. The second dimension above, the sectoral balance between urban ISI interests and rural tradeables, was probably less important. It may, however, help explain why pro-export reforms in Colombia did not have the same political significance they had in Argentina, where they would have delivered a short-term windfall to a small and politically isolated rural oligarchy. Perhaps for this reason, before 1971 proexport exchange reforms in Chile did not survive electoral competition, since they favored foreign mining companies.

The results of 1982 have also been analyzed in terms of the three dimensions noted above. On the condition of the external accounts, for all countries except Colombia the 1982 debacle represented the worst crisis since the 1930s. Overall, Latin American governments had little choice but to pay greater attention to export promotion, even in countries where the issue had been largely ignored before then. Though regional trade surpluses had more to do with recession than export promotion, and though the export sector was hampered by the overall decline in investment, exports became more diversified, and this could be taken to imply a broader set of interests supporting realistic exchange rates. Still, in the same way that several countries' abundant exports kept ISI policies largely intact until 1982, the exchange policy innovations that kept capital flight in check may also have helped extend the viability of a slightly modified ISI strategy during the 1980s, above all in Brazil. Because of the previous attention to exports, a wide range of producers could respond vigorously, which meant there was less of a cost in terms of the domestic demand.

---

appears to undermine this assumption: with its less-polarized distribution, Argentina should be characterized by a measurably lower degree of financial outwardness. Several things complicated this. Most obvious was the intervention of another factor, the political legacy of Perón, as already noted. But more to the point, Argentina's income distribution in the upper quintiles did not diverge as much from the Latin American norm as might be supposed; the big difference lay in the two lowest quintiles, which in Argentina enjoyed a much higher relative and absolute standard of living. Since it was consumer (and saver) behavior in the big wealth-owning upper quintile that is most important to the present argument, Argentina may be regarded as similar enough.

A. Latin America Versus East Asia Before 1982

	Latin America	East Asia
Exchange crises, export abundance (1950s–early 1960s)	Longer history of commodity export, more abundant resources	Most countries with few resources to export as of late 1950s
Sectoral balance between export and urban ISI interests (early 1960s)	ISI coalition stronger; rural tradeables interest politically isolated by 1950s	Rural tradeables sector larger, often due to post-WWII land reforms
Financial cosmopolitanism (Y,W dist + culture)	Early MNC presence: elites cosmopolitan and have more of national wealth; hence finance more globally oriented	Late MNC presence: elites largely share cultural insularity and command less of total wealth

B. Among Six Latin American Countries

1. Before 1982

Exchange crises, export growth (1950—mid 1960s)

Venezuela   Argentina
   Mexico   Chile   Colombia   Brazil
◄ – – more – – – – export growth – – – – – less – – ►
  fewer   – – exchange crises – –   more

Sectoral balance between export and urban ISI interests (before 1970s nationalization)

Venezuela   Brazil   Colombia
   Chile   Argentina   Mexico
◄ – – more – – · foreign or concentrated – – – less – – ►
  ownership in traditional export sectors

Financial cosmopolitanism

(assumed similar across the region)

2. After 1982

Exchange crises, export abundance

Debt service forces export orientation as imports compressed. Fiscal/payments crisis (domestic debt, arrears, hyperinflation, investment slump, foreign sector shortfall) aggravated by K flight

Sectoral balance between export and urban ISI interests

Shifts in favor of export interests with crisis and currency depreciations; tradeables expand as nontradeables stagnate. Rising mfg X by MNCs

Financial cosmopolitanism (expatr K/exports)

Expatriate funds place priority on policies to recover them (liberalization of DFI, privatization, combination of fixed exchange rates and free exchange mkt)
◄ – – greater – – – net expatr K/ X – – – – less – – ►
  Arg Mex Ven   Bra   Col   Chi

Fig. 6.1. Comparisons, time periods, and structural dimensions.

However, the third, financial dimension acted in a way that opposed the shift toward exporting. The foreign debt burden increased the importance of international financial links, empowering those who enjoyed them. A long drought in public and private investment militated for welcoming foreign funds. Billions of dollars of expatriate capital put a high priority on policies aimed at attracting it. Doing so often meant turning from exchange and credit policies centered on export promotion toward those that focused on the capital account. As I have argued, this was a familiar move in Latin America. As I noted in Chapter 3, the desire to attract foreign investment was a key motivation for fixed rates and free exchange markets in Chile in 1959–61, in Argentina in 1959–62 and 1967–70, and in Mexico during 1958–72—well before the years of easy borrowing (1977–81).

The Early 1990s: New Liberalism, Old Patterns

The contradiction between exports and finance emerged again in the early 1990s. Beginning around the time of the Brady Plan, reduced debt service, privatizations, relaxed regulations on foreign investment, and rapidly falling world interest rates all contributed to a virtuous cycle of enhanced creditworthiness, lower costs on the domestic debt, and improved fiscal balances in Latin America.[2] Flight capital first trickled and then poured back in, joining a tide of foreign-managed portfolio investments in newly liberalized or reorganized share and bond markets, and a great deal (especially in Argentina and Chile) of direct investment, mostly by foreign multinationals. Governments suddenly found themselves trying to manage large inflows of funds, a problem they had not faced for over a decade.[3] In

2. Andrés Velasco outlines a suggestive model whereby tax rates on domestic capital fall (rise) as the capital base expands (contracts), what has been called "fiscal increasing returns"; expectations about returns on capital repatriation become to this extent self-fulfilling. He concludes that under these conditions important signals for repatriation include "highly visible and symbolic" state actions. See "Animal Spirits, Capital Repatriation, and Investment," Economic Research Report 92-43, C. V. Starr Center for Applied Economics, New York University, New York, September 1992, p. 18.

3. With the portfolio flows, the decline of international interest rates was the main driving force. As for where the money landed, the main requirements seem to have been the presence (or at least the "emergence") of a capital market and some public discussion of liberal reforms (funds flowed to Brazil in its relatively unreformed state in similar magnitudes as they went elsewhere). For market operators, talking up a country presented all the advantages of talking up a stock, with none of the legal dangers. First,

the new international context, even more than during the previous borrowing boom, a critical issue of political economy facing Latin American countries involved whether exchange policy should respond to trends in the capital account or in the current account.[4]

The issue was political, too, because unless inflation were cut to practically insignificant levels, government policy could not respond to both foreign investors and exporters. The investor in financial assets wants stable future returns in terms of hard currency, while the price-sensitive exporter does best when he can expect the government to protect his future competitiveness by attending to the real exchange rate—which means adjusting the nominal rate as inflation and the trade balance require. Both investor and exporter need to trust the government to stick to a policy for the medium to long term. But over the relatively long period in question, a relatively rapid inflation rate will force the government to choose one interest or the other. Politics matters here—if only because the commitment to one will not be credible for long unless the government clearly absorbs the political cost of offending the other.

In recent years the political benefits to be derived from favoring the capital account have been obvious. As had been the case during the borrowing frenzy of the 1970s, after 1989 a fixed exchange rate made it easier for politicians to bring down inflation quickly, raise incomes across the board, and moderate the real burden of foreign debt service by riding a real currency appreciation that was supported by an influx

---

resident brokers with political contacts and other "local knowledge" make a favorable judgment, then word passes to the more adventurous international investment banks, tiny share markets rise rapidly across the board, the big profits begin to excite fund managers (while I-bank sources feed breathless press reports of a "turnaround"), the currency appreciates, adding to the windfall, and finally all the fuss brings in the individual investors. Regarding policy responses, one Latin American study is Patricia Correa with Ana María Herrera and Juan Pablo Trujillo, *Acumulación de Reservas Internacionales y Ajuste Macroeconómico en Siete Países Exportadores* (Bogotá: FESCOL/ ANALDEX/FEDESARROLLO, 1992), comparing seven countries. It concludes that reserves rise when, under high positive real interest rates, a current account surplus leads to expectations of revaluation, which is then confirmed by movements on the capital account (p. 98). It also concludes that for outward-oriented development a stable real exchange rate is necessary but not sufficient (pp. 103–4).

4. Jeffry Frieden has made this argument for industrial countries. He notes that a stable appreciated currency favors those investing abroad from an economy at the expense of tradeables producers; for those investing from the outside in, a currency is best that, relative to the investor's home currency, appreciates from a low base—assets bought cheap which then appreciate with the currency. See "Invested Interests: The Politics of National Economic Policies in a World of Global Finance," *International Organization* 45, no. 4 (Autumn 1991): 443–45 and 446 n. 46.

of foreign capital.[5] As in previous decades, here it was hard to separate the desire to light a beacon of stability from the invitation to speculate.[6] The results were familiar: highly popular anti-inflation policies; impressive income growth figures; finance ministers lionized in the foreign press; presidents staking their honor and credibility on the maintenance of the exchange rate; and isolated groups of industrialists and price-sensitive exporters who, when they complained, were told to get more productive.[7] In the same way that powerful urban ISI interests in Latin America were often overruled under IMF pressure in the 1960s and 1970s, so did new exporters in much of the region find it hard to overcome the international endorsement of stabilization plans that appreciated the real exchange rate.

As governments decided their priorities in the early 1990s, one could detect a pattern similar to that described in Chapter 3. In Colombia official hand-wringing about the real exchange rate seemed almost to have become a mark of economic patriotism. Even when in 1991 the government finally modified DL 444, it did so with a pledge to keep on promoting exports.[8] Later, as minor export interests worried

5. Eduardo Conesa in *La Prensa* (Buenos Aires), 26 February 1993, p. II–12; Roberto Gutiérrez, "El Endeudamiento Externo del Sector Privado Mexicano, 1971–1991," *Comercio Exterior* 42, no. 9 (September 1992): 864.

6. David Felix has argued that this is the familiar strategy of "pacifying foreign speculative capital." Reported in *Noticias* of The Latin American Program, Woodrow Wilson Center, Washington, D.C., Spring 1994.

7. In Argentina these concerns and the government response date back to mid-1991. See, for example, Daniel Sosa, "Seguí Mingo, Que Vas Bien," *Página 12* (Buenos Aires), 3 August 1991, p. 8. The most comprehensive critique of the Cavallo Plan is Eduardo R. Conesa, *La Crisis del 93: Una Agenda de los Riesgos que Enfrentará la Economía Argentina* (Buenos Aires: Planeta, 1992); on this point see p. 288. In May 1992 *Review of the River Plate* derided a visiting Rudiger Dornbusch's suggestion that the peso was overvalued. Blaming the debacle of 1981 on the devaluations undertaken by Martínez de Hoz's successor, it quoted Martin Feldstein (also visiting) in support of the fixed rate, as necessary to rid Argentina of its "inflationary culture." Unconcerned about the trade deficit, Feldstein said that "capital inflows would take care of this comfortably," though he did note that "at present the rate of investment is low, considering the potential of the economy." (Buenos Aires), 14 May 1992, pp. 257–58.

8. The reforms relaxed its exchange control provisions at a time when reserves were rising; the rate of devaluation was accelerated nonetheless, in order to counteract the effects of trade liberalization. The head of the central bank noted the balance-of-payments surplus and unexpected reserve accumulation of 1990 and early 1991, leading to "grave inflationary pressures." But in his speech to the main organization of exporters, he also pledged to keep the real exchange rate stable and described the export sector as having "definite priority." Francisco Ortega to the IX Congreso Asociación Nacional de Exportadores (ANALDEX), November 1991, "La Política de Estabilización y las Exportaciones," *Revista del Banco de la República* 64, no. 770 (December 1991): 17, 20. See also Germán Botero de los Ríos, "Las Exportaciones No Tradicionales y el Sesgo

about the effects of new oil discoveries, in October 1992 the general manager of the central bank assured a congress of exporters that "the basic guideline . . . has been to sustain the real exchange rate at levels that guarantee competitiveness."[9] In Brazil strong support remained for using the exchange rate to favor exports, even as international flows and the demands of stabilization made this harder to do. In 1990 FIESP came out strongly for a greater emphasis on export promotion by means of a depreciated exchange rate in order to make possible the reduction of government export subsidies—which would facilitate market access and reduce inflationary pressure.[10] With the real appreciation that accompanied the Plano Real in 1994–95, businessmen pressed for adjustment, and in the face of worsening trade figures the government obliged in early March 1995.[11]

But such considerations were less important elsewhere, especially in Argentina and Mexico. One could be struck with *déjà vu* upon reading Mexican or Argentine newspapers—especially before the fateful devaluation of December 1994 in the former and afterward in the latter—with headlines quoting trustworthy foreign or local experts to the effect that the currency was rock-solid and reserves were plentiful.[12] Policies in these two countries exemplified a kind of neoliberal-

---

Anti-Exportador," *Nueva Frontera* 885 [Bogotá], 1–7 June 1992, p. 5. Botero complained about the 15 percent real appreciation of the peso between the end of 1990 and mid-1992, even though his index placed the currency's value at its 1986 level (pp. 6–7). In the same issue the president of the main banking interest group, Asociación Nacional de Instituciones Financieras (ANIF), worried about the balance-of-payments effects of exchange freedom for the income from "personal services," which he saw as a window for capital of doubtful origin (p. 15). Although the magazine is edited by Carlos Lleras and could be expected to follow the ideas of the father of DL 444, this kind of concern by a banking industry representative shows the distinctiveness of Colombian ideas on this subject.

9. Speech of Francisco Ortega to Asociación Nacional de Exportadores (ANALDEX), 29–30 October 1992, *Revista del Banco de la República* 65, no. 780 (October 1992): 25, 28.

10. *Livre para Crescer: Proposta para um Brasil Moderno* (São Paulo: Federação das Indústrias do Estado de São Paulo/Cultura Editores Asociados, 1990), pp. 42–47, 180–81, 295. On Chile, see Matt Moffett, "Chile Stays Wary of Foreign Investment," *Wall Street Journal,* 9 June 1994.

11. *Latin American Weekly Report,* 26 January 1995, p. 27; 23 March 1995, p. 121; *Veja,* 15 March 1995, pp. 32–39.

12. Mitigating the importance of the real exchange rate in these countries, input costs were reduced by the liberalization of imports, export tax and free reductions, and other deregulations. In Mexico and Argentina the currency value became the central protagonist in the economic policy drama. Its stability became a matter of state, and openly questioning its stability took on overtones of treason. In April 1994 the Mexican government faced some thirty pension fund and mutual fund managers who petitioned for the government to avoid devaluing the peso until at least December 1995. Fernando

ism that contrasts with the East Asian export orientation. Despite the differences within each region, it can be said that, at this writing, Latin America's economic future is more dependent on the changeable currents of international finance.[13]

Choice and Constraint

In recent years arguments for the utility and legitimacy of structural, internationally focused explanations—such as a few of those advanced in this book—have usually prompted an obligatory critique, or dismissal, of dependency theory. Many of the critiques have been accurate. Yet an interesting thing has happened.

Barbara Stallings has observed that in the last two decades the influence of dependency theory appears to have varied almost *inversely* with Latin America's degree of constraint by international economic forces.[14] She has a point. Between 1982 and 1990 the region's terms of

Ortega Pizarro, "Acción Concertada del Gobierno para Cumplir la Exigencia de Inversionistas Extranjeros: No Devaluar," *Proceso* 913 (2 May 1994): 38.

13. In the wake of the peso collapse we should be mindful of the differences between 1982 and 1994–95, as well as the similarities. The funds in the 1990s went primarily to the private sector, and declines in stock market values could absorb more of the potential losses and thereby reduce the contingent burden on central banks. In addition, the flows of the early 1990s did not respond to rising commodity prices, a major cause of instability in 1980–82, nor were they likely to collide with falling demand for Latin American commodity exports. However, Latin America's total external debt rose substantially and its financial markets remained highly sensitive to international interest rates. On differences, see John Williamson, "Issues Posed by Portfolio Investment in Developing Countries," paper delivered to a World Bank symposium "Portfolio Investment in Developing Countries," 9–10 September 1993, Washington, D.C.; and John H. Welch, "The New Face of Latin America: Financial Flows, Markets, and Institutions in the 1990s," *Journal of Latin American Studies* 25, no. 1 (February 1993): 2. For historical background, see Albert Fishlow, "Lessons from the Past: Capital Markets During the 19th Century and the Interwar Period," *International Organization* 39, no. 3 (Summer 1985): 636–38. Three sources of potential instability stand out: (1) agents making projections based on debt-to-GDP or debt-to-fiscal-revenue ratios at exchange rates temporarily appreciated by capital flows; (2) international interest-rate sensitivity, mainly on the supply side; (3) the high level of foreign capital participation in financial markets, relative to the size of the external sector. On the third point, foreign participation in the markets of Argentina, Chile, and Mexico was estimated at 70–80 percent (*Financial Times*, 7 March 1994). It implies that the key risk indicator derivable from stock market capitalization is not its ratio to GDP (cf. *The Economist*, 26 February 1994, p. 84) but its ratio to exports.

14. By "dependency theory" I mean global, materialist theories of late development, mixing neo-Marxist and structuralist ideas, emphasizing the obstacles to enduring and

trade fell below Depression levels, as its net transfers to rich-country creditors amounted to the equivalent of (to use a favorite comparison) about six Marshall Plans in reverse.[15] Governments led by populists opted for "realism" and undertook neoliberal reforms. Or, facing panicked markets, they effectively renounced a remarkable amount of power over economic policy, or over their export revenues, in a bid for the confidence of international finance. Meanwhile, dependency theory became passé. Some scholars turned to analyzing states and internal class relations in developing countries; others, as I noted in the last chapter, came to view dependence more positively.[16] Among the many

---

equitable development, and favoring socialism (however defined) as a solution. See Barbara Stallings, "International Influence on Economic Policy: Debt, Stabilization, and Structural Reform," in *The Politics of Economic Adjustment: International Constraints, Distributive Conflicts, and the State*, ed. Stephan Haggard and Robert Kaufman (Princeton: Princeton University Press, 1992), pp. 41–43. Earlier critiques of dependency made similar points. See Tony Smith, "The Underdevelopment of Development Literature: The Case of Dependency Theory," *World Politics* 32 (1979): 240; Joseph L. Love, "The Origins of Dependency Analysis," *Journal of Latin American Studies* 22 (1990): 157.

15. On terms of trade, see Michael Bleaney and David Greenaway, "Long-Run Trends in the Relative Prices of Primary Commodities and in the Terms of Trade of Developing Countries," *Oxford Economic Papers* 45, no. 3 (July 1993). The authors reject the proposition of a trend against commodities before 1980 but show a significant decline after that date in agricultural commodities (but not metals). While arguing against generalization about the trend, they do suggest that the post-1980 fall in the aggregate index had to do with the debt crisis and the export promotion efforts undertaken by many debtors simultaneously (pp. 355–56). On transfers, the sixfold estimate comes from Osvaldo R. Agatiello, *Fuga de Capitales de la Argentina* (Buenos Aires: Editorial Belgrano, 1990), p. 117; a tenfold estimate can be found in Xabier Gorostiaga, "Latin America in the New World Order," in *Global Visions: Beyond the New World Order*, ed. Jeremy Brecher, J. B. Childs, and Jill Cutler (Boston: South End Press, 1993), p. 69. A cogent critique of World Bank and related estimates of net outflow from debtor countries is Rigmar Osterkamp, "Is There a Transfer of Resources from Developing to Industrial Countries?" *Intereconomics* 25 (September–October 1990). Such complaints about World Bank and ECLA estimates (cf. Robert Devlin, "Economic Restructuring in Latin America in the Face of the Foreign Debt and the External Transfer Problem," *CEPAL Review* 32, August 1987) are relatively rare, however.

16. The immediate successor to dependency in political science was an explosion of literature on the state and its effectiveness in the mid-1980s. One can begin with Peter Evans, Dietrich Rueschemeyer, and Theda Skocpol, eds., *Bringing the State Back In* (New York: Cambridge University Press, 1985), especially the articles by Rueschemeyer and Evans, "The State and Economic Transformation: Toward an Analysis of the Conditions Underlying Effective Intervention" and, closer to public-choice analyses, Charles Tilly, "War Making and State Making as Organized Crime." The new tack shared an older preoccupation of political modernization theorists as in Samuel Huntington, *Political Order in Changing Societies* (New Haven: Yale University Press, 1968). See Smith, "The Underdevelopment of Development Literature," pp. 261–82, for

empirical reasons for the demise of dependency theory, two relate closely to the themes of this book.

Many observers have repeated some version of the thesis that rapid and equitable East Asian capitalist development proves dependency theory wrong.[17] One often hears a tone of reproof ("East Asia is doing it, so why not the rest of you?") in which dependency theory appears as a self-made excuse for third-world failure.[18] More commonly and usefully the spotlight has fallen upon *policies* followed by East Asian states—measures to raise productivity in agriculture, to promote export-led industrial growth, to repress wages, to reduce birth rates, to spur private investment, and to educate the populace.[19]

Another line of critique arose from the fact that spectacular development failures often took place when the international system became more permissive rather than less. It was especially damaging to theories of surplus extraction to see that an abundance of capital did not solve a lot of important problems. This was evident during the borrowing spree of 1976–81 and in the behavior of rich oil-exporting countries. Terry Karl's study of Venezuela and scholarship on Middle Eastern "rentier states" have shown how oil wealth advanced redistribution and patronage rather than the organized provision of collective goods.[20] The distribution of income and life chances remained polar-

the connection between older and emerging concerns. Some of the most influential treatments of developing country states came from scholars of Africa. Here emerged the notion of the predatory state, extracting surplus from scattered and weak rural producers for the benefit of urban consumers and a ruling clique. See Goran Hyden, *No Shortcuts to Progress: African Development Management in Perspective* (Berkeley and Los Angeles: University of California Press, 1983), and Robert H. Bates, *Markets and States in Tropical Africa: The Political Basis of Agricultural Policies* (Berkeley and Los Angeles: University of California Press, 1981). An excellent summary of the issues is Joel S. Migdal, *Strong Societies and Weak States: State-Society Relations and State Capabilities in the Third World* (Princeton: Princeton University Press, 1989).

17. The landmark was Bill Warren, "Imperialism and Capitalist Industrialization," *New Left Review*, no. 81 (September–October 1973), pp. 3–44.

18. For example, David Landes, "Rich Country, Poor Country," *The New Republic*, 20 November 1989, p. 25; Douglass C. North, *Institutions, Institutional Change, and Economic Performance* (New York: Cambridge University Press, 1990), pp. 99–100.

19. The World Bank, *The East Asian Miracle: Economic Growth and Public Policy* (New York: Oxford University Press, 1993); *The Economist* survey of Asia (30 October 1993), especially pp. 5–9, "Why It Happened"; James W. McGuire, "Development Policy and Its Determinants in East Asia and Latin America," *Journal of Public Policy* 14, no. 2 (1994): 205–42.

20. "To the extent that policy-makers rely upon petrodollars instead of institutional or consensus-building mechanisms, there is a long-term diminution of state capacity." See "The Political Economy of Petrodollars: Oil and Democracy in Venezuela," Ph.D. dissertation, Stanford University, 1982, p. 629. On the circumventing of the civil service

ized, state discipline broke down, and with it so did the ability to formulate and carry out lasting solutions to dependency. Moreover, in a negative parallel to the model based on medieval European examples, in which economic necessity required the state to grant a voice to the civil society it was forced to tax, state-controlled oil rents often bankrolled despots.[21] Here were lessons for both dependency and statist theories: these states enjoyed both wealth and autonomy, yet they did not solve development problems well.

To assert the importance of economic crisis to reform is to make a related argument. Chapter 3 showed how easier conditions brought a worse result than did the export stagnation that helped provoke timely policy changes. It agrees with the durable political-science generalization that says states are strongest (and seen as most legitimate) when they act upon crises and threats.[22]

Still, to criticize dependency theory is not to ignore the exercise of power in international finance. I disagree with the notion that international financial agencies do not "compel national governments to do things that the latter do not perceive to be in their national interest."[23] The national interest in the presence of IMF conditionality,

---

law, see p. 227; on crisis, see p. 280. On this aspect of Venezuela see also Rexene Hanes de Acevedo, *El Clientelismo Político en América Latina: Una Crítica a la Teoría de la Dependencia* (Mérida: Universidad de los Andes, 1984). On the rentier state, see the Spring 1988 issue of *Arab Studies Quarterly* 10, no. 2, especially Samih K. Farsoun, "Oil, Ideology, and State Autonomy in the Middle East."

21. Farsoun, "Oil, Ideology, and State Autonomy in the Middle East," pp. 172–73. The same implication can be derived from Tilly, "War Making and State Making as Organized Crime," pp. 184–86.

22. Hence, though crises may often fail to bring about successful adaptations of policy, this should not be allowed to obscure the fact that they nevertheless present collective-action problems most insistently. A condition, though insufficient by itself, may still have a strong causal association with a particular outcome. On crisis and response, see Barbara Geddes, *Politician's Dilemma: Building State Capacity in Latin America* (Berkeley and Los Angeles: University of California Press, 1994), pp. 9–10. This does not obviate the need for a fuller description of crises if we are to comprehend their variety and the diversity of their effects. At the core of the concept of crisis as a creative moment, I believe, lies a historical connection between prototypical Western states and the conduct of war. The crises that concern us here obviously differ from the prototype in several ways, notably in their severity, on whom they impact, and whether they arise outside the country, within it, or from some connection between the two.

23. John Williamson, ed., *The Political Economy of Policy Reform* (Washington, D.C.: Institute for International Economics, 1994), pp. 24–25 and n. 13. The reasoning behind this assertion is either condescending or tautologous—the former if it assumes that the IMF knows the country's interest best (and anyone opposing the IMF recipe lacks a valid concept of it), and the latter if all policy decisions somehow reflect perceptions of the national interest. For a view that reflects the complexity of the external connection

with all this implies to the availability and terms of external financing, is very likely to differ from the national interest in its absence. Moreover, the national interest of a country in which a thousand internationally invested people control most of the assets is likely to differ from the national interest in a country in which such conditions do not obtain. Paul Volcker, for whom the "agony of the debt crisis" provided the "jolt necessary" for neoliberal reform, has observed that when Brazil's "feisty" finance minister Dilson Funaro suspended interest payments in 1987, the country lost more in capital flight than it saved in debt service. He remarks, "the difficulty with his approach is that failure to respect the rights of foreign creditors sends a chill down the spine of a country's affluent citizens, of which Brazil had many."[24]

Or consider the government rescues of private debtors in the wake of the 1982 crisis, undertaken out of the fear of depression and under pressure from foreign bankers.[25] Bankruptcies involving foreign creditors would have meant long litigation, liquidations that risked asset deflation, and unpredictable political costs; state takeovers kept distressed assets on the books as fully performing.[26] In Mexico a

---

better, see Bruce E. Moon, "Consensus or Compliance? Foreign-Policy Change and External Dependence," *International Organization* 39, no. 2 (Spring 1985): 306–7.

24. Paul A. Volcker and Toyoo Gyohten, *Changing Fortunes: The World's Money and the Decline of American Supremacy* (New York: Times Books, 1992), p. 210.

25. On Chile, see Carlos Díaz-Alejandro, "Good-Bye Financial Repression, Hello Financial Crash," *Journal of Development Economics* 19 (1985): 12; *Latin American Weekly Report,* 28 January 1983; Barbara Stallings, "Politics and Economic Crisis: A Comparative Study of Chile, Peru, and Colombia," in *Economic Crisis and Policy Choice: The Politics of Adjustment in the Third World,* ed. Joan M. Nelson (Princeton: Princeton University Press, 1990), p. 130. Arnold Harberger reports that earlier government bank bailouts (especially in late 1981) "served as the ostensible justification" for international creditor pressure. See "Lessons for Debtor Country Managers and Policymakers," in *International Debt and the Developing Countries,* ed. Gordon W. Smith and John T. Cuddington (Washington, D.C.: World Bank, 1985), p. 246. Several months later the banks withheld the final installment on their loan in order to force the government to guarantee private-sector debts (*Latin American Weekly Report,* 23 December 1983, p. 3). In Venezuela the government tried unilaterally in 1986 to cut debt service payments on private foreign debt while significantly reducing its rate subsidy through the FOCO-CAM program. Bankers, fearing financial losses, concerned about private-sector bankruptcies, and worried by the prospect of Argentina following suit, reportedly became "furious." They froze trade credits, threatened lawsuits, and summoned the country's finance minister and chief debt negotiator to New York—after which the government backed down until the end of Lusinchi's term. See Peter Simpson, "Venezuela Drives Bankers Crazy," *Euromoney,* September 1986, pp. 177–78.

26. For the same reasons, the foreign creditors reacted to the Mexican bank nationalization with relative equanimity. Darrell Delamaide, *Debt Shock: The Full Story of the World's Credit Crisis* (Garden City, N.Y.: Doubleday, 1984), p. 106; Karin Lissakers, *Banks, Borrowers, and the Establishment: A Revisionist Account of the International*

Finance Ministry publication later explained that because the private sector had to be encouraged to fill the investment gap left by the retreat of the state, its foreign debt burden needed to be alleviated.[27] The account added that state participation in resolving the private debt problem was "emphatically desired by debtors and creditors," and many of the latter refused participation in the 1983 "jumbo" loan until they were assured that the debt service of the Mexican private sector would be publicly guaranteed.[28] Across the region, while such bailouts of private debtors contributed to fiscal burdens, no government made a serious attempt to attach the foreign assets of domestic residents.[29] Without cooperation from recipient countries, this would have constituted a gesture both futile and costly to business confidence. At the

---

Debt Crisis (New York: Basic Books, 1991), pp. 182–83. See also the discussion in Carlos F. Díaz-Alejandro, "Latin American Debt: I Don't Think We Are in Kansas Anymore," *Brookings Papers on Economic Activity* 2 (1984): 356–58. As Felix notes, the neoliberal regimes of the Southern Cone had already experienced disruptive collapses of their domestic financial systems, so they had even less motivation for additional workouts. "Debt Crisis and Adjustment in Latin America: Have the Hardships Been Necessary?" Working Paper no. 170, Department of Economics, Washington University (St. Louis, September 1992), p. 15.

27. Secretaría de Hacienda y Crédito Público, *Deuda Externa Pública Mexicana* (Mexico City: SHCP/Fondo de Cultura Económica, 1988), p. 114. The private sector expressed its approval upon the extension of the guarantees in January 1984. *Latin American Weekly Report,* 27 January 1984, p. 2; *Excélsior* (Mexico City), 17 January 1984.

28. Secretaría de Hacienda y Crédito Público, *Deuda Externa Pública Mexicana,* pp. 114–16. In Mexico even before the blowup the chief of Bank of America's Mexican operations called for government intervention in the Alfa conglomerate on the grounds that the move would "save jobs for Mexicans." See Alan Robinson, "The Position of Alfa Is Delicate, Delicate, Delicate," *Euromoney,* June 1982, p. 49. In this period the government also rescued or took over Altos Hornos, Fundidora de Monterrey, and Mexicana de Aviación. See Rosario Green, *La Deuda Externa de México, 1973–1987: De la Abundancia a la Escasez de Créditos* (Mexico City: Nueva Imagen, 1988), pp. 97–98; Gutiérrez, "El Endeudamiento Externo del Sector Privado Mexicano, 1971–1991," pp. 855–59.

29. Governments proved reluctant to tackle even what should have been the easy cases, the notorious back-to-backs. Díaz-Alejandro and Felix both suggest that the authorities failed to take on the issue because it was politically too risky. Díaz-Alejandro ties this risk to the holding of foreign assets by the elite, as well as to its cultural proximity to debtor countries: "[T]he prospects of being cut off from their bankers abroad, or even from Disneyland, will make many members of the elite pause before risking near anarchy" ("Latin American Debt," p. 382). See also Felix, "Debt Crisis and Adjustment in Latin America," p. 25; Felix, "Half-Hidden Dimensions of Latin America's Debt Crisis," Working Paper no. 150, Department of Economics, Washington University (St. Louis, March 1990), pp. 20–23. In my conversations some Latin American economists and businessmen stressed the administrative as well as the political challenges, while others simply ridiculed the idea.

same time, however, prominent among the beneficiaries of this "free lunch" (courtesy of countries that "don't go out of business") were the leading international banks.

What's Left? Modeling International Financial Constraint

Might there be something left in dependency theory, broadly conceived, that can help us understand the "lost decade," the remarkable turn toward neoliberalism in Latin America, and the problems of 1994–95? In light of the arguments in this book, upon what basis can we anchor robust generalizations about the constraints of international finance on developing countries? Can we do so in a way that lets us comprehend differences among countries and over time? After discussing the limits of three critiques, I will suggest how a few of the arguments of this book might occupy at least some of the theoretical void whose existence Stallings implies.

One justification for the demise of dependency theory has practically disappeared. If one had argued against dependency theory only on the basis of the diversity of economic strategies in Latin America or the world (which would contradict any simplistic notion of external causation), one's objection would be substantially weaker today—as I implied in Chapter 4.[30]

As a critique of dependency theory, the East Asia line of argument misses at least some of its target. Any structural theory emphasizes the question of why good policies did not get chosen, or if chosen, why they were not effectively implemented. East Asian success stories differed from Latin America in some ways that even the old dependency theory thought important.[31] In these pages I have emphasized patterns of export concentration and asset ownership.

30. Jeffry Frieden rejects the "simple dependency view" on the basis of variation in policy choice and economic outcomes, in this case across five Latin American countries. *Debt, Development, and Democracy: Modern Political Economy and Latin America, 1965–1985* (Princeton: Princeton University Press, 1991), p. 237.

31. This objection does not apply to McGuire, "Development Policy and Its Determinants in East Asia and Latin America," with its long and judicious discussion of the determinants of policy choice. The best defense of the dependency position is that of Peter Evans. Looking mainly at Taiwan and South Korea as representatives of East Asia, he noted several differences between regions that could be traced to concerns familiar to dependency theory: the East Asian NICs were too small, poor, and threatened by "previously successful Communist armies" nearby, and MNC investment was mostly

The "problems of plenty" argument has its limitations, too. Bonanzas tend to obstruct institutionally settled social patterns of capital accumulation. I have already noted the issue of the "unbalanced productive structure," in which natural resources elevated exchange rates and made wages internationally uncompetitive. It has also been suggested that an economy based on narrowly owned natural resources tends to produce a particular mix of labor skills, reflecting how the elite molds the educational system to suit its own interests and the needs of resource exports.[32] Another part of the problem lies in the volatility of commodity-export receipts. Moisés Naim observes that since 1970 Venezuelan oil revenues varied year to year by an average of 6 percent of GDP. The booms would discourage nonresource exports, while the busts would bring devaluation, capital flight, tight credit, and fiscal stringency. By confounding expectations, such volatility encourages the search for quick, large profits domestically. Finally, it would be wrong to let our recognition of the constructive potential of crises become a dogma of "the worse, the better," perhaps to be perversely imposed upon countries in which millions live in precarious circumstances. Besides, as I argued in Chapter 2, observations about the perils of plenty apply just as well to international banks as they do to countries receiving capital inflows or oil rents.

It may be true that among rentier states, fiscal autonomy often underpins despotism. But although a financial crisis or some other market discipline may provide a remedy, power in asset markets is itself usually held quite narrowly. In the wake of the 1994 devaluation crisis, a Mexican banker observed that if "the relevant economic agents see the official attitude toward Chiapas as weak,

absent until relatively late in the industrialization process; given the strategic imperative to inoculate the countries against Communism, U.S. aid was used "not on behalf of traditional rural elites but on behalf of thorough land reform"; states were stronger there, for strategic (external threat) and historical reasons (inherited Japanese institutions and assets), especially with respect to "the absence of rural elite influence from the formation of state policy." See "Class, State, and Dependence in East Asia: Lessons for Latin Americanists," in *The Political Economy of the New Asian Industrialism*, ed. Frederic Deyo (Ithaca, N.Y.: Cornell University Press, 1987), pp. 206, 210, 212–13, 215, 221. Jeffrey Sachs's explanation of the divergence in industrialization policy between regions, discussed in Chapter 2, calls on similar structural elements. This is not to deny the recognition given by the World Bank to the political importance of land reform and mass education. It is quite explicit but superficial. See World Bank, *The East Asian Miracle: Economic Growth and Public Policy* (New York: Oxford University Press, 1993), pp. 159–67, 169.

32. Robert Wade, "East Asia's Economic Success: Conflicting Perspectives, Partial Insights, Shaky Evidence," *World Politics* 44 (January 1992): 311.

they will probably increase their pressure on the market."[33] As I argued in the last chapter, those who move markets may have no objection to formally unaccountable state power, as long as it is informally accountable to them. Beyond this, policies that respond to economic crisis survive politically if they solve the collective-action problems of capital accumulation, which means the problems of the propertied: saving the Chilean bourgeoisie from socialism; diversifying the crops of the Brazilian *fazendeiro;* or fortifying South Korea or Taiwan economically against nearby Communist rivals. Conversely, in Brazil during the late 1980s the state could postpone its Armageddon by creating indexed assets and lending overnight, making inflation profitable for banks and the rich, keeping home a lot of capital that otherwise would have fled, and thereby weakening the sense of political urgency about ending inflation—while the poor got poorer. An underlying assumption about the practical benefits of "embedded autonomy" is that the social networks in which state actors are embedded put a high value on the tasks that autonomy makes possible.[34]

Let us now contemplate Stallings's paradox in a more constructive spirit. Why are some countries more vulnerable to international financial power than others? Two obvious variables are the current account and the public-sector balance. Deficits create the possibility of sudden, internationally provoked disruption. Although it has been said that developing countries are supposed to import capital, we would be justified, I think, in considering these two variables to be characteristics more of policy than structure, since deficits are still amenable to routine political action.

But there *is* a structural side to this vulnerability. Its foundation might be the well-known idea of "structural dependence," which holds that without any business collective action or ideological congruence between politicians and capitalists, governments remain beholden to the investment power of private capital if they hope to oversee eco-

---

33. *Proceso* 947, 26 December 1994, p. 15.

34. Cf. Geddes, *Politician's Dilemma,* p. 9; the latter phrase comes from Peter Evans, "The State as Problem and Solution: Predation, Embedded Autonomy, and Structural Change," in *The Politics of Economic Adjustment: International Constraints, Distributive Conflicts, and the State,* ed. Stephan Haggard and Robert Kaufman (Princeton: Princeton University Press, 1992). The issue of support and implementation after the decision to reform is taken up in Merilee Grindle and John Thomas, *Public Choices and Policy Change: The Political Economy of Reform in Developing Countries* (Baltimore: Johns Hopkins University Press, 1991).

nomic growth and win popular approval.[35] Although one of the best expressions of this model deals with taxes, we can say that in countries where fewer questions are settled the contested issues might range from intellectual property rights to labor legislation to exchange control. This view agrees with the analysis in Chapter 4: rather than looking for an organized "financial fifth column" behind decisions to favor bondholders or the IMF, we should consider the interests of politicians and the alternatives open to them. However, although it posits a rational basis for the preferences of state actors, this basic proposition does not give us a means to distinguish among countries.[36] To do so we can call upon Albert Hirschman's classic analysis of asymmetrical interdependence.[37]

Despite the fact that international capital mobility clearly limits the economic options of rich countries, it is reasonable to suppose that it binds smaller, poorer countries even more strongly. Hirschman's analysis of power and trade asks us to conceive of the gain from trade as that which is in the power of the trading partner to take away. This implies a relation of asymmetry between an economically large country and a small one, because the former has, relative to its total trade, much less to lose by ending the trade relationship than does the latter.[38] Now, let us posit a financial analog to this relationship. One way to do so would be to define size as financial market size (say, total capitalization of asset markets). Holding the risk and expected return on assets in the periphery constant, small changes in the average rate

35. Adam Przeworski and Michael Wallerstein, "Structural Dependence of the State on Capital," *American Political Science Review* 82, no. 1 (March 1988): esp. 17–18, 20. In their view states can avoid structural dependence when they inherit a high tax on consumption (or, in the case of foreign investment, remittance) out of profiles—as the authors put it, the state escapes dependence in a "static" sense. In more dynamic situations, that is, when the state wishes to raise taxes or attract new investment, dependence follows. See also Duane Swank, "Politics and the Structural Dependence of the State in Democratic Capitalist Nations," *American Political Science Review* 86, no. 1 (March 1992); Claus Offe, "Two Logics of Collective Action," in *Disorganized Capitalism: Contemporary Transformations of Work and Politics* (Cambridge, Mass.: MIT Press, 1985), pp. 191–93; Fred Block, "The Ruling Class Does Not Rule: Notes on the Marxist Theory of the State," *Socialist Revolution* 33 (1977): 6–28. A clear direct motive for government accommodation derives from the politician's desire to reduce the cost of servicing the domestic debt.

36. Jeffry Frieden has complained that dependency theories fail because they lack "firm microfoundations" (*Debt, Development, and Democracy*, p. 239).

37. Albert O. Hirschman, *National Power and the Structure of Foreign Trade* (Berkeley and Los Angeles: University of California Press, 1945).

38. Ibid., pp. 18–26, 29.

of return on comparable assets in the center would produce flows large enough to swamp, or else to strand, small peripheral economies. The effects of changes in key world interest rates would be magnified and perhaps quite costly in their destabilizing effects.[39] (In the face of the massive inflows of the early 1990s an IMF study called developing-country policy options "limited."[40])

Another side of asymmetry would emerge in bargaining. Finance has the advantage of approximating the stock bargaining model (dividing up a sum of money) more closely than does trade. There are obvious problems with framing the model as a negotiation between two governments, one the source of investment and the other the destination, because we effectively assume away the independence of IFIs and international private banks. If we do so for the sake of argument, however, one result is clear. As Harrison Wagner shows, even without the interpersonal comparison of utilities between bargainers, we can conclude that the richer bargainer will come away with more than half the sum, by virtue of his lower discount rate on future benefits.[41]

Interestingly, Hirschman's own later reservations about his model of asymmetrical trade interdependence may not apply to finance. Looking back at his model, he posited a disparity of attention between

39. See Guillermo Calvo, Leonardo Leiderman, and Carmen M. Reinhart, "Capital Inflows and Real Exchange Rate Appreciation in Latin America," *IMF Staff Papers* 40, no. 1 (March 1993), who conclude that "the importance of external factors suggests that a reversal of those conditions may lead to a future capital outflow, increasing the macroeconomic vulnerability of Latin American economies" (p. 108). See also the response in the Argentine markets after the first Fed tightening of 1994, summarized in Marcelo Zlotogwiazada, "Los Dólares Dan Media Vuelta," *Página 12* (Buenos Aires), 26 February 1994, p. 12.

40. The current domestic debt load makes sterilizing the capital inflows with more government debt risky also, especially given the small relative size of the capital markets. On these issues, see "Capital Inflows, Hot or Cool?" *Outreach* 8 (Washington, D.C.: World Bank Policy Research Department, February 1993); on capital controls, see Donald J. Mathieson and Liliana Rojas-Suárez, *Liberalization of the Capital Account: Experiences and Issues,* Occasional Paper 103 (Washington, D.C.: International Monetary Fund, March 1993), secs. III and IV. A judicious summary of this problem, one that does not rule out taxes or controls on inflows (if used along with many other tools), is Williamson, "Issues Posed by Portfolio Investment in Developing Countries," pp. 10–12. The quote is from Calvo et al., "Capital Inflows and Real Exchange Rate Appreciation," p. 108.

41. This assumes the same discount curve for both bargainers, so that the richer would be dealing with a more gently sloping portion of the curve. If we assume interpersonal utility equivalence at equal levels of wealth, the result will be strengthened. See R. Harrison Wagner, "Economic Interdependence, Bargaining Power, and Political Influence," *International Organization* 42, no. 3 (Summer 1988): 466–68.

large and small, one that made concentrated efforts and thus the relative advance of the small economy possible, much as a small, nimble firm might outperform a slow giant.[42] This may well describe important aspects of international investment in emerging markets: local investors more savvy than foreign ones about local risk; and the key to sustained growth, patient capital, being patient insofar as it is ignorant. More likely, however, is that the disparity of attention will aggravate the disruptive cycles of boom and bust. One day foreign investors underestimate some risks because Latin America is "the place to be," only the next day to exaggerate the risks or to attribute them wrongly to an entire region—as was the regrettable pattern in 1982 and 1994–95.[43] The Brazilian foreign minister commented that the most important lesson of the 1994–95 crisis was that "being different is not enough; appearing to be different is also necessary."[44]

So far we still cannot distinguish usefully among countries of roughly equal size. To do so we adapt another part of Hirschman's classic description of power and trade, which considered the domestic interests favoring the maintenance of any given trade relationship. The relative strength of these interests was taken to approximate the relative importance of the relationship to the country's entire foreign trade.

I noted in Chapter 2 that Latin America has historically been more open to international finance than have the larger countries of East Asia, and that this point is often overlooked when observers character- ize East Asian economies as "open" during their periods of most rapid growth. I argued further that the two regions differ in what I have called their degree of financial cosmopolitanism, with Latin American private wealth being both more concentrated and more outward-ori- ented.

This suggests a way to think about why some countries are more vulnerable to the volatility and constraints of international finance. Let us assume that some proportion of domestic capital uses the

42. Hirschman's doubts are expressed in *Essays in Trespassing: Economics to Politics and Beyond* (New York: Cambridge University Press, 1981), pp. 30–33. It might be objected that today, with long and detailed lists of Super 301 violations coming from the U.S. Commerce Department, the idea of disparity of attention on trade looks less plausible.

43. On the "tequila effect" of the Mexican crisis on emerging markets, especially in Latin America, see "Latin America in the Fallout Zone," *The Economist*, 7 January 1995, pp. 59–60; Floyd Norris, "Mexican Shadow Falls on Emerging Markets," *New York Times*, 1 February 1995, D1.

44. Luiz Felipe Lampreia, cited in *Latin American Weekly Report*, 9 March 1995, p. 104.

expected outcome of international market signals, or negotiations, as a guide to its own investment. Like the Brazilian rich in Paul Volcker's account, such investors are neither organized nor consciously antinational, just attentive to foreign signals and rational maximizers of their wealth. They know that when governments lose, they have to devalue, default on domestic bonds, or raise taxes. But while each domestic agent knows that others are also attentive to the international sphere, no coordination among them is possible. Thus, each knows that the decisions of other domestic agents will accentuate the result of international signals or bargains. Moreover, to the extent that the decisions of foreign fund managers move the domestic market, it does not matter if their views contradict local investors' assessments of the situation. There will always be a big incentive for the locals to anticipate the decisions of the foreigners.

If the concept of the orientation of wealth seems too woolly, we can refer back to the reasoning in Chapter 2. Begin by assuming that as a household is richer, it devotes a greater proportion of its consumption to imports. Next assume that households structure their asset portfolios in line with their consumption profiles—dollar assets to pay for dollar-priced goods, yen assets for yen goods, and local-currency assets for domestically made goods. (This amounts to saying that we ignore speculative transactions.[45]) A country with narrower distribution would hence find more of its privately held wealth in foreign assets.

Before proceeding, let us speculate about another implication of wealth and income distribution for international capital movements. Even after thorough liberal reforms, return flows of flight capital to Latin America, and the pattern of capital flows in general, may turn out to be disappointing.[46] Why? To the reasoning about consumption patterns and asset portfolios above, add two recent trends in Latin

45. Here I adopt a portfolio-balance framework similar to that of Jeffrey Frankel, "In Search of the Exchange Risk Premium: A Six-Currency Test Assuming Mean-Variance Optimization," *Journal of International Money and Finance* 1 (1982): 255–74, in which a "minimum-variance portfolio" mirrors consumption patterns (p. 259). Although for Frankel it corresponds to the extreme of risk aversion, I use the minimum-variance portfolio as a proxy for long-run demand for foreign assets, where net expected profit from speculation (here, from transactions into and out of domestic currency) goes to zero.

46. Stanley Fischer has suggested that since capital flight may have achieved a more optimal portfolio balance for its holders, the scale of its return may prove much smaller than that of its exit. "Sharing the Burden of the International Debt Crisis," *American Economic Review* 77, no. 2 (May 1987): 168. While there are problems with this idea (the greatest outflows came from countries in which capital controls had been absent, presumably allowing optimization well before the flight took place), his conclusion may be sound as a result of the trends noted here.

America: rising income and wealth polarization on one side, and the liberalization of trade on the other. Hence import consumption among rich households rises; their asset portfolios follow the new shape of spending, with a larger foreign component; and their portfolios represent an even larger proportion of aggregate (national) wealth. The overall result: Latin American countries will have, in the aggregate, an increasing demand for foreign assets, as a proportion of all assets, while these trends of polarization and trade liberalization hold.[47] (The figures also suggest that it may be common to see periods in which U.S. investment in liberalizing Latin America is balanced, not by trade deficits with the United States, but by equally large Latin American foreign investments.)

None of this need imply an investment drought or an end to growth. It only says that foreign funds will have to play a larger role well into the future, if growth is to be sustained. Moisés Naim has observed that one of the subtle and destructive results of capital flight was to turn a large part of the domestic business class into satisfied rentiers, in "the neutering of the entrepreneurial impulses" of many private wealth holders.[48] We may see an aspect of this by comparing estimates of the return of flight capital to the imputed annual interest on the accumulated net stocks of this capital (Figures 1.1A–F and Table 4.4, above). In the early 1990s holders of overseas assets brought back amounts of the same magnitude as their interest income on the assets, leaving principal relatively intact. Later, in the wake of the Chiapas uprising and uncertainty about the peso, a Mexican stock analyst noted that Mexican investors had already sold most of their holdings in the Mexican market: "foreigners have been looking at Mexico longer term than the Mexicans."[49]

Clearly, a lot is missing here. Apart from the current-account and public-sector balances noted above, I have not considered the terms or currency denomination of debt, the liquidity of capital markets, the structure and ownership of commercial and industrial firms, the health of the banking system, or even the reserve situation of the

---

47. The argument is not undermined by the fact that consumer goods may make up only around 10 percent of total imports (the approximate Mexican figure for 1992). The weighted average ratio of wealth to consumption among the households buying imported consumer items is presumably well above unity.

48. *Paper Tigers and Minotaurs: Economic Policy Reform in Venezuela* (Washington, D.C.: Institute for International Economics, 1994), p. 86.

49. Stephen Fidler and Damian Fraser, "Shock Waves Hit the Latin Markets," *Financial Times,* 7 March 1994.

country.[50] Still, if we now step back and consider structural dependence, international asymmetry, and domestic wealth-holding patterns together, these conclusions follow. For any given degree of financial distress or need for investment, the structural dependence of financially small states on international capital will be greater than that of large states. And for any given financial size of states, other things being equal, the power of international forces will be magnified, the narrower the distribution of domestic private wealth.

I would like to close by expanding on the theme of democratic legitimation in an age of mobile capital. It has been said that during the debt crisis Latin American asset holders who placed their capital abroad acted for the most part "in the way that is posited as rational by economic theory and accepted as normal in industrial countries."[51] This is true. Yet I also believe it correct to say that corrupt officials and embezzling presidents behaved more or less in the way expected by public-choice theory. While Latin America may recently have suffered from a surplus of leaders who acted according to the latter kind of rationality while castigating the former, this does not mean that the tension between national identity and individual market incentives will dissolve as Latin America embraces neoliberalism. On the contrary.

Adam Przeworski has written that "while reproduction of capital is organized today at the transnational level, reproduction of consent continues to be a national problem."[52] A financial circuit that passes offshore before coming back is not necessarily bad. It will probably improve the efficiency of intermediation and may raise the quality of a country's capital stock. But since governments play a crucial role in enforcing the private accumulation that feeds this financial circuit, they have to establish credibility as defenders of common, national interests. This often leads to a divergence, especially acute in countries that are highly unequal economically, between what is required to make profits safe and what is required to obtain popular consent.

We can see this in the way politicians talk about capital accumula-

50. See also Robert W. Cox, "Global Perestroika," in *Socialist Register 1992,* ed. Ralph Miliband and Leo Panitch (London: Merlin Press, 1993), pp. 28–29.

51. Donald R. Lessard and John Williamson, "The Problem and Policy Responses," in *Capital Flight and Third World Debt,* ed. Donald R. Lessard and John Williamson (Washington, D.C.: Institute for International Economics, 1987), p. 201.

52. "Class Compromise and the State: Western Europe and Latin America," University of Chicago, June 1980, photocopy, p. 30. Published in Spanish in Norbert Lechner, ed., *El Estado y Política en América Latina* (Mexico City: Siglo 21, 1981).

tion. They commonly attempt to soothe the poverty of the majority with visions of material progress, promising that sacrifices made today will be repaid with prosperity tomorrow. The metaphor of country-as-household is the standard one (unsurprising in matters of *oikonomia*), in which citizens scrimp along together and, under wise leaders and their economic experts, apply their savings to build a modern future, much as they would apply the family's savings to buy a washing machine. For obvious reasons international capital mobility periodically complicates this story. Mobile capital may still justify itself politically (as we could see in the PAN's platform of the mid-1980s) as a way of protecting national savings from arbitrary government. However, once liberal reforms have "put the house in order" (as long and publicly sought by international finance), it may be harder to blame a bad government for the next disappointment.

Referring to the United States, Robert Reich has asked: "What do we owe one another as members of the same society who no longer inhabit the same economy? The answer will depend on how strongly we feel that we are, in fact, members of the same society."[53] In Latin America this sort of question raises itself insistently. Today more than ever Latin American societies are composed of islands of first-world wealth and sophistication in the midst of third-world seas. Even if the latter renounce all socialist dreams, what they still need from the former is productive investment; but their very presence may be taken more as a danger than an opportunity. In these circumstances a recovery of private investment is a collective-action problem that governments may try to solve by appealing to the norms of the big household, to national solidarity.[54] In effect, they describe private investment as a public good.[55]

53. Robert B. Reich, *The Work of Nations* (New York: Vintage Press, 1991), p. 303.

54. On the collective-action issue, see Raúl Laban and Holger C. Wolf, "La Inversión con Reformas Increíbles," *El Trimestre Económico* 59, no. 233 (January–March 1992): 4. On national solidarity as a motive for investment, for example, in 1985 the *Wall Street Journal* told of a wealthy Mexican businessman "torn between conflicting senses of duty to family and to country." The man compromised, he told the reporter, by "putting money in the States for security and putting money in Mexico to prevent an explosion." Ricardo's famous demonstration of comparative advantage depended on capital staying put. He assumed that it would do so for reasons of supervision, information, and trust (much as did Smith), but also because of an independent preference for national assets—based on feelings that, Ricardo declared, he "should be sorry to see weakened." David Ricardo, *Principles of Political Economy and Taxation* [1821] (London: George Bell and Sons, 1908), chap. 7, sec. 47, pp. 116–17.

55. In Latin America as in the United States, the public-good side of private assets is a phantom. Usually private business strenuously denies the public character of investment (and wishes all trustworthy governments to agree). But when bankruptcy looms,

However, especially where the symbols and discourse of nationalism have been appropriated by twentieth-century popular movements, government calls for private investor solidarity may scare capital away. In 1986 *The Wall Street Journal* quoted the editor of the Mexico City daily *Excélsior,* who sought to expose *sacadólares,* people "who have failed in giving their solidarity to Mexico." The *Journal*'s reporter commented, "it is precisely words like 'solidarity' that scare the big owners of Mexican capital. To them, the *Excélsior* campaign to shame the sacadolares exemplifies the very attitude that made them send their money out of Mexico in the first place."[56]

There are old and fundamental issues here, and they bear on the possibility of stable political agreements on which to base the orderly progress of capitalist development. But there are newer ones as well, relevant not only to Latin America but to any place desperate for investment. It appears sadly anachronistic to hold capital to norms of good citizenship and reciprocity when it can change jurisdictions so rapidly. The "virtual senate" of mobile money can enforce the claim that property rights are one of those to which few responsibilities ought to attach.

---

the public side of the enterprise suddenly steps into the light. Across Latin America the bailouts of 1982–83 proved that major private investments, especially in manufacturing and banking, are at least contingently public goods.

56. 14 March 1986.

Index

Page numbers in *italics* refer to figures and tables.